MW00335059

Academic and Behavior Supports for At-Risk Students

The Guilford Practical Intervention in the Schools Series

Kenneth W. Merrell, Founding Editor
T. Chris Riley-Tillman, Series Editor

This series presents the most reader-friendly resources available in key areas of evidence-based practice in school settings. Practitioners will find trustworthy guides on effective behavioral, mental health, and academic interventions, and assessment and measurement approaches. Covering all aspects of planning, implementing, and evaluating high-quality services for students, books in the series are carefully crafted for everyday utility. Features include ready-to-use reproducibles, lay-flat binding to facilitate photocopying, appealing visual elements, and an oversized format.

Bullying Prevention and Intervention: Realistic Strategies for Schools
Susan M. Swearer, Dorothy L. Espelage, and Scott A. Napolitano

Conducting School-Based Functional Behavioral Assessments, Second Edition:
A Practitioner's Guide
Mark W. Steege and T. Steuart Watson

Evaluating Educational Interventions:
Single-Case Design for Measuring Response to Intervention
T. Chris Riley-Tillman and Matthew K. Burns

Collaborative Home/School Interventions: Evidence-Based Solutions
for Emotional, Behavioral, and Academic Problems
Gretchen Gimpel Peacock and Brent R. Collett

Social and Emotional Learning in the Classroom:
Promoting Mental Health and Academic Success
Kenneth W. Merrell and Barbara A. Gueldner

Executive Skills in Children and Adolescents, Second Edition:
A Practical Guide to Assessment and Intervention
Peg Dawson and Richard Guare

Responding to Problem Behavior in Schools, Second Edition: The Behavior Education Program
Deanne A. Crone, Leanne S. Hawken, and Robert H. Horner

High-Functioning Autism/Asperger Syndrome in Schools: Asessment and Intervention
Frank J. Sansosti, Kelly A. Powell-Smith, and Richard J. Cowan

School Discipline and Self-Discipline:
A Practical Guide to Promoting Prosocial Student Behavior
George G. Bear

Response to Intervention, Second Edition: Principles and Strategies for Effective Practice
Rachel Brown-Chidsey and Mark W. Steege

Child and Adolescent Suicidal Behavior:
School-Based Prevention, Assessment, and Intervention
David N. Miller

Cognitive Therapy for Adolescents in School Settings
Torrey A. Creed, Jarrod Reisweber, and Aaron T. Beck

Motivational Interviewing for Effective Classroom Management: The Classroom Check-Up
Wendy M. Reinke, Keith C. Herman, and Randy Sprick

Positive Behavior Support in Secondary Schools: A Practical Guide
Ellie L. Young, Paul Caldarella, Michael J. Richardson, and K. Richard Young

Academic and Behavior Supports for At-Risk Students: Tier 2 Interventions
Melissa Stormont, Wendy M. Reinke, Keith C. Herman, and Erica S. Lembke

RTI Applications, Volume 1: Academic and Behavioral Interventions
Matthew K. Burns, T. Chris Riley-Tillman, and Amanda M. VanDerHeyden

Coaching Students with Executive Skills Deficits
Peg Dawson and Richard Guare

Enhancing Instructional Problem Solving:
An Efficient System for Assisting Struggling Learners
John C. Begeny, Ann C. Schulte, and Kent Johnson

Academic and Behavior Supports for At-Risk Students

Tier 2 Interventions

MELISSA STORMONT
WENDY M. REINKE
KEITH C. HERMAN
ERICA S. LEMBKE

THE GUILFORD PRESS
New York   London

© 2012 The Guilford Press
A Division of Guilford Publications, Inc.
72 Spring Street, New York, NY 10012
www.guilford.com

All rights reserved

Except as indicated, no part of this book may be reproduced, translated, stored in a retrieval system, or transmitted, in any form or by any means, electronic, mechanical, photocopying, microfilming, recording, or otherwise, without written permission from the publisher.

Printed in the United States of America

This book is printed on acid-free paper.

Last digit is print number: 9 8 7 6 5 4 3 2 1

LIMITED PHOTOCOPY LICENSE

These materials are intended for use only by qualified professionals.

The publisher grants to individual purchasers of this book nonassignable permission to reproduce all materials for which photocopying permission is specifically granted in a footnote. This license is limited to you, the individual purchaser, for personal use or use with individual clients or students. This license does not grant the right to reproduce these materials for resale, redistribution, electronic display, or any other purposes (including but not limited to books, pamphlets, articles, video- or audiotapes, blogs, file-sharing sites, Internet or intranet sites, and handouts or slides for lectures, workshops, webinars, or therapy groups, whether or not a fee is charged). Permission to reproduce these materials for these and any other purposes must be obtained in writing from the Permissions Department of Guilford Publications.

The authors have checked with sources believed to be reliable in their efforts to provide information that is complete and generally in accord with the standards of practice that are accepted at the time of publication. However, in view of the possibility of human error or changes in behavioral, mental health, or medical sciences, neither the authors, nor the editor and publisher, nor any other party who has been involved in the preparation or publication of this work warrants that the information contained herein is in every respect accurate or complete, and they are not responsible for any errors or omissions or the results obtained from the use of such information. Readers are encouraged to confirm the information contained in this book with other sources.

Library of Congress Cataloging-in-Publication Data

Academic and behavior supports for at-risk students : tier 2 interventions / Melissa Stormont ... [et al.].
     p. cm. — (The Guilford practical intervention in the schools series)
   Includes bibliographical references and index.
   ISBN 978-1-4625-0304-9 (pbk.)
   1. Problem children—Education.   2. Learning disabled children—Education.   3. Problem children—Behavior modification.   4. Learning disabled children—Behavior modification.
5. Remedial teaching.   I. Stormont, Melissa.
   LC4801.A32 2012
   371.93—dc23
                                                          2011043574

In memory of Dr. Ken Merrell,
a cherished mentor, colleague, and friend
who inspired a generation of school psychologists and special educators.
His spirit will live on in this influential book series.

About the Authors

Melissa Stormont, PhD, is Associate Professor in the Department of Special Education at the University of Missouri. Dr. Stormont has published extensive research related to the educational and social needs of young children who are vulnerable for failure in school, including children with behavior problems, children with attention-deficit/hyperactivity disorder, and children who are homeless. She spent 3 years as a preschool teacher and has conducted extensive field research in Head Start and early childhood settings. She has focused the majority of her research efforts on factors contributing to early behavior problems in young children. Dr. Stormont has published more than 60 articles, books, and book chapters related to the needs of children at risk for failure.

Wendy M. Reinke, PhD, is Assistant Professor in the Department of Educational, School and Counseling Psychology at the University of Missouri. Dr. Reinke is the Founder and Co-Director of the Missouri Prevention Center and Co-Investigator for the Johns Hopkins Center for Prevention and Early Intervention. She has published extensively on supporting teachers with classroom management and on prevention and early intervention of disruptive behavior problems in children; is coauthor of the books *Coaching Classroom Management* and *Motivational Interviewing for Effective Classroom Management*; and has trained hundreds of school-based coaches around the country to deliver her teacher consultation model. Dr. Reinke is on the editorial boards of the *Journal of School Psychology, School Psychology Quarterly,* and the *Journal of Applied School Psychology.* Dr. Reinke currently is the Principal Investigator on two federally funded grants totaling over $3.6 million, including a large-scale group randomized efficacy trial funded by the Institute of Education Sciences.

Keith C. Herman, PhD, is Associate Professor in the Department of Educational, School and Counseling Psychology at the University of Missouri and Co-Director of the Missouri Prevention Center. In addition to his training in counseling psychology, Dr. Herman completed respecialization training in school psychology at the University of Oregon. He presents nationally and has published over 60 peer-reviewed articles and book chapters. Much of his work focuses on the prevention and early intervention of internalizing disorders and on working with teachers and families to promote effective environments for children.

Erica S. Lembke, PhD, is Associate Professor in the Department of Special Education at the University of Missouri, a trainer for the National Center on Response to Intervention, and Vice-President on the national board of the Division for Learning Disabilities of the Council for Exceptional Children. Dr. Lembke currently serves as the state of Missouri and University of Missouri student advisor for the Student Council for Exceptional Children and received the Susan Phillips Gorin Award for advising at the 2011 national conference of the Council for Exceptional Children. She is currently co-Principal Investigator on a federally funded Institute of Education Sciences grant examining the use of handheld devices to conduct mathematics progress monitoring and administer mathematics diagnostic interviews. Dr. Lembke has numerous publications on the topics of curriculum-based measurement and response to intervention. She has made over 100 national, international, and state presentations on the topics of progress monitoring and response to intervention. Her research interests include designing and implementing curriculum-based measures in elementary and secondary grades and developing strategies to improve elementary students' academic performance.

Preface

Response-to-intervention (RTI) prevention-based tiered models have become widely accepted and adopted frameworks for supporting student learning and development in schools. Partly fueled by dissatisfaction with test-and-place approaches to special education and also by legislative reforms, most school practitioners are now being asked to be knowledgeable about implementing RTI approaches for both academic and behavior problems (see Gresham, 2005).

Although there are various tiered preventive models, they all share some features. First, they are preventive methods grounded in public health approaches to disease management. Second, these methods give high priority to the delivery of a continuum of services based on student need. The number of tiers along this continuum may differ across models, but all have at least three tiers: (1) universal supports that are given to all students, (2) more selective and generally group-delivered supports given to students unresponsive to the universal supports, and (3) more intensive and individualized supports reserved for those fewer students who are unresponsive to the selective supports. Third, data-based decision making is a hallmark of these methods. Careful and efficient assessment is needed for screening and progress monitoring to aid decision making at each tier. Ultimately, these assessment and intervention methods were proposed to aid in the diagnostic decision making for entry into special education.

Good evidence has emerged indicating that schools and school-based practitioners trained in these methods are able to provide effective universal (Tier 1) schoolwide academic and behavior supports (Nakasato, 2000; Scott, 2001; Stormont, Lewis, Beckner, & Johnson, 2008). Additionally, much literature is available to support school efforts to deliver individualized supports to students at Tier 3. However, much less has been written about how well schools are able to meet the needs of students in the middle—those who are not fully responsive to the universal supports but whose problems are not severe enough to warrant the intensive supports of Tier 3.

WHO BENEFITS FROM TIER 2 INTERVENTIONS?

In schools where universal, evidence-based academic instruction and behavior supports are in place, a number of students continue to struggle. Some of these students will benefit from additional supports that prevent the academic or behavior problems from escalating to more severe levels. Identifying and intervening with these students before serious problems develop and more costly services are needed is advantageous. Tier 2 interventions are specifically designed for these students who need a bit more support than is offered universally to all students, but whose problems are not severe enough to require individualized Tier 3 supports.

WHAT IS THE PURPOSE OF THIS BOOK?

This book fills the void of knowledge about effective Tier 2 assessments and interventions. In particular, within a single resource we have compiled strategies for Tier 2 supports for both academic and behavior problems. Many students exhibit problems in both areas, making the distinction between these problems less than useful to school practitioners. In fact, the root of behavior problems for some students stems from academic deficits (see Chapter 3). This is an important topic, as little guidance is available in the literature to support practitioners in (1) determining which students need Tier 2 supports, (2) selecting interventions that are the most promising for these students, (3) differentiating Tier 2 and Tier 3 supports, and (4) determining which students proceed to a Tier 3 level of support. This book includes a comprehensive presentation of programs and interventions to support students who are at risk for negative academic and/or behavior outcomes.

This book narrows the research-to-practice gap regarding students who are at risk for failure by providing information that will allow school professionals to be more supportive of these students. For children who qualify for Tier 2 supports, some will need assistance across all areas and some in just one area. We provide a comprehensive review of academic and behavior supports because academic and behavior problems co-occur and behavior problems and family needs co-occur. Thus, when teams are increasing their capacity to meet the needs of more children at the Tier 2 level, they can utilize the recommendations from various chapters for different problems. Chapter 2 includes ecological considerations for ensuring that schools use culturally sensitive practices, and it discusses the importance of, and practical strategies for, supporting increased family involvement for children at risk for failure. Chapters 3 through 6 include information on Tier 2 strategies in the following areas: externalizing behavior problems (Chapter 3), internalizing behavior problems (Chapter 4), reading difficulties (Chapter 5), and mathematics difficulties (Chapter 6). Chapter 7 provides information on laying the foundation for Tier 3 supports. Chapters 3–6 all include the following information:

- Overview (what the problem is).
- Theoretical foundations for intervening in the problem.

- How to identify children with the problem.
- Review of evidence-based practices for intervening in the problem.
- Review of evidence-based programs for intervening in the problem.
- Use of data to inform intervention and monitor progress.

FOR WHOM IS THIS BOOK WRITTEN?

This book is written for all school personnel (general education teachers, special educators, behavior specialists, school psychologists, counselors, and others), given that all professionals work with students at risk for failure. However, this book is particularly appropriate for school personnel who are part of Tier 2 schoolwide positive behavior support and RTI teams who have the task of designing effective academic and behavior support systems and resources.

Acknowledgments

We are indebted to the innovative educators and psychologists who developed and evaluated the response-to-intervention models and practices over the past few decades. Most of the methods described in this book are grounded in the work of many brilliant people, and we appreciate the opportunity to bring all these wonderful ideas together in a single resource.

In addition, we would like to thank Heather Klemp for her diligent editing and positive feedback. We also would like to thank our families for their encouragement and patience, especially our children, Kennedy, Carter, Michael, Danielle, Philip, Samantha, and Taylor Faye, for allowing us to learn and grow and helping us to become better at all we do.

Contents

CHAPTER 1

Laying the Foundation
for Tier 2 Interventions

Anthony

It is November, and it is clear that Anthony is struggling in his kindergarten class-room. Anthony is impulsive, hyperactive, and sometimes aggressive with his peers. He has received three office disciplinary referrals in the past month and goes to the safe spot and buddy room almost every day. Due to budget cuts, the school no longer has a behavioral consultant, and the teacher does not have the knowledge or skills to develop an intervention plan to meet Anthony's needs. The school-based positive behavior support (PBS) team has not received adequate training in the area of Tier 2 supports and has called on an outside consultant to provide some professional development for the school. In the meantime, what will happen with Anthony?

Olivia

Olivia is struggling in reading. As a second grader, she is reading at the kindergarten level. She has moved three times in the past 3 years. Two of her former schools did not use a systematic evidence-based approach for working with children's reading skills. In her current school, they do use evidence-based core instruction and reading strate-gies. However, she is so far behind that her teacher is concerned that she may have a learning disability and is going to refer her for an evaluation for special education and related services.

José

José is a fourth grader who has behavior problems and is struggling academically. His teacher is concerned that his family may be struggling to meet their basic needs. José frequently comes to school too late to eat the free breakfast for which he is eligible, and he has been caught on several occasions stuffing food in his pockets at lunch. His

1

behavior has gotten worse over the past year; this is the first year he has not completed and returned homework assignments. The school counselor and his teacher have communicated with José's mother, who seems overwhelmed due to various family stressors. José's father recently lost his job, and the family is on the brink of homelessness.

In schools today, students who are at risk for failure, like Anthony, Olivia, and José, are often the rule rather than the exception. The number of students who struggle in school behaviorally and/or academically is staggering (Donahue, Voelkl, Campbell, & Mazzeo, 1999; Institute of Medicine, 2009). The multiple problems children face and the need for early intervention across school and home contexts is also clearly illustrated by research. For example:

- According to the World Health Organization (2004), as many as one in five children have social, emotional, and behavioral needs for support, and if they receive any services, they receive them in school.
- As early as kindergarten, many children struggle significantly in school. Some children in kindergarten are already at a disadvantage compared to their peers in terms of early literacy and self-regulation skills (Stormont, Beckner, Mitchell, & Richter, 2005).
- Approximately 14% of young children have both academic and behavior issues, and these children have the poorest outcomes when compared to peers with either behavior or academic problems (Reinke, Herman, Petras, & Ialongo, 2008).
- Early behavior problems predict risk for later academic problems and, similarly, early academic risk predicts later social and emotional problems, including depression (Bohanon et al., 2011a; Herman, Lambert, Reinke, & Ialongo, 2008).
- The American Academy of Child and Adolescent Psychiatry (2010) reports that about 5% of children and adolescents in the general population suffer from depression at any given time; depression can have a significant impact on children's academic, social, and emotional functioning.
- Data from the U.S. Department of Education (2007) indicated that 43% of grade 1 students were below proficient in reading (based on fluency outcome measures); without early intervention, children are at great risk for never reading on grade level.
- Despite efforts to improve student performance in mathematics, the National Center for Education Statistics (2010) reported that 62% of fourth-grade public school students scored at basic or below-basic levels in mathematics achievement in 2009. The number of students identified with mathematics disabilities has increased by over 25% since 1990 (National Mathematics Advisory Panel [NMP], 2008).
- Many economic challenges face families today. Due to increases in unemployment/ underemployment and decreasing housing options and wages for low-income individuals, more and more people are at risk for poverty and homelessness (Stormont & McCathren, 2008).
- Families represent 40% of the homeless population, and children represent 25% (Stormont & McCathren, 2008). Most children are young, and half of these children

are under the age of 6. Children who are homeless may miss, on average, 3 weeks of school every 3 months, which can significantly diminish their success in school. Children from low-income backgrounds are also at increased risk for social, emotional, and physical health problems as well as academic failure.

Many children who are at risk have a number of factors that are influencing their ability to be successful in school. Regardless of the reasons behind a child's risk for failure, research has clearly shown that there is a window for prevention of social, emotional, and early academic problems. If problems remain when children reach the upper primary grades, they are likely to be sustained, and children are then at risk for a host of additional negative outcomes, including association with deviant peers, school failure, dropping out of school, and incarceration (Kauffman & Landrum, 2009; Reid, Patterson, & Snyder, 2002).

Thus, schools must build the capacity to address the many different types of problems that at-risk children will manifest, including academic and behavior problems. It is also important that schools implement approaches to working with children that are culturally sensitive and that support and partner with families as much as possible. For many students who are at risk, relatively simple, and often temporary, interventions can have a large impact (Rathvon, 2008; Reinke & Herman, 2002; Reinke, Lewis-Palmer, & Martin, 2007; Stormont, 2007). For other students, more extensive and individualized interventions are needed. Within the context of a continuum of supports, or a three-tiered model, students' needs are determined by their responsiveness to intervention (Lembke, McMaster, & Stecker, 2009; OSEP Center on Positive Behavioral Interventions and Supports, 2004; Stormont, Lewis, Beckner, & Johnson, 2008). Tiered prevention approaches are designed to support all students' academic achievement and/or successful social behavior in an intentional, systematic, and data-driven manner that often includes changing the way schools operate. The two prevention models discussed in this text have the same overall problem-solving approach and similar essential features. Many researchers have called for increased integration of prevention models for academic and social behavior problems (e.g., Kalberg, Lane, & Menzies, 2010; Sugai, 2011). However, given the fact that professionals reading this text are from schools, districts, and states in various stages of implementing one or both of these models, we have chosen to discuss them separately.

> **Regardless of the reasons behind a child's risk for failure, research has clearly shown that there is a window for prevention of social behavior and early academic problems.**

One of the two models discussed in this text is RTI, which includes assessment and intervention practices that have a long history in education (e.g., precision teaching, direct instruction). RTI has also been cited in the Individuals with Disabilities Education Improvement Act (2004) as an optional process for identifying students with learning disabilities (Stecker, 2007; Sugai, 2007, 2011). The second three-tiered model discussed in this text is a schoolwide posi-

> **Tiered prevention approaches are designed to support all students' academic achievement and/or social behavior success in an intentional, systematic, and data-driven manner that often includes changing the way in which schools operate.**

tive behavior intervention support (PBIS) system; both models have a foundation in public health.

Within both three-tiered prevention-based models, evidence-based interventions are implemented at a universal level for all students and followed by more intense interventions for students requiring a second (Tier 2) or third level (Tier 3) of support. Figure 1.1 presents the approximate percentage of students that would be in need of each type of preventive intervention provided within the continuum if the system were functioning well for students in the school. "Functioning well" means that the core academic and/or behavioral system in place is meeting the needs of the majority of students in the school.

If core instruction is functioning well for the majority of students in the building, we would expect a schoolwide screening in academics to reveal that at least 80% of students fell into Tier 1, meaning that these students do not need additional academic or behavioral interventions (Sugai, 2011). In terms of primary prevention for social behavior problems, 80% of students respond to school and classwide systems in place to support all students across all settings. Extensive research has been conducted on the overall effectiveness of schoolwide universal academic and behavioral supports (e.g., Horner & Sugai, 2005; Nakasato, 2000; Scott, 2001; Stecker, 2007), and most educators and school-based clinicians are aware of a variety of preventive interventions.

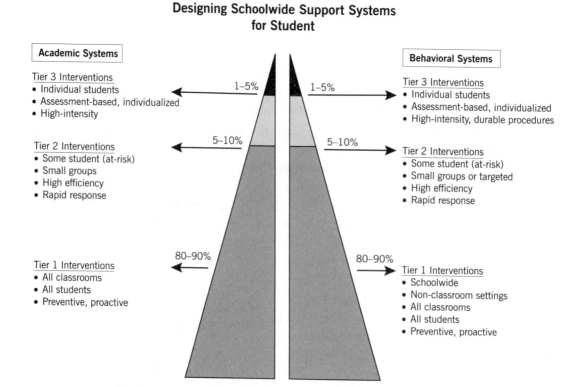

FIGURE 1.1. Tiered prevention models and the percentage of students that responds to each tier. From *pbis.org*. Copyright 2011 by *pbis.org*. Reprinted by permission.

A vast amount of social behavior research has also been conducted on more individualized interventions for the 1–5% of students who need Tier 3 levels of support (e.g., Bambara & Kern, 2005). However, less academic research has been conducted on targeted interventions for students who need Tier 3 interventions, and most of the academic research has been restricted to reading (Stecker, 2007). Tier 3 supports are designed for students who have intensive needs that require extensive supports. Laying the foundation for Tier 3 supports is discussed in Chapter 7.

The middle part of the triangle, Tier 2, has not received very much attention in the literature. Tier 2 represents a large percentage of students who struggle or have traditionally "slipped through the cracks." Even though this is a large group of students, many practitioners are not aware of interventions that are appropriate for this group, and school-based systems may not be clearly structured to provide needed identification systems and infrastructure to support these students and/or the staff. Hill Walker (2004) states: "There is perhaps no field in which there is a greater discrepancy between the availability of empirically developed, evidence-based practices and their adoption and use than in K–12 education" (p. 399). This is most certainly true for Tier 2 students. However, school reform, increased attention to student outcomes, and use of evidence-based practices clearly support the need for schools to work smarter, not harder. Although the general principles guiding both RTI and PBIS are fairly straightforward, implementing the systems pieces, which are foundational for success, can be quite an extensive undertaking, depending on a school's current practices. Commitment to adopting new models may also require significant changes in what adults in schools are expected to do. All of the essential features work in tandem, so that resistance to adopting one piece (e.g., progress monitoring) will influence the effectiveness of the whole system.

The remainder of this chapter lays the foundation for Tier 2 supports. First, the key universal features of Tier 1 need to be in place and implemented with integrity. If they are not, then the focus should be directed to building capacity at this level. Second, decision-making rules need to be established for determining which students are in need of Tier 2 supports. Third, resources need to be allocated to focus specifically on children in need of Tier 2 interventions. These resources include a team charged with carefully monitoring the progress of individuals receiving Tier 2 supports. Resources also need to be allocated for professional development on the types of interventions available to support children in Tier 2. It is vital that professionals who intend to use specific interventions are prepared to implement them with a high degree of integrity.

UNIVERSAL SUPPORTS ARE IN PLACE

To maximize social behavior and academic learning for all learners, including those at risk, a solid core of evidence-based instruction must be in place. Thus, before schools implement Tier 2 interventions, they need to verify that they do indeed have sound core instruction in place (Burns, Griffiths, Parson, Tilly, & VanderHayden, 2007; Richter, 2008; Sandomierski, Kincaid, & Algozzine, 2007; Stormont et al., 2008). For academic areas such as reading and mathematics, research has identified core curricula and practices that must be included at the universal level to be able to identify students who need more support. Research in reading has been particularly extensive; many evidence-based curricula have been developed and are available for schoolwide adoption (Burns et al., 2007). Evidence-based programs in reading include the foundational practices of building phonemic awareness, phonological skills, fluency, vocabulary, and comprehension (National Institute of Child Health and Human Development, 2000). Although there hasn't been the amount of research in mathematics as there has been in reading, recommendations provided by the NMP (2008) and the Institute on Educational Sciences' report on the use of mathematics interventions in RTI (Gersten, Beckmann, et al., 2009) add considerably to the research on mathematics interventions.

Within PBIS systems, evidence-based universal practices to teach and support social behavior are not packaged in a core curriculum, unlike in the case of reading. Within a schoolwide PBS-tiered model, social behavior is taught systematically, but the specific social behavior varies and is determined by individual schools or districts and supported by school-based teams. The foundational social skills promoted within a schoolwide system of PBS are typically delineated on a matrix that is agreed upon by the majority, preferably all, of staff and widely disseminated. Figure 1.2 includes a sample matrix, and Forms 1.1 and 1.2 (in the Appendix) include the steps involved in creating a matrix and teaching plan. Matrices include agreed-upon behavioral expectations—such as be respectful, be responsible, be safe—and specific behavioral illustrations of what each expectation looks like in a classroom, hallway, cafeteria, playground, bus, and other settings.

Once the behavioral expectations and rules are agreed upon, they are taught explicitly and then supported through prompts, behavior-specific praise, and incentives. As occurs with academic subjects, some children will learn specific skills fast, whereas others will need more practice and support. Some children may need minor supports, such as reminders (e.g., "Remember to *walk* to get the scissors"), and others may need more extensive support that can be delivered individually or in small groups. The latter more typically involves students who need Tier 2 behavioral supports.

UNIVERSAL SUPPORTS ARE IMPLEMENTED WITH INTEGRITY

Often when RTI or PBIS systems are not effective in supporting student growth, it is because the infrastructure is not fully in place. Both tiered systems of support require significant commitment, resources, and capacity to support various kinds of changes in response to data. Such changes may include providing adults with more support to teach behavioral expectations by sending coaches to classrooms to model how to teach specific expectations. In another case, a new teacher may need support in continuing to use the progress monitoring data he or she is collecting to determine who is responding to the core curriculum. Just as children need a continuum of supports, often teachers and other staff will need support as well. Traditional professional development does not support the generalization

Setting	I can be respectful:	I can be safe:	I can be a learner:
All Settings (These expectations apply to all specific locations discussed below.)	• **I can show respect for others. This means I will:** • Use polite language, tone, and volume. • Use polite body language. • Treat others as I want to be treated. • **I can allow others to work undisturbed. This means I will:** • Put materials where they belong. • Put trash in trash cans. • Ask permission to use the property of others. • **I can accept responsibility for my own behavior. This means I will:** • Be honest. • Accept the consequences for my choices. • **I can cooperate with others. This means I will:** • Allow others to resolve their own conflicts.	• **I can allow others to work undisturbed. This means I will:** • Keep my hands, feet, and objects to myself. • **I can manage personal and school property. This means I will:** • Use materials and equipment for intended use. • Push in my chair after use. • **I can follow rules and directions. This means I will:** • Go directly to my destination with a pass. • Walk in the building at all times.	• **I can listen attentively. This means I will:** • Listen when others are speaking. • Raise my hand to share when appropriate. • Give appropriate responses or ask appropriate questions. • **I can cooperate with others. This means I will:** • Work appropriately with others in small groups. • Be a problem solver. • **I can follow rules and directions. This means I will:** • Work independently after directions are given. • Complete the task without frequent reminders. • Respond to the universal attention/quiet signal. • **I can stay on task. This means I will:** • Do my work until it is completed. • Begin and complete assignments on time. • Give my best effort. • **I can manage personal and school property. This means I will:** • Keep my materials organized and prepared for learning. • **I can participate in discussions and activities. This means I will:** • Contribute ideas or suggestions to my group/class.
	I can be respectful. This means I will:	I can be safe. This means I will:	I can be a learner. This means I will:
Hallway	• Wait for a teacher's signal to pass other lines. • Keep my hands to myself and off the walls and student work.	• Walk on the right side in a single-file line • Stop at stop signs. • Walk through doorways on the right-hand side.	• Greet others with a quiet wave.
Bathroom	• Allow privacy for others. • Flush the toilet. • Turn off faucets when finished.	• Wash my hands with soap and water and dry with a paper towel before leaving. • Keep the floor dry and clean.	• Return to class promptly when I am done.

(cont.)

FIGURE 1.2. Rock Bridge Elementary (RBE) PBS matrix of expectations. From RBE PBS. Copyright 2008. Reprinted by permission.

Setting	I can be respectful. This means I will:	I can be safe. This means I will:	I can be a learner. This means I will:
Cafeteria	• Handle and eat food appropriately. • Take only what I can eat. • Stop speaking when the yellow light flashes.	• Eat only my own food. • Put my lunchbox in classroom basket. • Wipe up my table space. • Keep my coat with me. • Bring only appropriate belongings.	• Remember my PIN and lunch. • Make healthy food choices.
Playground	Line up quickly at the first signal. Invite others to play. Share/take turns when using school equipment.	Leave rocks, sticks, and wood chips on the ground. Participate in school-approved games only. Play in approved areas.	Follow the rules of school-approved games. (See *RBE Expectations* for detailed rules and procedures for playground games.)
Buses	Keep food and drinks in my backpack or lunchbox until I get off the bus.	Stay out of the street while waiting for the bus. Remain seated in my assigned spot on the bus. Wait my turn to exit the bus. Cross in front of the bus.	Be on time to the bus stop in the morning. Follow the driver's directions. Listen for my bus number to be called after school.
Parent Pick Up	Walk in the hallway safely to the parent pick-up area. Keep food and drinks in my backpack or lunchbox.	Remain seated in my assigned spot. Stay on the sidewalk until an adult gives permission to go. Ask permission to go back into the building.	Be on time to parent pick-up area in the afternoon. Watch for my ride.
Assemblies	Applaud appropriately to show thanks. Stay seated flat on my pockets, legs criss-cross.	Stay with my teacher and class.	Keep comments and questions on topic.

FIGURE 1.2. *(cont.)*

of skills into classroom settings. Adults need practice in context and feedback. Some professional educators may assume that educators will have the skills, knowledge, and supports to independently implement recommended practices. These assumptions contribute to the research-to-practice gap in schools.

Professional development needs will change depending on where individual schools are in the change process. Some schools may need support implementing universal supports or features for several years, whereas others may have a fairly sound foundation after 1 year. Professional development tends to occur across phases that include awareness building, initial implementation, full implementation, and institutionalization with ongoing opportunities for review of skills and practice (Stormont et al., 2008). Too often, schools report that they are working to establish Tiers 2 and 3 systems of support when they have not fully

> **Just as children need a continuum of supports, often teachers and other staff will need support as well.**

established the structures and systems to support Tier 1. Therefore, at a minimum, schools implementing tiered systems of support need to ensure that the following universal supports are in place before moving to secondary levels of supports (Burns et al., 2007; Richter, 2008; Sandomierski et al., 2007; Stormont et al., 2008):

- *Buy-in.* At least 80% of the school staff needs to be onboard and supportive. Staff members may be more willing to accept new practices if they are provided with the support and professional development they need. Sharing data, including successes, and involving staff in reviewing and providing feedback may also support buy-in.

- *Team-driven process.* Schools must have a representative team driving the process of establishing the key features of the tiered approach and educating other staff on these features. Teams frequently conduct needs assessments to determine if certain needs exist in their schools and then devote time and resources, or even create resources, to meet those needs. Many tools are available online at *pbis.org* and at *rti4success.org* for teams to assess their needs and guide goals and/or action plans.

- *Administrator support and commitment.* Teams could not devote the time and resources required for successful implementation of tiered supports without the support of their administration. Administrators need to ensure that (1) the support is available both short- and long-term, (2) that resources are allocated, and (3) the implementation of RTI and/or PBIS is a priority. At a minimum, schools can expect that efforts to support change will not be fully realized for 3–5 years. Universal supports need to be in place for a period of time before Tier 2 and 3 levels of support can be implemented.

- *Evidence-based curriculum, instruction, and practices.* As discussed in the previous section, it is essential that all students be provided with effective instruction and core foundational practices.

- *Data-based decision making.* Data need to be collected to carefully monitor every step of the way, even though full implementation and the subsequent changes will take several years. Data collected on the implementation of universal features for supporting social behavior or on the core curriculum in academic areas can be used to show the impact of interventions at that level, which is then used to guide further decision making. Data gathering to determine if an intervention is effective is, in itself, an evidence-based practice. The use of objective data for decision making is often much more common in special education and school psychology than in general education. Accordingly, general educators may need more support in learning and implementing systematic data collection and progress monitoring practices.

- *Problem solving.* Using data to guide problem solving is a foundational feature of PBIS and RTI. Ascertaining the interface among practices, data, and system needs are all part of this process (Sugai, 2011). The lens for failure is not focused on students but rather is wide, encompassing all possible factors that are influencing success. Figure 1.3 illustrates these essential, interrelated features (Sugai, 2011).

- *Technical assistance/training needs.* As noted above, one of the unique features of using RTI and PBIS systems is that data are constantly informing the needs for professional development.

> **Data gathering to determine if an intervention is effective is, in itself, an evidence-based practice.**

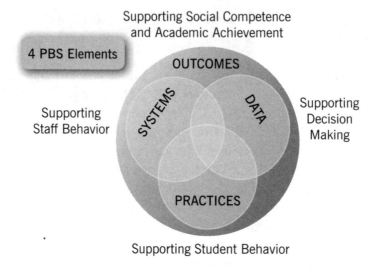

FIGURE 1.3. Essential features of SWPBS and RTI. From *pbis.org*. Copyright 2011 by *pbis.org*. Reprinted by permission.

The question is not whether schools need technical assistance or specific training but rather *what* assistance and training they need. The answer is provided by needs assessment data—that is, data collected on students and/or staff. School staff, at a minimum, "need to understand the priorities of what to teach, how to teach, and when to teach it. Problems occur when the priorities are not communicated or there are competing demands on staff time" (Bohanon, McIntosh, & Goodman, 2011, p. 3).

• *Family involvement.* Family involvement is critical to support the effectiveness of any intervention. Chapter 2 provides an overview of the importance of, and specific practices to use to increase, family involvement. It is clear that when families are involved in their children's education, they can be more supportive at home. When school professionals and families have more trusting relationships, school professionals also have the opportunity to share school and community resources with families.

• *A system of schoolwide screening/benchmarking and progress monitoring that is technically adequate.* This key feature is introduced in the following section and then covered in greater detail in each of the intervention chapters.

• *Data management and frequent communication.* It is important to devote time and resources to training selected members of school teams on data management and analysis (Sugai, 2011). People need to be trained on the types of data that are useful for specific purposes, data management systems, data entry, and data analysis. Administrators need to ensure that people who are trained also have time allocated for data management and analysis tasks. It is equally important that teams report findings back to staff and families and to publicly acknowledge any improvements that children are making in specific areas. Data reports can also summarize survey data or show increases in family involvement in specific homework activities (see Chapter 2). Commonly used data management systems include the School-wide Information System (SWIS) for social behavior and AIMSweb for academic and social behavior. Additional academic data management systems are discussed in Chapters 5 and 6.

ASSESSMENT OF UNIVERSALS

Given the problem-solving orientations used within RTI and PBIS systems, it is vital that time and resources are devoted to establishing systems of schoolwide screening and progress monitoring. It is important that PBIS and RTI teams meet often and regularly use data to inform their decision making and that the school is supportive of team efforts and willing to make changes that need to be made to support success (Stormont et al., 2008). In terms of specific data used for decision making, multiple sources of information, including informal and/or descriptive data, are often valued and used; however, it is important that the screening and progress monitoring evaluation systems also include measures that have strong reliability and validity.

Many tools are available with which to assess the implementation of universal features of PBIS and RTI. The most often used evaluation for assessing implementation of universal features of PBIS is the School-wide Evaluation Tool (SET; Sugai, Lewis-Palmer, Todd, & Horner, 2001). SET data are used to assess key features of PBIS, determine goals for the year, monitor efforts from year to year, and evaluate processes and needs for improvement. Multiple data sources are used when administering the SET, including school data (e.g., discipline handbook), student data (e.g., office disciplinary referrals; ODRs), and teacher data (e.g., social skills lesson plans). Data are also collected from a minimum of 10 staff and 15 students to assess the integrity of implementation. A SET score of 80% or higher indicates that a school is implementing the universal features of PBIS with integrity. The original SET has been revised and is available online at *www.pbis.org*.

There are similar integrity measures for RTI that help districts and school teams assess the effectiveness of implementation. For instance, on *rti4success.org* an entire section of the library is devoted to fidelity in maintaining the RTI process. Fidelity of implementation is addressed and tools are provided (e.g., see Johnson, Mellard, Fuchs, & McKnight, 2006). However, these fidelity tools need more research to document their technical characteristics.

Additional survey data can also be collected and used to ensure that universals are sound prior to instituting Tier 2 supports. An example located at the PBIS website is the Effective Behavior Support Self-Assessment Survey (Sugai, Horner, & Todd, 2000), which can be used by school staff members to determine their current implementation across different systems of support as well as where they need improvement. Data from the survey are then used to create an action plan. A similar type of assessment is available for schools to use to assess core reading practices. Kame'enui and Simmons (2003) created the Planning and Evaluation Tool for Effective Schoolwide Reading Programs. School teams can also collect observational data (e.g., percentage of students on task, number of students in the hallway when bell rings) and additional survey data depending on the information they feel is important for decision making.

DECISION RULES FOR TIER 2

Which children need Tier 2 supports? They represent a large number of students (approximately 15%) who do not respond to evidence-based universal social behavior or academic instruction (e.g., Burns et al., 2007). But, who they represent in a given school will vary in relation to school professionals' decision rules for identifying who is struggling and how much or how long students struggle before they are provided with more resources. Research can provide some direction in terms of how academic and social behavior risk has been defined in the context of tiered prevention-based models.

Screening decision rules have been established within the academic areas of reading and math. These are covered in more depth in Chapters 5 and 6. Who is at risk within a PBIS model has not been standardized for social behavior as well as it has been for academic behavior. In an exhaustive investigation of the existing published peer-reviewed literature, Mitchell, Stormont, and Gage (in press) reviewed research that has been conducted using Tier 2 social behavior interventions within the context of a three-tiered prevention model, such as PBIS. The 13 articles that met inclusionary criteria included different strategies for identifying children who needed Tier 2 interventions. Students were identified through three main methods: nomination, student data, and behavioral screening. In the research student referrals for Tier 2 interventions have included (1) teacher nomination based on a perception of the need for more support (Campbell & Anderson, 2007; McIntosh, Campbell, Russell-Carter, & Dickey, 2009), (2) increased classroom behavior problems (Fairbanks, Sugai, Guardino, 2007), and/or (3) the existence of a behavioral support plan (McCurdy, Kunsch, & Reibstein, 2007). Administrator nomination has also been used as one part of the identification process.

The most commonly used student data to identify students who need Tier 2 behavioral interventions are ODRs. Researchers have used different numbers of ODRs as criteria for participation; two ODRs were used in one study, whereas another study used five. Other researchers have also considered the number of ODRs within a time frame (e.g., one or more within the first 4 months of school). However, it is important to note that the use of ODR data alone has not been common in the research in this area. Typically researchers have used a combination of student behavioral and academic data and perceptions of need according to teachers, administrators, or behavioral support teams. In 3 of the 13 studies, a behavioral screening instrument was utilized to identify students in need of Tier 2 interventions. Two studies used the Social Skills Rating Scale (SSRS; Gresham & Elliot, 1990) and one study used the Systematic Screening for Behavior Disorders (SSBD; Walker & Severson, 1992). Research methodologies have varied in terms of who is screened and when, with some using the criteria that students are screened after schoolwide prevention efforts are in place, whereas others recommend screening all students as part of the implementation of schoolwide prevention efforts. One of the benefits for using the schoolwide

> **Which children need Tier 2 supports? Who they represent in a given school will vary in relation to school professionals' decision rules for identifying who is struggling and how much or how long students struggle before they are provided with more resources.**

behavioral screening is that students who have internalizing problems can also be referred for more support. Another benefit of screening all students is that some of the research in this area has used subjective criteria for inclusion (e.g., teacher perception of increasing problems) and behavioral screening instruments that have been standardized provide more objective data that can be used for decision making. Chapters 3 and 4 more thoroughly discuss measures and methods that can be used to screen for children with externalizing and internalizing problems. Chapters 3, 4, 5, and 6 also include data and processes that can be implemented for progress monitoring and for determining students who need more intensive Tier 3 supports. Forms 1.3, 1.4, and 1.5 (in the Appendix) include sample nomination and referral forms and cumulative record reviews that teams can use.

TIER 2 RESOURCES

Just as schools must be committed to providing universal supports if they are to be effective, they must also be committed to ensuring the success of Tier 2 efforts. A Tier 2 team consisting of individuals with expertise in working with students at risk for academic and social behavior failure should be established to support efforts. The team should be charged with determining Tier 2 readiness, as described earlier in this chapter, as well as selecting the specific assessment tools and interventions to be used.

The Tier 2 team members should ensure that communication with staff is open, and they should promote buy-in by soliciting feedback from staff on proposed data collection methods and interventions. The team should also make sure that home–school communication is firmly set in place and it should determine specific interventions and practices that may or may not fit with the culture of any given school (Crone, Hawken, & Horner, 2010). It is important that the administration support this team by providing the time and resources needed for its success. Depending on the team's composition, some team members may need to receive additional training in specific interventions. This training may be available through professional development opportunities at local universities, webinars, or state or national workshops. The team may want to self-assess its school regarding the specific needs presented in this section and to develop action plans to determine appropriate starting points (McIntosh, Bohanon, & Goodman, 2010; see Form 1.6 [in the Appendix] for an example).

> **Just as schools must be committed to providing universal supports if they are to be effective, they must also be committed to ensuring the success of Tier 2 efforts.**

TIER 2 SUPPORTS AND PROGRESS MONITORING

Too often in schools today, children are not provided with an appropriate intervention, and many times this is because educators don't know what their options are and/or how to determine which children need what type of intervention. Another potential barrier for implementing effective Tier 2 practices is that some educators may not believe that specific roles fit with their current job responsibilities. We recently conducted two surveys of special and general educators related to supporting children with emotional, behavioral, and social needs (Reinke, Stormont, Herman, Puri, & Goel, 2011; Stormont, Reinke, & Herman, 2011; Stormont, Reinke, & Herman, in press). Some relevant findings include the following:

- Forty-five percent of educators reported that they had not heard of the term *evidence-based practices.*
- Only 43% of educators agreed or strongly agreed with the statement *I am confident that the interventions/practices I use have the desired impact on students.*
- Both RTI and PBIS require that classroom teachers systematically collect data to inform instruction and needs for support. However, teachers reported they thought it was more the role of school psychologists than teachers to conduct behavioral assessments.
- Special educators were more likely than general educators to agree that evidence-based social behavior practices were indeed evidence-based; general educators were more likely than special educators to agree that non-evidence-based behavioral practices were evidence-based.
- Of 10 evidence-based programs used to support improvement in social behavior, only PBIS was acknowledged as an evidence-based program by the majority of teachers.

TIER 2 PLANS

It is also recommended that children who need Tier 2 interventions receive support plans to guide systematic planning based on their needs and progress monitoring data. Such a plan would include:

- Identification of specific needs for support
- Identification of a target intervention or interventions
- Identification of the data to be utilized for progress monitoring
- Determination of who is in charge of data collection
- Scheduling of meetings to monitor progress
- Frequent ways of supporting home–school communication
- Determination of additional needs for support

A sample completed plan is provided in Figure 1.4. A reproducible blank plan is available in Form 1.7 in the Appendix. The sample plan includes examples of evidence-based practices and programs as well as appropriate progress monitoring mechanisms (discussed in this book). It is vital that this level of depth and clarity in intervention planning and progress monitoring is achieved with Tier 2 children if optimal results are to be obtained. Tier 2 children have been selected because of their need for extra supports that are not provided to everyone. At the Tier 2 level, a small number of supports and interventions are typically

Student: <u>Jackson Miller</u>

Support needs	Interventions currently in place in school	Person responsible	Data to monitor progress
Literacy—needs extra support for identifying rhyming words, letter naming, and naming the first sounds when a word is spoken aloud	Intervention time 30 minutes daily in a small-group setting using the peer-assisted learning strategies program	General education teacher	Individual growth and development indicators (IGDIs) to include rhyming, alliteration, and picture naming given weekly for 1 minute each
Attention—has attention problems and thrives on adult attention	Check-in/Check-out	Counselor	Meets 80% of behavior goals, 4 weeks
Anger management—difficulty thinking about other choices besides verbal aggression (when upset, yells, screams); this has improved but may be an issue especially with more children, more structure, and more challenging work	Small social skills group Visual reminder	School psychologist	Direct observation data and teacher ratings
Impulse control—blurts out answers during large group	Use prompts and cues, proximity, and immediate reward (sticker) every day child meets a specific goal	Teacher	Direct observation data; number of days child meets goal
Home–school communication—increase communication to family about progress	Family preference is e-mail	Counselor	One summary of progress every week

(cont.)

FIGURE 1.4. Tier 2 support plan.

Notes:

Data management system: The school psychologist will create an Excel spreadsheet to keep track of all data to monitor progress. Each support need will have a column and the data collected will be given to the school psychologist on a weekly basis.

Meeting for progress review: Monthly

Discuss any family support needs: Mother is in between jobs and struggling with some health issues. The school counselor will email the progress report once a week and also offer support in terms of resources available in the community. Counselor will also phone before monthly meetings to determine if there are any barriers for participation and will determine ways to help overcome barriers (e.g., child-care, need for voucher for transportation).

FIGURE 1.4. *(cont.)*

> It is recommended that children who need Tier 2 interventions receive support plans to guide systematic planning based on their needs and progress monitoring data.

chosen to allow for greater integrity of implementation. Interventions can be delivered to small groups or to individuals with similar needs in a one-on-one setting. Although interventions can be delivered to individuals, they are not as highly individualized as are Tier 3 supports. The interventions are often scripted, and research has supported their effectiveness for students with specific characteristics (Hawken, Pettersson, Mootz, & Henderson, 2009; McIntosh et al., 2011). When supports require extensive individualization, time, resources, and expertise to implement, they are typically considered to be Tier 3 supports (Stecker, 2007).

SUMMARY

This chapter provided an overview of the reasons that universal supports need to be in place if we are to effectively identify students in need of Tier 2 supports. Tiered prevention models for academics (RTI) and for social behaviors (PBIS) were reviewed as well as how to determine if the universal systems for each model are in place. Recognizing the need to monitor the progress of student outcomes as well as to monitor the integrity of implementation of interventions is necessary to ensure effectiveness and for determining when to modify, fade, or intensify supports. This chapter highlights these important issues to ensure that schools can create teams that effectively identify and intervene with students in need of Tier 2 academic and behavioral supports. Chapter 2 provides an ecological context for providing Tier 2 supports and Chapters 3–6 present specific evidence-based practices and interventions that can be used as Tier 2 supports for students with externalizing problems, internalizing problems, and reading and math deficits. The book concludes with a chapter on determining when children may need Tier 3 supports.

The Ecological Context
of Tier 2 Supports

Much attention has been given to the contextual fit of interventions in RTI models. *Contextual fit* refers to how well an intervention matches the setting in which it occurs. In particular, Benazzi, Horner, and Good (2002) define it as "the extent to which the behavior support plan reflects the values, skills, resources, and administrative support of the school personnel" (p. 168). As shown by this definition, the focus is often on how the intervention matches the contextual features within the school environment. Much less has been written about the match between interventions and other contextual features of the community or of the sociodemographic characteristics of the children and staff within the building. In this chapter, we consider two sometimes neglected elements of contextual fit: the cultural responsiveness of the intervention and the involvement of the student's family in the intervention plan. Attention to these elements is needed if school support teams are to reach the goal of being truly culturally responsive.

CREATING CULTURALLY RESPONSIVE TIER 2 SUPPORTS

The growing diversity of students and staff in the nation's schools requires that behavior support teams be mindful of the cultural context of their interventions. Culturally and linguistically diverse (CLD) students continue to be overrepresented in special education (Artiles & Trent, 1994; Coutinho & Oswald, 2000; Skiba et al., 2008). These students are also disproportionate recipients of school disciplinary practices such as ODRs and suspensions (Bradshaw et al., 2010; Krezmien, Leone, & Achilles, 2006; Skiba, Michael, Nardo, & Peterson, 2002). Despite concern about these problems over the past decade, little progress has been made in reducing the disparities.

Some have suggested ways that RTI models could be part of the solution to reduce the disproportionality problem (National Center for Culturally Responsive Education Systems, 2005). A basic premise of a schoolwide tiered approach is that effective behavior and academic supports must reflect sensitivity to the contextual fit of all interventions. Given that RTI approaches, like PBIS, are not rigid curricula, they allow for the flexible development of effective supports to match child

> **The growing diversity of students and staff in the nation's schools requires that behavior support teams be mindful of the cultural context of their interventions.**

and school needs and contexts. Moreover, RTI approaches emphasize data-based decision making, which is key for improving outcomes for all students.

The flexibility of RTI models can be a strength when it comes to cultural adaptation efforts. However, it is no guarantee that school behavior and academic support teams will, in fact, be attentive to the cultural context of their students and families. Consider that ODRs are a primary tool for determining responsiveness to intervention in PBIS models, and research has shown that children of color are most likely to receive them. Without attention to these disparities by actually disaggregating data by culture variables, as recommended by Skiba et al. (2002), well-intentioned school teams may inadvertently perpetuate the disparity problem.

Elements of Cultural Responsiveness

The National Center for Culturally Responsive Educational Systems (NCCRESt, 2011) defines cultural responsiveness as the "valuation, consideration, and integration of individual's culture, language, heritage, and experiences leading to supported learning and development." A guiding assumption of the NCCRESt framework is that the current focus on "the student's response to intervention or interventions shift to an emphasis on the importance of the interventions as responsive to the child" (Harris-Murri, King, & Rostenberg, 2006, p. 9). Culturally responsive educators design instruction and interventions to match their students' life experiences (Boesch, 1996; Ladson-Billings, 1992). Culture intersects with all subsystems within a school: schoolwide, classrooms, students. Within each subsystem, at least three aspects of culture interact: the cultural qualities that all participants bring with them into the setting, the aspects of culture that are depicted in the setting (e.g., the structure, artwork, language, signs that appear in each setting), and the work and interactions that take place in the setting.

Academic and behavior support teams are likely to create culturally responsive supports only to the extent that each of its members is culturally competent; in other words, they are able to interact successfully with persons from cultural backgrounds that differ

from their own. In turn, cultural competence is largely defined by intrapersonal aspects of culturalism. Common elements of cultural competence include awareness, attitudes/beliefs, knowledge, and skills to interact in culturally competent ways (Vasquez, 2010). A prerequisite of cultural competence is the ability of participants to self-reflect and to

> **Academic and behavior support teams are likely to create culturally responsive supports only to the extent that each of their members is culturally competent—that is, able to interact successfully with persons from cultural backgrounds that differ from their own.**

monitor their own beliefs and biases before they can make progress in learning about other cultures and developing skills in interacting with them. Vasquez refers to this awareness and appreciation of cultural diversity as *cultural sensitivity*. Fundamental to cultural sensitivity is perspective taking. Knowledge about diversity and the cultural practices of other groups is also helpful, but it is insufficient for full competence. Knowledge without self-awareness can be misapplied, as when school staff members overgeneralize cultural group characteristics and use them to guide their understanding of all people from that cultural group. Thus, a process model of competence is emphasized, not a static content knowledge of cultures (Whaley & King, 2008).

Cultural skills are those interpersonal skills that allow a person to comfortably communicate cultural beliefs and misunderstandings in ways that leave others feeling respected and understood. One key aspect of cultural skills is cultural empathy, which is the ability to convey an emotional connection to others (Vasquez, 2010). A related skill, described by Tseng and Streltzer (2004), is cultural guidance, which involves assessing cultural factors

> **Knowledge without self-awareness can be misapplied as when school staff overgeneralize cultural group characteristics and use them to guide their understanding of all people from that cultural group.**

that may be part of the problem and creating interventions sensitive to these factors. Thus, culturally responsive schools are defined by the presence of a high number of culturally competent and sensitive school personnel who value, consider, and integrate cultural variations to support student learning and development.

Methods for Assessing Culturally Responsive Schools

Much like the tiered approach to providing effective supports to students, schools and districts can approach their cultural responsivity by considering how attentive each tier is to providing a welcoming cultural context for all students and staff. Several tools have been developed to assist in this process.

The NCCRESt (2005) created an online tool for districts to use to self-evaluate their special education referral systems. This tool divides the cultural responsiveness of schools into five domains: (1) school governance, organization, policy, and climate; (2) family involvement; (3) curriculum; (4) organization of learning; and (5) special education policies and procedures. Within each domain the items guide areas for improvement. The tools are available at *www.nccrest.org/publications/tools/assessment.html*. In addition, the center has a variety of tools, presentations, and trainings to help guide schools in addressing any deficiencies that their self-assessment identifies (see *www.nccrest.org*).

An additional resource to support district-level self-reflection and evaluation of diversity issues is offered by the Center for Multicultural Education at the University of Washington. Their *Diversity Through Unity* guidebook (*education.washington.edu/cme/DiversityUnity.pdf*) concludes with an Essential Principles Checklist to help school personnel self-assess how well their building is attending to diversity issues. The authors of this guidebook identify 12 principles of diversity, divided into five categories: (1) teacher learning; (2) student learning; (3) intergroup relations; (4) school governance, organization, and equity; and (5) assessment. Through self-assessment and team discussion this tool can help school and district personnel reflect on the strengths of their current diversity efforts as well as pinpoint areas for continued refinement and growth.

> **Much like the tiered approach to providing effective supports to students, schools and districts can approach their cultural responsivity by considering how attentive each tier is to providing a welcoming cultural context for all students and staff.**

One final brief tool tailored to behavior support teams that may be of help is the Rubric for Examining Cultural Responsiveness of Academic and Behavior Support Teams (see Form 2.1 in the Appendix). The rubric asks team members, either collectively or individually, to consider how well they address four domains of cultural responsiveness when they design interventions: understanding the cultural context, awareness of personal assumptions, ongoing collaboration, and specific cultural adaptations. Results can guide group discussions about improving attention to each of these domains.

Methods for Building Cultural Competence of Academic and Behavior Support Teams

Building a culturally responsive RTI or PBIS system begins with self-reflection and assessment. Individual members of a behavior support team, and ideally all school personnel, can reflect on their own cultural sensitivity, knowledge, empathy, and skills. Additionally, assessment of the cultural responsiveness of individuals and systems within a district and school is needed to identify strengths and areas of growth. The tools described above provide a useful framework for conducting these assessments.

Particular areas of consideration for evaluating, assessing, and improving responsiveness are the systems for identifying and placing children in special education (Harris-Murri et al., 2006). When properly used, a problem-solving model, inherent in most RTI models, includes many of the critical elements of cultural responsiveness defined above. Problem-solving models emphasize gaining an ecological understanding of the problem through systematic assessment across settings and systems. As such effective teams that use problem-solving models do not operate from a within child-deficit perspective. Rather the assumption is that problematic academic or social behaviors arise in response to an interaction between the child and various systems. For instance, a first step in a problem-solving model, after identifying a child who might benefit from additional academic support, is to examine the current instructional context to determine strengths and weaknesses of the classroom that may be contributing to the problem.

Sometimes missing from these ecological assessments, however, is the cultural sensitivity of instructional content, the classroom environment, and the cultural context of the student's home life. For instance, rarely do support teams examine cultural aspects of pedagogy that may be related to children's academic and behavior problems, such as institutional policies and values; personal cognitive and emotional processes communicated by teachers and staff to students; and the cultural appropriateness of instructional materials, strategies, and activities (Richards, Brown, & Forde, 2007). Thus, an important step for even well-functioning support teams is to be sure that these aspects of culture are regularly considered when assessing and creating intervention supports for students.

Finally, a critical area for improvement in the cultural responsiveness of interventions is professional development, particularly training teachers and support personnel in culturally responsive classroom practices. Hershfeldt et al. (2009) proposed a model of cultural proficiency called "Double Check," which emphasizes culturally proficient teaching and classroom management. This model dovetails with SW-PBIS and features the following core elements: (1) reflective thinking about children and their "group" membership, (2) effective communication, (3) authentic relationships, (4) connection to curriculum, and (5) sensitivity to students' cultural and situational messages. The Double Check model served as the framework for the creation of a professional development series, which is a core element of the program. Professional development seminars to promote cultural competence among school staff should include each of these five domains.

> **An important step for even well-functioning support teams is to be sure that these aspects of culture are regularly considered when assessing and creating intervention supports for students.**

STRATEGIES FOR WORKING WITH FAMILIES OF CHILDREN AT RISK FOR FAILURE

A particularly important aspect of children's cultural environment is their family. Understandably, because RTI models were developed in schools with the priority of improving educational outcomes for youth, most interventions within these models focus on the school environment. However, abundant literature makes clear that family involvement in education and in support plans is critical for intervention success. The remainder of the chapter focuses on the current challenges faced by families and ways for school support teams to maximize family involvement.

Overview of Family Involvement in Support Plans

Today many families are struggling to meet their most basic needs. Families of children who are at risk for failure tend to struggle even more than other families (Stormont, 2007; Turnbull, Turnbull, Shank, Smith, & Leal, 2006). As educators, it is critical to remember that education is only *one of the needs* families are trying to meet for their children, and they may need to juggle other responsibilities in order to become more involved in their children's education (Stormont, 2007; Turnbull, Turnbull, Shank, et al., 2006). Through building positive relationships with families, professionals can help support greater involvement in their children's education in ways that fit with current family needs and challenges (Esler, Godber, & Christenson, 2002; Swick, 1995). It is clear that when families are involved in their children's education, children do better in the short and long term (Dearing, Kreider, Simpkins, & Weiss, 2006; Hill & Craft, 2003; International Reading Association, 2002; O'Donnell, Schwab-Stone, & Muyeed, 2002). Research also shows the following:

- As children get older, families tend to be less involved in their education (Epstein, 1995). However, providing positive experiences early on may help sustain involvement.

- Exploring characteristics that influence involvement in children's education is important for outreach efforts. Parents' educational level and family form (two-parent vs. single-parent) are associated with the amount and type of family involvement (Fantuzzo, Tighe, & Childs, 2000). This does not mean that parents with lower educational levels or single-parent families care less about their children's education; rather it is likely that they have more barriers to becoming more involved and/or sustaining involvement.

- Research indeed supports the premise that families of children from low-income backgrounds have more barriers to becoming involved in school when compared to families of children from middle to high income backgrounds. Professionals need to make extra, and sometimes different, efforts to increase low-income families' school involvement (Epstein, 1995; Turnbull, Turnbull, Erwin, & Soodak, 2006).

- Barriers to involvement include parenting stress, work responsibilities, daily household management tasks, and stress related to meeting basic needs (McWayne, Hampton, Fantuzzo, Cohen, & Sekino, 2004). Even when two parents are active in a child's life, increasingly both parents are working; research shows that the parents of 60% of preschool-age children and 70% of school-age children are in the labor force (Children's Defense Fund, 2008).

- Again, it is important to remember that education is only one of the areas that families are trying to address. When finances are stretched, families may be spending more and more time trying to ensure sufficient food and shelter for all members.

- Homelessness is an increasing concern for low-income families. One predictor of homelessness for female-headed households is lack of support. Staying in school is a buffer for children living in homeless circumstances (Stormont and McCathren, 2008).

- Families and children have greater access to resources to help them meet their needs if children are attending school and if school personnel are knowledgeable about families' needs and the supports available in the school and the community. This chapter includes strategies for partnering with families and increasing their access to community resources.

- Focused interventions that target increasing family involvement in school have been shown to be effective (e.g., Kaminski, Stormshak, Good, & Goodman, 2002). Accordingly, the end of this chapter includes a systematic step-by-step process for increasing family involvement.

- Family involvement in school predicts reading achievement for children of mothers with either low or high education levels. In fact, the children of mothers with low education levels who were involved in their children's education did not differ in reading achievement from children of mothers with higher education levels (Dearing et al., 2006).

For children who are at risk, fostering collaborative relationships with their families is a critical need if ultimate success in school and in life is to be achieved. Experts in the field of educational collaboration and parent involvement highlight specific opportunities for partnerships with families and specific practices to use when establishing and maintaining those partnerships (Epstein, 1995; Turnbull et al., 2006).

Essential Partnership-Building Practices

Within the context of the specific opportunities that are discussed later in this chapter, the following practices are considered essential in forming and sustaining collaborative relationships with families (Epstein, 1995; Esler et al., 2002; Ortiz & Flanagan, 2002; Overton, 2005; Stormont, 2007; Turnbull et al., 2006): knowing families and honoring cultural diversity, communicating positively, and demonstrating commitment and competence. *These practices are important to remember when implementing interventions with family components* to support children with specific problems (e.g., externalizing behavior). Through use of these practices, trust can be established, which is a key element to sustainable positive relationships (Fish, 2002; Ortiz & Flanagan, 2002).

Knowing Families and Honoring Cultural Diversity

A good definition of family is "two or more people who regard themselves as a family and who carry out the functions that families typically perform" (Turnbull et al., 2006, p. 7). Accordingly, if professionals understand who is part of a student's family, then they can work to involve those family members in different capacities. For example, almost 6 million grandparents are living in households with one or more grandchildren; 42% of those grandparents are serving as the primary caregiver (U.S. Census, 2000). In other cases an aunt and older cousins may be available to help with children's homework in the evening or on the weekend while their parent is working. It is also important to understand cultural perspectives and how these influence views and beliefs related to education. Often, families' cultural perspectives do not align with those of the schools', and this difference can create a barrier to collaboration if educators don't understand different cultural perspectives (Derman-Sparks, 2003; Kea, Campbell-Whatley, & Richards, 2004; Turnbull et al., 2006; Weinstein & Mignano, 2003).

Finally, *knowing families* also means that professionals understand unique or special challenges through which families could be going. In the case example of David, in Figure 2.1, the lack of knowledge of a family's circumstances creates more stress for this family. If David's teacher understood his current home situation, however, she may be more understanding of his behavior and more supportive of his emotional needs during an uncertain time. The negative notes home and reactive stance (without proactive supports) will likely exacerbate his behavior in both home and school settings.

Communicating Positively

Ask parents how often a school professional has contacted them unexpectedly with positive information about their child. The majority will likely say never or not very often. It is vital that professionals make a point to communicate more positive information than negative information about a child and that they keep information on their number of contacts with families to monitor communication. This is especially important for families of children at risk who may not have had many positive contacts with school professionals. Fortunately,

Little David entered school with his backpack on his back and a lot on his mind. His kindergarten teacher noticed he was slow to put his things in his locker and line up against the wall. David accidently bumped into a little girl, who then shouted at him. He snapped out of his fog and pushed her, which caused her to fall. His teacher reprimanded him and immediately sent him to the office. The morning bell hadn't even rung and his day was pretty much over.

David went home with a note regarding his behavior. He gave it to his grandmother, who sighed and said, "Well, your mom won't like this." His grandmother sent him to the bedroom he was currently sharing with his three cousins to do his homework and think about his behavior at school. He hadn't been home for 5 minutes and his evening was pretty much over.

David's mother, Brittany, is currently working two jobs to try to save enough money to move them into a two-bedroom apartment. They lost their low-income housing and became homeless because Brittany made too much money. She is currently living in a small house with her elderly mother, her sister and brother-in-law, and their three children. When she gets negative notes about David, it is very stressful for both of them. David misses having his own room and is worried about his mother because she is so worried and tired all the time. David's teacher, Mrs. Smith, knows nothing about his current living situation but is worried about his increased behavior problems. Mrs. Smith has asked to meet with the school psychologist to discuss a possible referral for evaluation for special education and related services. David's risk for continuing to have behavior problems would be greatly reduced if his family and his teacher had a positive relationship.

FIGURE 2.1. Fostering resilience through knowing families.

with an increased emphasis on schoolwide approaches to support appropriate behavior and higher achievement, these contacts are more likely to happen. When positive home communication is tied to universal practices and specific intervention plans, children do better than when no home connection is made. For example, in a meta-analysis of home–school collaboration interventions, Cox (2005) determined that the most effective interventions were those on which parents and school personnel worked together to implement an intervention and had ongoing communication. Furthermore, when families feel they are treated as equals in implementing interventions for their children, they may feel empowered to help their children be more successful, *and* they feel more comfortable participating in their children's education in the future (Cox, 2005).

Additional specific practices educators can use to demonstrate positive and respectful communication with families include the following (Berger, 2000; Esler et al., 2002; Stormont, 2007; Swick, 1995; Turnbull et al., 2006):

- Share some personal information with families. Often we expect families to open up and provide personal information when they know nothing about the people with whom they are meeting. Appropriate personal information could include, for example, number and ages of children and reasons for becoming a teacher or educator. Figure 2.2 provides an example of one father's experience of feeling personally connected to a teacher after a "Meet the Teacher" group activity.
- Determine family preferences for amount of communication (daily, weekly, etc.) and type of communication (e-mail, phone, brief conversation in person when student is picked up) and try to respect these preferences.

My husband was a single father raising three children when we were dating. He called one night after a parent open house at the beginning of the year. He told me he was very impressed with his son's teacher. I asked him to be more specific because he is not very easily impressed. He said the parents were seated, uncomfortably, at their children's desks, and the teacher introduced herself and added some personal details. She discussed why she originally wanted to be a teacher, what she learned on her journey teaching older children, and why she returned to teaching younger children. In only 15 minutes, she was able to reach my husband, in a group setting, no less, by being personal. My husband felt she was approachable and committed to her job. He said he not only felt that his son was in good hands but that he could go to this teacher if he needed anything. That peace of mind was a big deal, given that he was juggling a lot of family needs at the time.

—Melissa Stormont

FIGURE 2.2. Building trust through sharing.

- Hold informal gatherings that families can attend and interact with educators and other families, and educators can share successes and gather information.
- Ensure access to interpreters when needed.
- Be friendly, honest, and use jargon-free language.

Overall, through effective and positive communication with families, educators can build trusting relationships (Adams & Christenson, 2000). When there is trust in a relationship, children's needs are much more likely to be met because everyone is working toward a common goal and negativity does not permeate interactions.

Demonstrating Commitment and Competence

When communicating respectfully and positively with families, it is important for professionals to also demonstrate their competence and commitment to the children they share. The following strategies can be used to demonstrate commitment and competence (Barbour, Barbour, & Scully, et al., 2005; Fish, 2002; Landsverk, 1995; Resnick & Hall, 1996; Riley, 1994; Stormont, 2007; Turnbull et al., 2006):

- Be persistent in communication attempts. If a family member does not respond to one attempt, ensure that the mode of communication used is indeed the preferred method. A note home indicating interest in communicating about something specific (e.g., current behavior plan, need for more math practice at home) and good times to return calls (with the desired phone number listed) may also help support communication.
- Explore solutions to involvement barriers for specific groups of parents and work to overcome these barriers and increase involvement.
- For presentations that families cannot attend, create another way for them to access the presentation (e.g., CD-ROM, video) and make sure that they have the required technology.
- Be a good problem solver. The first thing that is important for problem solving and addressing issues is to define the problem. Often professionals and families differ on their

perspectives regarding what constitutes a problem. Family members will be more likely to feel commitment from a professional who takes the time to first explain problems objectively, and then moves toward creating a plan to resolve problems.

> **When there is trust in a relationship, children's needs are much more likely to be met because everyone is working toward a common goal and negativity does not permeate interactions.**

- Be committed to solutions that *feel* right. If families or teachers are struggling to come up with a plan that feels right at home or at school, it is important to state that brainstorming should continue until a plan is reached that everyone feels is appropriate.
- Think outside the box. Exploring ways in which other professionals have resolved problems or met the needs of children and families in similar situations is important to support thinking outside the box.
- Be a lifelong learner and share current opportunities in the community and additional activities with families. It is impossible for professionals to know everything; however, it is appropriate to have a disposition that embraces lifelong learning. This is this something that can be modeled for children and families. For example, professionals can say, "I don't know, but I will try to find out." When professionals do this, it is important to remember to write down the names of individuals and dates indicating that they told someone they would look into something. This needs to stay in an "inbox" until information is obtained. Every week or few weeks, a follow-up contact with families is appropriate to let them know the status of information-gathering attempts.
- Demonstrate a willingness to be open to feedback from families. Many families do not feel heard in professional settings. Accordingly, it is important to not only demonstrate willingness to receive feedback but to also solicit feedback.

Opportunities for Partnership

The opportunities for family involvement with schools that are presented in this chapter include sharing information and resources to support parenting and learning at home, volunteering, decision making, and tapping community agencies and resources (Epstein, 1995). Resch et al. (2010) found that parents of children with disabilities did not feel they had established partnerships with educators and did not feel supported as parents or included in their schools or communities. Families of children who are at risk may also feel disconnected and unsupported (Stormont, 2007). Thus, for children at risk, collaboration with families through specific opportunities for involvement is critical. Each of these opportunities is discussed further in the following sections.

Support for Parenting and Learning at Home

When compared to children who aren't at risk for behavior and academic problems, children at risk tend to have more frequent challenges related to their daily care (e.g., parenting). When educators build relationships with families, they are more likely to be able to influence children's home-learning context and support family members' use of effective parenting practices. Many parents are doing the best they can with the resources they possess. Educators can vastly influence the amount and type of support parents provide their children at home.

As stated previously, it is important for educators to understand who is part of the family and available to provide support for learning at home. Parents should focus their efforts on fostering positive conditions at home to support learning (Ingram, Wolfe, & Lieberman, 2007). Teachers can provide guidance and support for family members to assist children at home with homework assignments and other school-related learning activities (Ingram et al., 2007). Teachers can include checklists that have very clear instructions that can be used to help support completion of homework assignments. To help support family members who are working with children on their homework, educators could also use electronic guidelines on a class webpage, a homework line, or tape-recorded instructions.

It is also important to help families find a fit between homework and their busy lives. A few minutes after dinner to read a book and complete some problems together may be the best time. In other cases, integrating more homework into the weekend may be easier for families to accomplish if key family members work two jobs during the week. It is equally important to try to include school activities within the context of families' existing routines. Especially for young children, early literacy and math activities are easy to integrate into family routines such as grocery shopping, banking, shopping for clothes, cooking together, etc. See Form 2.2 in the Appendix for an example of a family homework survey.

For behavioral support, families may need more structured homework assignments. For children with Tier 2 behavior support plans, it is vital that families understand specifically what is being worked on in the school setting and how they can support the same behavior in other settings (see Form 2.3 in the Appendix and Figure 2.3 for examples).

Support for Volunteering

Families can learn strategies that work well in school settings that could also enhance learning at home by volunteering at school. It is important to have flexible times for families to visit school. Some families can't make lunch or specific party times, but perhaps they have time to come and help with afternoon snack or morning reading time. It is also essential to have a variety of ways in which families can be involved. Some families may not be able to attend class activities, but perhaps they could cook for a party or volunteer to make something with their child to bring to the party. Form 2.4 in the Appendix includes different involvement options from which families can choose.

Support for Decision Making

Families are often called to come into the school setting and help solve school-based problems. As such, families may need educators to help them understand the specifics related to the type and extent of the problem, and this context can then help them make decisions. To provide this context, educators should collect and use data to help describe the problem. This data-oriented approach to decision making can then be continued when families and professionals are monitoring the effectiveness of strategies. Family members may want to

---

Dear family of **Shania**

Your child is working on: **Keeping hands to self**

The specific behaviors related to this skill include:

- Understanding personal boundaries
- Knowing appropriate places to keep her hands (by sides, in pockets, crossed arms with hands under armpits, on top of head)
- Staying respectful of other individuals and their belongings
- Politely asking permission to share or borrow another's materials or supplies

Please work on this skill when you are in a location, such as a store, where you want your child to keep her hands to herself (i.e., not touching sale items, other individuals).

At school, I do the following when working with your child:
- **Remind** her of what she should do—see above.
- **Watch** her behavior.
- **Remind** her of what she should be doing if she makes a mistake.
- **Praise** her when she uses the skill correctly!
- **Understand** that this is something that requires teaching and support, just like academic subjects.

FIGURE 2.3. Homework for social behavior: Shania.

observe their child in the specific settings in which they are struggling to help them understand both the behavior problem and potential supports that may work for their child. Video or audio recording, if schools allow it, is another potential way to provide families with information on their child's behavior.

Decision making should also include a commitment to honor family preferences and should be conducted in an atmosphere that supports parity in relationships with families. Families should not feel rushed to make a decision, and educators need to be sensitive to communication from families before, during, or after decisions are made that indicates discomfort with the process and/or decisions. It may be helpful if professionals do the following for families when partnering for decision making:

- Preview what decisions are going to be made.
- Indicate what information will be reviewed to support decision making.
- Review who will be present.
- Determine if families would like additional information or people to aid in decision making.
- Determine if families are comfortable with decisions.
- Determine if educators are comfortable with decisions. For example, perhaps a family member does not want a specific consequence or intervention to be used with his or her child but the teacher does not know what to do instead.
- Set a follow-up date for determining or reviewing decisions (depending on preferences and whether an initial decision was made).

> Decision making should also include a commitment to honoring family preferences and should be conducted in an atmosphere that supports parity in relationships with families.

Support for Accessing Community Resources and Agencies

Families of children at risk need access to more community (and state and national) resources than families of children without risk; often they require resources related to meeting their more basic needs (Fowler & Corley, 1996; Turnbull et al., 2006). Schools can provide resources to assist families in obtaining health, nutrition, employment, and adult education services, and they can act as liaisons to community resources (e.g., libraries, museums, zoos) whereby parents can help their children learn outside of school (Ingram et al., 2007). Table 2.1 lists potential community resources.

TABLE 2.1. Community Resources Available to Meet Families' Needs

Family need	Community resources
Economics	Family assistance programs Local charities Civic organizations Salvation Army Public housing authority Special utility fund Social Security office Local food bank
Health care	Local public health center Medicaid/Medicare Free or reduced-cost care Children's Health Insurance Program (CHIP) Dental care support
Continuing education	Local community colleges Federal student financial aid High schools with daycare services available Online support through the local public library Adult literacy classes
Employment	Temporary employment agencies Community job counselors Online job search websites Paid internships Local job fairs and career fairs Public library assistance for accessing information on jobs School postings for employment opportunities
Parenting stress	Local crisis centers for children and families Stress management techniques Student–parent center within university/college setting Parent support group Local parents' day- or night-out programs offering free respite Easter Seals—childcare at free or reduced cost

Systematic and Focused Efforts

It is also important to be systematic about increasing family involvement (Epstein, 1995; Kaminski et al., 2002). Prior to the implementation of specific strategies, it is vital that professionals think about where they are currently and what their vision is for increasing family involvement (Epstein, 1995). Figure 2.4 illustrates a process for increasing family involvement in a systematic fashion. Districts, individual schools, a team of educators within a school, or individual teachers can use this framework.

1. Determine a vision for increasing family involvement, including types of families that may be specifically targeted. For example, schools may feel they have a specific group that is not very involved, such as grandparents, fathers, single parents, or foster parents.
2. Determine a baseline—that is, where the school is currently. Teachers could complete surveys or checklists to collect data on how frequently they communicate with specific types of families.
3. Set goals for the year based on the discrepancy between points 1 and 2. The

> **It is also important to be systematic about increasing family involvement.**

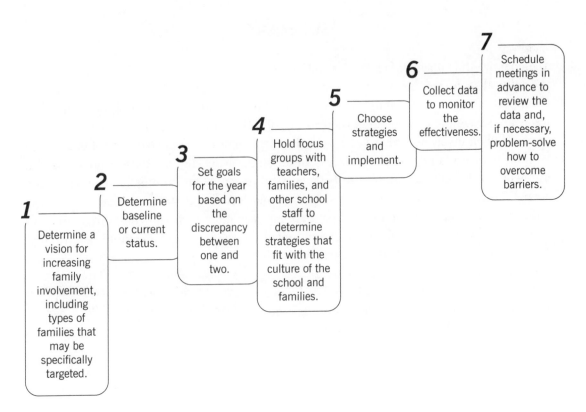

FIGURE 2.8. A seven-step framework to guide the process of targeting and working to increase family involvement.

goals should be based on social validity data, including what teachers feel they can accomplish.

4. Conduct focus groups with teachers, families, and other school staff to determine strategies that fit with the culture of the school and its families. Strategies can include a combination of specific practices from this chapter or from other sources.

5. Choose strategies and implement. Some examples from this chapter include increasing positive communication with families, developing family-centered events to increase involvement, and accounting for and overcoming barriers to involvement.

6. Collect data to monitor the effectiveness of strategies. Examples of data that could be collected include number of contacts before–after strategies are implemented, percentage of families who attended events that are planned in a different way, and families' satisfaction with amount and type of school communication. It is important to make this information public so that families and professionals can see the progress made in specific areas.

7. Schedule meetings in advance (i.e., already on the calendar) to review the data and, if necessary, problem-solve how to overcome barriers. Include families from diverse backgrounds to help in the problem-solving process and to add their unique perspectives to ways involvement can be increased.

SUMMARY

To maximize the impact of Tier 2 interventions, school support teams need to be attentive to the cultural context of their interventions. Moreover, intervention effects will be maximized if support teams involve families every step of the way. However, because many families today are struggling to meet all of their responsibilities, often there are barriers that interfere with their involvement in school. School professionals need to make extra efforts to find ways to increase family involvement for all children, especially for those who are at risk and who will need more support to be successful in school and ultimately complete high school. Through building partnerships, families and schools can work together and support children in an abundant number of ways. Perhaps the most profound commitment schools can make to students is to show understanding of their culture and a commitment to their families—to those individuals who will be with them much longer than any one teacher or school. "The ways schools care about children is reflected in the way schools care about the children's families" (Epstein, 1995, p. 1).

> Intervention effects will be maximized if support teams involve families every step of the way.

CHAPTER 3

Tier 2 Interventions
for Externalizing Behavior Problems

Each year, children arrive in school classrooms showing signs of exposure to numerous risk factors and completely unprepared for, and unfamiliar with, the demands of the schooling process. Failure to adapt to these academic and behavioral demands sets the stage for additional problems later in life (Kellam & Rebok, 1992). Exposure to risk factors such as poverty, abuse, neglect, and lack of school readiness sets up the potential for the development of externalizing behavior patterns in youth (Patterson, Reid, & Dishion, 1992). Externalizing behaviors manifest themselves in the form of defiance, restlessness and hyperactivity, aggression, disruptive classroom behaviors, and lack of self-regulation (Walker et al., 1998) and have a negative impact on student educational progress. A substantial body of research has shown that early-onset externalizing problems during elementary school are associated with increased risk for subsequent severe behavior and academic problems (e.g., Reinke et al., 2008). In the absence of preventive interventions, many students who exhibit externalizing problems in the early grades (K–3) go on to develop more significant antisocial behavior patterns by upper-elementary and middle school grades (see Reid et al., 2002; Reinke et al., 2008). Therefore, intervening before externalizing behavior problems become severe is vital.

Despite this need, teachers feel inadequately prepared to support students who exhibit challenging behaviors in the classroom (Reinke, Stormont, Herman, Puri, & Goel, 2011). Teachers who have children with behavior problems in their classroom may find that the misbehaviors tend to control the social interactions they have with these students, making working with them difficult and unpleasant (Shores et al., 1993). A common response to handling students with externalizing behaviors is to remove them from the classroom, thereby limiting their access to instruction and reducing their involvement with classroom peers. In fact, nationwide, disruptive and aggressive behaviors are the most common reasons for ODRs, suspensions, and expulsions (Walker, Horner, Sugai, & Bullis, 1996). The use of suspension and expulsion does not adequately address the needs of these students, however. This lack of exposure to schooling content and socialization limits the ability of these students to learn prosocial or adaptive behaviors for successful development. Further, the use of exclusionary discipline practices may paradoxically reinforce students' externalizing behaviors, especially with students who do not like, or have little interest in, school (Atkins et al., 2002). To effectively support students exhibiting externalizing problems, schools need to implement alternative strategies that can promote the development of adaptive behaviors that lead to successful schooling experiences. The use of Tier 2 interventions is particularly promising because these interventions are focused on supporting students who exhibit early signs of externalizing behavior problems, potentially remediating maladaptive behaviors before they become severe.

The purpose of this chapter is to describe and provide an overview of several evidence-based practices and interventions that can be utilized with students who demonstrate externalizing problems and who are therefore in need of additional support to be successful in the school setting. Prior to the presentation of specific practices and interventions, the theoretical foundation upon which these interventions are based is discussed. Understanding how externalizing problems develop and are maintained is an important prerequisite to choosing the appropriate Tier 2 intervention when working with students who exhibit externalizing problems. Last, this chapter provides a list of resources that can be used to support efforts to identify students, intervene with students, and monitor the progress of the Tier 2 interventions implemented in response to externalizing problems.

> **Tier 2 interventions are particularly promising because they support students who have early signs of externalizing behavior problems, potentially remediating maladaptive behaviors before they become severe.**

THEORETICAL FOUNDATIONS FOR INTERVENING IN THE PROBLEM

When identifying Tier 2 supports for elementary students exhibiting externalizing problems, our approach is guided by a combined social learning and behavior analytic perspective. Social cognitive theory (Bandura, 1986) suggests that interpersonal contexts contribute to the development of externalizing symptoms in youth. The key assumption is that social behaviors are learned. These behaviors are mediated by the child's expectations, attributions, and cognitions, and are reinforced by the environment. A behavior analytic perspective adds the notion that behavior has a function or purpose, and that interventions are most likely to be effective when they take those functions into consideration (see Crone & Horner, 2003; O'Neil et al., 1997). For instance, we use the classic example of a child in a grocery store in want of the candy lining the check-out aisle. The child asks his mother for the candy, and the mother refuses. The child thinks to himself, "This is not fair—I never get what I ask for," and begins to whine. The mother says more sternly, "No!" The child begins to yell, "I want the candy!" The mother shouts back, "I said *no!*" The child drops to the ground, yelling more loudly, making a scene. The mother, feeling embarrassed by her child, quickly purchases the candy and hands it to him. The yelling stops immediately. If the purpose of the child's behavior (whining and yelling) is to obtain the candy, what then did the child learn from this interaction?—that if he yells loud enough, he will get what he wants. The grocery store example highlights the interactional nature of cognition, social behavior, and the environment in the development of externalizing problems in children. Although biological risk factors have also been linked to externalizing problems, this chapter focuses on identifying malleable risk factors that can be manipulated in a school environment to reduce children's risk for ongoing externalizing difficulties.

Guiding Principles

Several key principles guide how we intervene to support children with externalizing problems. First and foremost, intervening *before* externalizing behavior problems become severe is optimal. Assumed within a tiered model is the belief that we can prevent externalizing problems and the impact they have on students. A host of research supports the notion that by establishing universal practices that reduce externalizing problems and by intervening at school and with caregivers, we can prevent externalizing disorders in children (National Research Council and Institute of Medicine, 2009). Second, children learn effective coping thoughts and behaviors through both explicit instruction and natural encounters with the environment. Thus, effective supports to prevent externalizing problems in youth need to capitalize on the situations and experiences that occur in the natural environment to embed these opportunities in the daily experiences of all youth. Third, because externalizing behavior problems are functional, effective interventions must address the function of the problem behaviors. Every behavior that occurs repeatedly serves a purpose. Some externalizing behaviors are maintained by adult or peer attention or to obtain something that the child wants. Other externalizing behaviors are maintained by escape or avoidance of unpleasant or unpreferred situations (e.g., difficult academic content). To be effective, Tier 2 supports must attend to the function or purpose of the behavior.

The following sections highlight the link between externalizing problems, academic and social behavior deficits, and maladaptive cognitions. The purpose is to bring to the forefront important areas in which Tier 2 interventions can target and support students who display externalizing behavior problems.

Link between Externalizing Behavior Problems and Social Behavior Deficits

Students who enter school with poor social skills and externalizing problem behaviors are likely to continue this pattern unless they receive intervention (Kellam, Ling, Merisca, Brown, & Ialongo, 1998; Reid et al., 2002). Students who have social skills deficits may be aggressive with peers or disruptive in the classroom in their efforts to gain teacher attention. Without the experience of effectively interacting with adults or peers, these students may receive ODRs early in the school year for problem behavior related to inappropriate attempts at obtaining or escaping social interactions. Teachers and peers may find their interactions with these students to be aversive, leading them to avoid these students.

Rejected by their peers, students with externalizing problems tend to develop friendships with one another. This pattern leads to a lack of socialization with prosocial peers, further limiting the ability of these students to learn adaptive behaviors for interacting with others (Patterson et al., 1992). Tier 2 interventions for these students focus on explicit social skills instruction and reinforcement for successful experiences with adults and peers in applying these new skills.

Link between Externalizing Behavior Problems and Academic Deficits

Students who enter school with academic deficits and do not respond quickly to universal academic instruction tend to fall behind their peers academically. If the academic deficits faced by these students are not remediated, a pattern of continued failure can lead to externalizing problem behaviors (Hinshaw, 1992; Maguin & Loeber, 1996). In this pattern, academic and problem behaviors become closely linked because the student finds it aversive to perform academic tasks. If problem behavior is reinforced through removal of the aversive work, the student may increasingly use externalizing problem behavior to escape tasks. The result may be an unintended cycle in which the teacher provides an academic task demand, the student engages in problem behavior, and then the teacher removes the task from the student or the student from the task (e.g., placed in time-out or sent to office). Within this scenario, the student's externalizing behavior is reinforced by escaping academic tasks (Lee, Sugai, & Horner, 1999; Roberts, Marshall, Nelson, & Albers, 2001). This pattern is particularly detrimental because students will prevent themselves from accessing the instruction they need to learn effectively. Therefore, effective Tier 2 interventions for these students must target academic supports as well as reinforce incremental increases in completion of academic tasks in the classroom.

The above sections highlighted two potential sources of externalizing problems in children (i.e., social skills deficits and academic deficits). However, it is both possible and realistic that a student exhibiting externalizing behavior problems suffers from both. Therefore, it is important to thoroughly evaluate the underlying issues when identifying children who would benefit from Tier 2 supports for externalizing problems. The following section summarizes another consideration when building supports for students who exhibit externalizing problems.

Link between Externalizing Behavior Problems and Poor Social-Cognitive Processing

As academic failure and negative social interactions with adults and peers continue, students with externalizing behaviors may develop poor social-cognitive processing, demonstrating deficiencies in how they interpret social situations or problems. For instance, some students who display externalizing problems interpret benign encounters with others as hostile, increasing the likelihood that they will use aggressive behavior in these encounters. This tendency to view the actions of others as hostile is referred to as *hostile attribution bias* (Dodge, 2006). For example, suppose a student is walking down the hallway. Another student bumps into this student, knocking his books from his hands. The student could view this action either as an accident or as intentional. The student who views it as intentional is more likely to react in a retaliatory manner. Experiences that foster hostile attribution bias include modeling of hostile attributions by adults and peers and failure of major life tasks (Dodge, 2006). Students with externalizing problems often experience school failure and peer rejection, leading to the development of hostile attributions and poor coping thoughts. Effective Tier 2 interventions can support these students by providing explicit instruction and practice in effective social problem solving, perspective taking, and coping strategies. The following section describes methods for identifying students in need of Tier 2 supports.

HOW TO IDENTIFY CHILDREN
WITH EXTERNALIZING BEHAVIOR PROBLEMS

In today's classroom it is not uncommon to find one or more students who, on average, are more inattentive and impulsive, have less self-regulation, are aggressive, or who are more defiant than others. However, as noted in the first chapter, universal supports must be solidly in place before students in need of additional supports can be identified appropriately. When screening classrooms, it is important to note if teachers are employing effective classroom behavior management strategies. Classrooms without effective management in place have higher numbers of students displaying disruptive and off-task behavior. This makes it difficult to distinguish which students would benefit from additional supports. If a teacher is struggling with management issues, the initial focus should be on supporting the teacher toward incorporating effective classroom behavior management strategies (see Reinke, Herman, & Sprick, 2011). Once these strategies are in place, those students needing more support can be more easily identified by using the universal screening procedures described in the next section.

Schools can use several strategies to identify children with externalizing problems who would benefit from Tier 2 supports. First, using a tiered model of behavioral support, schools identify students who are not responding to universal supports using data commonly collected in school settings, such as ODRs, suspension data, attendance, and tardiness. Tier 2 teams use a predetermined decision rule (e.g., two or more ODRs within a given time frame) to identify students who may need additional supports. The second approach uses a proactive, systematic universal screening process by which students at risk for serious behavior problems are identified early. Both approaches have strengths and weaknesses. For example, ODRs are easily collected and summarized by schools. However, ODRs are not considered a perfect measure of risk, and they involve waiting for problem behaviors that warrant a discipline referral to occur before supports are provided. In contrast, using universal screening strategies, such as teacher nomination, can allow for earlier identification of students in need of additional supports, but these strategies are also often more time consuming and labor intensive than using readily available data (e.g., ODRs). The following material provides a description of measures commonly used for identifying students in need of Tier 2 behavioral supports. This is not an exhaustive list by any means, but rather a starting guide for determining ways in which to measure behaviors that place students at risk for serious externalizing behavior problems.

Office Discipline Referrals

ODRs are typically documented by forms that the adults referring students to the office complete. These forms may be called incident forms, discipline tracking forms, or behavior log entries (Tobin, Sugai, & Colvin, 2000). If the ODR forms specify useful information about the incident and are used systematically and consistently, they represent existing data that are uniquely valuable for efficient and effective decision making regarding students in need of additional supports (Horner, Sugai, & Todd, 2001; Sugai, Sprague, Horner, & Walker, 2000; Wright & Dusek, 1998). School personnel complete ODRs when they determine that the observed behavior warrants a referral (Sugai, Sprague, et al., 2000). Once completed, ODRs are typically entered into a computer program for tallying, summarizing, and graphing to answer questions about student behavior (Cordori, 1987).

School teams may set criteria with which to identify students who are not responding to the schoolwide intervention and who require more support to be successful (Tobin et al., 2000; Wright & Dusek, 1998). The most common criterion is receiving two or more ODRs in 1 year (Horner, Sugai, Todd, & Lewis-Palmer, 2005). This threshold has been validated in research, showing that students with two or more ODRs have significantly higher ratings of problem behavior on scales such as the *Behavior Assessment Scale for Children–2* (BASC-2; Reynolds & Kamphaus, 2004) and the *Social Skills Rating Scale* (SSRS; Gresham & Elliott, 1990) than students with zero or one ODR (McIntosh, Campbell, Carter, & Zumbo, 2009; Walker, Cheney, Stage, & Blum, 2005).

However, it is important to consider possible threats to the reliability of ODR data. For instance, considering the ethnic disproportionality in punishment and representation in special education (Skiba et al., 1997), it is important to consider whether students receive different rates of ODRs based on bias and not actual behaviors. As mentioned in Chapter 2, disaggregating data by race or gender can provide invaluable information about potential bias in any of the data used for identifying students in need of Tier 2 supports.

Multiple-Gating Screening Measures

Multiple-gating screening measures are systems of progressively intensive measures to identify students at risk for negative outcomes (Lochman, 1995; Patterson et al., 1992; Sprague et al., 2001). Multiple-gating measures include a series of stages. The first stage (or gate) of such a gating system involves a relatively inexpensive screening that is conducted schoolwide. Only the students identified in this initial screening progress to the next stage, which includes more intensive screening. At each stage, although the assessment becomes increasingly more expensive and time consuming, there is a decrease in the number of students assessed (Sprague & Walker, 2005).

One commonly used multiple-gating screening measure in school settings is the *Systematic Screening for Behavior Disorders* (SSBD; Walker & Severson, 1992). The SSBD is used to identify elementary school students with elevated risk for either externalizing or internalizing behavior disorders (a version for use in preschools is also available; Feil, Severson, & Walker, 1998). The SSBD's multiple-gating procedure consists of three stages: (1) teacher ranking, (2) teacher rating, and (3) systematic direct observation. In the first stage, general education teachers rank students in their classrooms according to level of concern in two categories: externalizing behaviors and internalizing behaviors. In stage 2, teacher's complete checklists of adaptive and maladaptive behaviors for the top three ranked students from stage 1. Students who exceed the normative cutoff points on these checklists move on to stage 3, in which a trained observer (e.g., school psychologist) records the target students' engaged academic time and peer social behavior in both classroom and playground settings. Students who move through two stages are candidates for Tier 2 interventions, and those moving through all three stages are candidates for Tier 3 interventions.

Brief Universal Screening

Several additional brief screening measures have been developed more recently and can be used through multiple-gating procedures to identify students in need of additional supports. *The Social Skills Improvement System (SISS) Screening Guide* (Elliott & Gresham, 2007) provides a classwide screening of social skills to identify the level of performance for each student in the classroom, using criterion-referenced performance continua for social behaviors and motivation to learn. Using this screening measure, students' skills are compared to grade-level expectations. The measure can be completed for an entire classroom in approximately 20 minutes. Students who fall in the at-risk range for social behavior on the SISS can then be further assessed using the *Social Skills Improvement System (SISS) Rating Scale* (Gresham & Elliott, 2007). The *SSIS Rating Scale* measures social skills, problem behavior, and academic competence for children ages 3–18. Similarly, the *BASC-2 Behavioral and Emotional Screening System* (Kamphaus & Reynolds, 2007) was designed to provide a systematic screening of large groups of children and adolescents (classrooms, grades, age groups) for behavioral and emotional problems. Teacher, parent, and child measures are available for use and differentiate students with elevated or extremely elevated risk for problems. Students with elevated risk move to the second stage, which includes a more comprehensive assessment involving behavior rating scales such as the BASC-2 (Reynolds & Kamphaus, 2004). Across both screening systems described above, the students with scores indicating risk for behavior problems enter stage 3, where they are provided Tier 2 behavioral supports with ongoing progress monitoring. Students who do not adequately respond to the Tier 2 intervention may be identified for Tier 3 supports.

Regardless of how schools measure and determine students in need of Tier 2 behavioral supports, the process needs to be formalized and systematically utilized. A systematic approach will include a team comprised of a variety of personnel who bring different skills and expertise to the process (see Chapter 1 for information about the team process). This team will identify students using a predetermined data decision rule. The Tier 2 team then completes a full review of new referrals. An important part of this process for identifying supports for students with externalizing behavior problems is that the team conducts a brief functional assessment to determine the function or purpose of the behaviors identified as problematic. Once an appropriate Tier 2 intervention is identified and implemented, the team collects ongoing progress monitoring data that can be used to evaluate success and modify the Tier 2 supports when necessary (see Chapter 1 for a sample plan). The following material provides a review of evidence-based practices that can be used by schools for students with externalizing behavior problems in need of Tier 2 supports.

REVIEW OF EVIDENCE-BASED PRACTICES FOR INTERVENING IN EXTERNALIZING BEHAVIOR PROBLEMS

As noted earlier in the chapter, the theoretical model that guides effective Tier 2 supports for externalizing problems is one that operates from social-cognitive and behavior analytic perspectives. Therefore, the practices overviewed below are aligned with this perspective. Interestingly, students exhibiting externalizing problems in need of Tier 2 supports benefit from the same universal strategies that work with all students (e.g., contingent praise, positive adult relationships, clear expectations, effective instruction, structured routines). We simply need to be more purposeful in their application. As such, this section focuses on effective strategies or practices that can be used by schools to provide Tier 2 supports for students. The purpose of this information is to help give schools and Tier 2 teams the tools to build feasible and effective Tier 2 supports. In addition to the practices highlighted in this chapter, a host of well-established comprehensive programs has been developed as Tier 2 interventions, some of which we review following this section. Last, we provide a list of additional resources at the end of this chapter, as previously noted.

> **Students exhibiting externalizing problems in need of Tier 2 supports benefit from the same universal strategies that work with all students (e.g., praise, positive adult relationships, clear expectations, effective instruction). We simply need to be more purposeful in their application.**

Conducting a Brief Functional Assessment: The First Step in Identifying Tier 2 Interventions for Students with Externalizing Behavior Problems

The first, perhaps most important, step in supporting students displaying externalizing problems is to determine the function or purpose of the problem behaviors before deciding upon a Tier 2 intervention. In other words, begin by understanding the reason why the student continues to display the problem behavior. Typically, individuals only continue using behaviors that serve a purpose. If a student continues to use aggression in the classroom, this means that it is serving as an effective strategy for getting something the student wants or needs. For instance, a student may become aggressive with another student on the playground to obtain the basketball they are using. Or, a student may become aggressive with a teacher by throwing objects at him or her when presented with a math assignment as a means of escaping the task. In yet another scenario, a student may hit another student during circle time so that the teacher pulls her aside and discusses the

> **Behaviors that recur, even problem behaviors, serve a purpose. Tier 2 interventions work best when they address this purpose.**

incident, thus gaining teacher attention. Ultimately, before we can determine which Tier 2 interventions will be most effective for a particular student, a good hypothesis regarding the function of the behavior needs to be considered through the completion of a brief functional assessment. In particular, students who use externalizing behaviors to gain attention versus to escape something aversive respond very differently to interventions. Therefore, when describing effective supports for students with externalizing behaviors, it is important to identify students based on the type of problem behavior observed. Generally, there are two main categories of problem behavior: attention maintained and escape maintained. Figure 3.1 provides a guide to the information a Tier 2 school team could gather for the brief functional assessment and how to develop this hypothesis. Figure 3.2 presents an example of identifying the function of a problem behavior in order to provide the appropriate Tier 2 supports (see blank Form 3.1 in the Appendix).

We have differentiated between interventions for students with attention-maintained problem behavior and escape-maintained problem behavior because, as previously noted, every behavior that is repeated serves some purpose. Therefore, Tier 2 interventions work best when they address this underlying purpose. For instance, if a student displays aggres-

---

In order to ensure that the Tier 2 intervention selected is a good match for the target student, a hypothesis about the function of the behavior problem must first be developed.

The following provides a guide for identifying the information needed to make this determination. Figure 3.2 provides an example using the function hypothesis development and planning form. A reproducible blank form is available in the Appendix.

The Science Behind Behavior Change: Behavior is affected by events that happen immediately before it (antecedents) and events that happen following it (consequences).

By changing the variables affecting behavior, we can increase or decrease the behavior. This means that we can change student (and adult) behavior by altering these variables.

Identifying behaviors that could replace the problem behavior is helpful toward putting supports in place to make this happen.

Step 1. Identify the behavior(s) to decrease. What is the specific behavior that is problematic? What exactly does it look like?

Step 2. Identify the antecedent. What happens before the problem behavior occurs?

Step 3. Identify the consequence. What happens after the problem behavior occurs?

Step 4. Identify the function of the behavior. What is our best guess of the purpose of the behavior? The most likely functions are to gain attention (adult or peer), to obtain something, or to escape or avoid something (activity, social interaction, or place).

Step 5. Identify the behavior(s) to increase. What behavior(s) can the student increase to be successful?

Once the function has been identified, match the student with a Tier 2 intervention that will support the student in decreasing the problem behavior and increasing the use of effective behaviors.

FIGURE 3.1. Guidelines for determining the function of behavior to inform Tier 2 interventions.

Student: _China_   Date: _1/20/11_

Antecedent	Behavior	Consequence	Possible Function/Purpose
What happens before the problem behavior?	What does the problem behavior look like?	What happens after the problem behavior?	Does the student receive **attention, obtain something,** or **avoid/escape** something?
Asked to read out loud.	_Slams down book, puts head on desk, will not talk or read._	_Sent to time-out or to office. Does not read._	_Avoids reading._
Students are reading silently at desk.	_Gets out of seat, walks around talking to peers._	_Told to sit down and read. Peers talk to her. She isn't reading._	_Although getting some attention, she is primarily getting to avoid reading._
Student Supports Needed (check off all that apply):	☐ Adult attention ☐ Peer attention ☑ Avoid aversive activity ☐ Avoid aversive social interaction	☑ Academic support ☐ Support with organizing ☑ Choices ☑ Reinforce replacement behavior	☑ Teach social behavior ☑ Teach cognitive coping ☑ Teach problem solving ☑ Home–school communication
Behavior(s) to Increase: What behavior(s) will replace the problem behavior to support student success?	_Use a pass to avoid task._ _Complete more assignments._ _Use words to communicate._	Tier 2 Intervention: What Tier 2 intervention(s) was selected to support the student? Intervention provides needed supports? ⓨ **N** (If no, how will needs be met?)	1. _Choose to Pass._ 2. _Participate in PALS reading group._ 3. _Participate in small-group social skills instruction._ 4. _Send daily note home to parents._

FIGURE 3.2. Function hypothesis development and planning form.

42

sive behavior in order to gain attention from his or her peers, then an effective Tier 2 intervention will support this student in gaining attention from his or her peers but in a more appropriate manner. Likewise, if a student is using defiant behavior to be removed from the classroom for the purpose of avoiding difficult academic materials, we want to support him or her in finding appropriate ways to ask to be released from difficult material and provide academic supports to foster successful experiences with the challenging content.

Additionally, we have included a section on supports for teaching prosocial behaviors. These Tier 2 supports will likely benefit all students exhibiting externalizing problem behaviors because the focus is on using small-group instruction to teach appropriate social behaviors. Furthermore, students who display externalizing behaviors often do so because they do not have appropriate ways in their behavioral repertoire to express themselves. Thus, small-group social skills instruction can target the ineffective cognitions and attributes that mediate and increase externalizing problem in some students. It is important to note that effective Tier 2 interventions can be layered to maximize outcomes for students. For instance, a student with attention-maintained problem behaviors may benefit from a Tier 2 intervention that increases positive adult attention and participation in group-based social skills training. Teaching students effective social behaviors, similar to teaching academics, is a powerful intervention. In fact, most, if not all, of the Tier 2 interventions described below include some form of explicit instruction in appropriate social behavior. With this being said, Figure 3.3 provides guidelines for effectively teaching appropriate

Students benefit from being taught social behaviors. The following provides a step-by-step guide for teaching social behaviors to students. Teaching students positive replacement behaviors can be incorporated into most, if not all, Tier 2 interventions for students with behavior problems.
Step 1: Identify the positive replacement behavior. For instance, if the student hits others when angry, the positive replacement behavior may be for the student to walk away and go to a designated spot in the classroom to calm down.
Step 2: Identify an adult to teach the behavior(s) to the student.
Step 3: Identify a time to meet with the student to teach the behavior.
Step 4: Meet with the student and explain the purpose of the meeting. For example, "We are meeting today because your teacher mentioned that you sometimes hit your friends. We are going to talk about what you could do instead so that you and your friends can be safe."
Step 5: Teach the positive replacement behavior by explaining it verbally and then modeling it. It is helpful to model the behavior for the student so that he or she knows exactly what it looks like when done correctly.
Step 6: Ask the student to show you the new behavior. For example, "OK. Now let's practice. Pretend that I am your friend and I said something you didn't like. Show me what you will do."
Step 7: Role-play, with the student as the teacher and you as the student. Display correct and incorrect variations of the new behavior. Ask the student to tell you if you did it correctly and, if not, what you should have done instead.
Step 8: Set up a system to reinforce the student for displaying the new behavior (e.g., verbal praise, sticker, token economy).
Step 9: If the student is successful in using the new behavior, identify a time to review. If the student struggles, immediately incorporate a time for review and practice.

FIGURE 3.3. Explicit instruction for social behaviors.

social behaviors to students. Social skills groups provide more intensive instruction in areas that are likely to benefit students with externalizing problems.

Each Tier 2 intervention described is accompanied by a rubric that outlines what types of supports are offered within the intervention. This rubric allows for easy mapping of the student needs identified using the function hypothesis development and planning form (see Figure 3.2) with interventions that can effectively meet these needs.

Effective Practices for Supporting Students with Attention-Maintained Problem Behaviors

The following material provides a description of supports that are most effective for students with attention-maintained problem behaviors. Many of the practices outlined below incorporate the teaching of expected behaviors and how to reinforce these behaviors with adult and peer attention. This combination can be particularly effective in working with students who have had a history in which both adults and peers have repeatedly rejected them due to their inability to effectively engage in positive social interactions. The supports described can be feasibly and systematically offered by schools for students with externalizing problems.

Group-Based Contingency Programs

Group contingencies involve setting common expectations for a group of students and then providing a common positive outcome when the students engage in the expected behavior. Token economies are used when students earn tokens (e.g., points, stickers, chips) contingent on the performance of the expected behavior, which can then be redeemed for a reinforcer (e.g., desired item, preferred activity). Group contingencies and token economies are both supported by research and are often used in combination (Barrish, Saunders, & Wolf, 1969; Jones & Kazdin, 1975; Yarborough, Skinner, Lee, & Lemmons, 2004). The following provides a description of establishing a Tier 2 group contingency program. The program involves the development of a daily behavior card and a menu of classroom-level rewards. This program can be used by Tier 2 teams to support several students across classrooms, and it can be used when there is more than one student in a given classroom in need of additional supports.

Group Contingency Intervention Rubric

Student Supports Targeted:	☑ Adult attention	☐ Academic support	☑ Teaching social behavior
	☑ Peer attention	☐ Support with organizing	☐ Cognitive coping
	☐ Avoid aversive activity	☐ Choices	☐ Problem solving
	☐ Avoid aversive social interaction	☑ Reinforce replacement behavior	☑ Home–school communication

Common to many Tier 2 supports for student behavior problems is the use of a daily behavior card, also referred to as a *daily progress report* (DPR) (see Crone, Horner, &

Hawkin, 2004). For each student in the program, a set of three to five behavioral goals is identified. If a schoolwide discipline system is in place, such as PBIS, the goals can be directly aligned with schoolwide expectations (e.g., be safe, be respectful, be responsible). For example, if a student is identified for Tier 2 supports because of aggressive behavior with peers on the playground and in the classroom, one of the student's goals might be to "Be safe." Each goal should have a specific expectation stating exactly what the student should be doing. The specific expectation for this student would be to keep his or her hands and feet to self. The card is then fashioned to provide the student with ongoing feedback throughout the day as to whether he or she is successfully meeting the goals. For instance, the card can be broken down by academic subject or classroom period (see Figure 3.4 for a sample daily behavior card and blank Form 3.2 in the Appendix, including directions for teachers). At the end of each period, the teacher takes a few minutes to review the goals with the student and provides him or her with information on performance. The student then earns points based on the degree of his or her success in meeting the goals, and is informed of how many points or percentage of points must be earned in order to receive a reward for self and class. At the end of the day, the points are tallied. This daily behavior card can be sent home for a parent signature, further supporting home–school communication. If at the end of the day the student has earned the predetermined number of points or percentage of points, then a reward is provided to *all* students in the classroom. The reward is selected from a menu of teacher-approved classroom rewards. The reward could be randomly selected (i.e., slip of paper with reward written on it pulled from a hat), selected by the student, or by the teacher. Figure 3.5 provides a list of common and inexpensive classroom-level rewards for students in elementary school.

WHY DO ALL STUDENTS IN THE CLASSROOM EARN THE REWARD?

Students with externalizing problems often have few friends and their peers tend to avoid them. Including classroom peers in the reward creates a positive association with the student receiving the Tier 2 support. Students with attention-maintained problem behaviors are often eager to please adults and peers. This allows the student to gain attention for meeting his or her goals, reinforcing the likelihood that he or she will continue displaying the appropriate expected behavior. Additionally, peers can be prompted to model appropriate behavior and can be encouraged to provide positive feedback to the student for successful school behaviors. The overarching goal is to increase the student's use of effective behaviors while interrupting the cycle of peer rejection.

TWO OR MORE STUDENTS IN THE SAME CLASSROOM ON THE PROGRAM

If two or more students have been identified for a Tier 2 intervention for attention-maintained behaviors, the percentage of points for the reward can be based on the overall mean of points earned by this group of students. For instance, in a classroom in which two students are receiving the daily behavior card Tier 2 intervention, at the end of the day, the points are added for each student, combined, and then the overall percentage of points available is

Student: Ryan	Date: January 24, 2011
☺ 3 = Great	Goal: 80% of points earned
☺ 2 = OK	Points Earned:
☹ 1 = Needs work	Goal Met? (Y) or N If yes, reward earned? Simon Says Game

Goals & Expectations	Subject Math	Subject PALS	Subject Specials	Subject Spelling & Writing	Subject Lunch & Recess	Subject Read aloud & SS	Subject Reading	Total Points
Goal 1: Be Safe 1. Keep hands and feet to self 2. Use materials properly	3	3	1	3	2	3	3	18
Goal 2: Be Respectful 1. Follow directions first time 2. Use quiet voice in classroom	2	3	1	3	2	3	2	16
Goal 3: Be Responsible 1. Come prepared to learn	3	3	3	3	2	3	2	19
Total Points Earned								53
Total Points Possible								63

% Earned Today: 53/63 = 84%

Parent Signature _____

FIGURE 3.4. Example of daily behavior card targeting externalizing symptoms.

46

Rewards should be brief, easy, and affordable. The following is a list of potential rewards that meet these criteria and that can be delivered to all students in the classroom.

1. Brief games: Simon Says, Thumbs up 7 up, I Spy, Hangman, tic-tac-toe, musical chairs
2. Hokey Pokey song and dance
3. Make a silly face
4. Stickers
5. Popcorn at desk
6. 5 minutes of free time
7. Robot dance for 30 seconds
8. Using an inside voice, crow like a rooster
9. On the count of 3, everybody laugh out loud
10. Talk to a neighbor for 5 minutes
11. Blow bubbles
12. Play music

FIGURE 3.5. Ideas for classroom-level rewards.

totaled. This way, the goal is met only if the combination of the two students is enough. If the goal is 80% of total points, then the reward is provided to the class only if the combined total points for the two students are enough to meet the 80%. Take the following example: Student 1 earns 13 out of 15 points and Student 2 earns 11 out of 15 points, for a total of 24 out of 30 points, or 80%. If tallied separately, Student 1 would meet the 80% goal, but Student 2 would not. This would cause a problem for classroom-level rewards if one student earned the reward and the other did not. Combining the efforts of the students avoids this problem as well as highlights the use of teamwork to reach a common goal.

THINGS TO REMEMBER WHEN IMPLEMENTING

First, in order for students to be successful in meeting goals, they need to understand the expectations. Therefore, at the start of the intervention, review the expectations with each student, explain why these expectations are important (e.g., "It is important to keep your hands and feet to yourself so that everyone is safe and no one gets hurt"), model the expectation by showing the student what it looks like, and have the student practice the expected behavior (see Figure 3.3). This process ensures that the student understands the expectation and what it looks like to meet this expectation.

Second, explain to each student how to earn the reward, including how points are earned per period and how many total points he or she will need to earn the classroom reward. Be sure that the percentage of points needed to earn the reward is reasonable. If the percentage is too high and the student is not able to reach the goal, he or she will quickly revert to gaining attention using the problem behaviors that were successful in the past. A good rule of thumb is to set the percentage a bit lower from the start and increase the number as the student is successful over time. Gathering data on the baseline rates of problem behavior can help in determining a goal that maximizes the likelihood of success while still increasing appropriate behaviors.

Third, prepare the peers in the classroom by explaining that the student is earning points for the class by using his or her best behavior. Remind them that they too need to be using their best behaviors to help show the student what it looks like. Explain to them what rewards can be earned, when the reward will happen (i.e., right before the end-of-day dismissal), and get them excited about helping the student meet the goals. To head off the possibility of peers being negative toward the student if he or she is not earning enough points, precorrect for the issue by teaching them to give the student praise for trying his or her best. Further, prosocial peers can be included in the program. For example, rotate randomly selected peers to use a behavior report card to earn points along with the student needing Tier 2 supports, making it more of a team game.

Last, the reward must be delivered consistently and within a short time frame of meeting the goal. Otherwise, the reward will lose its value, making the intervention less effective. For older students, the tallying of points can be a brief math lesson in which they are involved in dividing the total number of points earned by the total possible. In all classrooms where points are earned, the teacher and peers should provide positive attention for the accomplishment to the students working to improve their behavior. When the points are not earned, the teacher should simply make a statement like, "We will try again tomorrow." If a student is consistently not earning enough points, then additional supports or more explicit instruction in the expected behaviors may be necessary.

Positive Adult Attention and Mentoring

Students with externalizing behavior problems often have negative interactions with others, including adults in the school setting. When these students do receive attention from adults, it is often in response to misbehavior and therefore disciplinary in nature. As such, finding ways to build positive adult relationships that provide attention to prosocial behaviors can be an effective Tier 2 intervention for students with attention-maintained problem behaviors. Students can be assigned an adult mentor who meets with them on a daily or weekly basis to check in, see how the student is doing in school, and provide him or her with positive feedback for successes and encouragement for working toward goals. The primary emphasis is on building a positive relationship. Mentoring as an intervention can sometimes be perceived as an easy, inexpensive intervention. However, relationships are very complex, and relationships with goals of improving developmental, behavioral, and academic outcomes for at-risk youth have even deeper layers of complexity. Mentoring programs that have a strong systemic infrastructure to implement research-based practices are more likely to foster positive outcomes for students (DuBois, Holloway, Valentine, & Cooper, 2002; Herrera et al., 2007; Stormont et al., 2008). For instance, screening and identification of adults within or outside the school setting who can meet with students regularly is essential. Additionally, creating a time and space for meetings to occur, determining activities that are engaging and supportive of student growth, and having enough structure to the meetings so that the student does not engage in behaviors that have created negative adult relationships in the past are necessary. Guidelines for developing effective school-based mentoring programs are available (see Smith & Stormont, in press).

Adult Mentoring Rubric

Student Supports Targeted:	☑ Adult attention	☐ Academic support	☑ Teaching social behavior
	☐ Peer attention	☐ Support with organizing	☐ Cognitive coping
	☐ Avoid aversive activity	☐ Choices	☐ Problem solving
	☐ Avoid aversive social interaction	☑ Reinforce replacement behavior	☐ Home–school communication

Impulse Control Training

Some students who exhibit disruptive classroom behaviors, such as persistently calling out or interrupting instruction, can benefit from strategies that make them more aware of these behaviors while encouraging them to inhibit these behaviors in the future. One example of an evidence-based intervention that uses a similar strategy is the Good Behavior Game (see Barrish et al., 1969). In this intervention, students receive points for misbehavior, with teams winning a reward if they have less than a set number of points. Similarly, a simple Tier 2 strategy that can be used is to have the classroom teacher or other adult point out the problem behavior when it occurs while the student tracks the behavior. To use this strategy, a simple tracking form is placed on the student's desk. Then, each time the student calls out or disrupts instruction the teacher calmly states, "That's a mark." The student then makes a tally on the tracking form each time this occurs (Form 3.3 in the Appendix is a reproducible tracking form). For students who do not respond well to teacher redirection, a signal can be agreed upon that indicates to them that a tally mark should be made. For instance, a teacher we worked with who used this strategy would place her finger next to her nose, showing the student that he or she had talked out and needed to make a mark.

At the end of each day, the number of marks indicating the number of times the problem behavior occurred is totaled. A goal is selected based on the initial number of times the student talks out (or disrupts the class). So for a student who talks out 30 times per day, an initial goal of talking out only 20 times per day may be set. The goal is for the number of talk-outs or verbal disruptions to progressively decrease over time. An example might be that once a student meets the initial goal two or more times, the teacher would then decrease the number of tallies to earn the reward to 15, then 10, then 5, and so on. Each time the student meets the goal, he or she receives a reward.

Typically, call-outs or verbal disruptions in the classroom are attention-maintained behaviors. Therefore, identifying a reward that is aligned with receiving attention appropriately can be very effective (e.g., 5 minutes of time with teacher, taking a special note to the office to present to the principal). By making the student more aware of the problem behavior, he or she can then decrease the behavior. However, it is also necessary to teach the student a replacement behavior (e.g., raising a hand, flipping a card to indicate a question). Whatever the replacement behavior, the student will need to be taught this behavior as well as the procedures for knowing when to make a mark and for how to earn a reward. See Figure 3.3 for effective teaching of social behaviors.

Impulse Control Training Rubric

Student Supports Targeted:	☑ Adult attention ☐ Peer attention ☐ Avoid aversive activity ☐ Avoid aversive social interaction	☐ Academic support ☐ Support with organizing ☐ Choices ☑ Reinforce replacement behavior	☑ Teaching social behavior ☐ Cognitive coping ☐ Problem solving ☐ Home–school communication

Effective Practices for Supporting Students with Escape-Maintained Problem Behaviors

The following material provides a description of supports that are most effective for students with escape-maintained problem behaviors. Many of the practices outlined below incorporate teaching expected behaviors and reinforcing these behaviors with allowing the student to avoid an aversive task or situation. It may feel counterintuitive to allow a student who is struggling behaviorally to avoid work or a particular situation. However, students displaying problem behaviors that are escape-maintained are already avoiding tasks or situations. Teaching students to display appropriate behaviors that serve the same function, while simultaneously reinforcing incremental increases in task completion, will lead to successful school experiences and positive outcomes for these students. Tier 2 teams should consider whether academic supports and/or social skills training will benefit students with escape-maintained problem behaviors. For instance, a student who displays aggressive behavior to avoid a social situation may benefit from small-group social skills training, whereas a student who displays defiant behavior to avoid academic tasks may benefit from academic supports. The supports described below can be feasibly and systematically offered by schools to support students with escape-maintained externalizing problems.

Allowing the Student to Avoid Some Academic Activities

Students who find academic tasks or other activities aversive will benefit from a Tier 2 support that allows them to avoid certain tasks. Therefore, Tier 2 teams can implement a program that allows students to avoid portions of an academic activity. Many students with externalizing behavior problems who are frequently allowed to avoid unpreferred or difficult academic tasks are missing out on a large portion of academic work, setting the cycle for future or continued academic failure. Using a strategy that allows a student to avoid some work while reinforcing incremental increases in task completion can begin to break this cycle. Ideally, the student simultaneously receives academic support for content he or she is avoiding. The following section provides a description of a program that could be used as a Tier 2 support for students with externalizing problems who are avoiding academic tasks.

CHOOSING TO PASS WITH RESPONSE COST

One strategy to support students who find activities or certain academic tasks so aversive that they exhibit externalizing problems as a means of escaping them is to allow them to avoid the task, but within limits. One approach is to set up a system in which the student is allowed to pass a certain number of times when asked to complete the activity he or she is attempting to avoid. For instance, a student may be allowed a total of three passes per day. When the student wants to avoid an activity, he or she can choose to pass on—get out of—doing the task. Although the student can choose to complete the task or use a pass, once the passes are used up, the expectation is that the student completes the task even if only a portion. It is important to set up this intervention with care. For the intervention to be effective, it needs to be more efficient and effective for the student to use a pass to avoid the aversive task than to display the problem behaviors.

To begin, the student must be taught the appropriate replacement behavior (i.e., choosing to use a pass by raising hand and telling the teacher politely), using the procedures outlined in Figure 3.3. The student needs to be taught what it means to use a pass to avoid an unpreferred task or activity. The following needs to be detailed:

1. When can the pass be used? Making clear when the pass system can be used will prevent overspill into other activities. For instance, when teaching the student the new behavior, indicate what specific times of the day the pass system can be used (i.e., the times when significant behavior problems occur), what will happen if the student asks to use a pass outside that time (i.e., the teacher will tell the student that he or she cannot use a pass at this time, and if the student complains, he or she loses points).

2. When the student uses a pass, what will he or she do instead? Having a packet of preferred activities that the student can complete in place of the activity will prevent behavior problems associated with lack of structure.

3. What will the pass look like? The pass could be a piece of laminated paper labeled as *Pass* that is handed to the teacher, or it could be a tally system that is used to track the number of passes used each day. In either case, it is helpful to have some visual representation of the number of passes both used and remaining. Figure 3.6 provides an example of a pass system (a blank Form 3.4 is provided in the Appendix).

4. How will the student inform the teacher that he or she would like to use a pass? Giving the student a sentence to use or having a procedure set in place for choosing to use a pass will avoid confusion (e.g., raising hand and marking a tally when the teacher comes to desk).

5. What will happen if the student uses all the passes available and refuses to complete work? Thinking about potential pitfalls can prevent significant problems. Giving a teacher some way to manage the instance when the student wants to pass despite having already reached his or her limit for the day is proactive: (a) Identify the minimum amount of work that the student will need to complete. It is best if this amount is less than all of the work, particularly in the initial phases of the intervention. (b) Have the teacher indicate this amount to the student. For example, the teacher may simply state, "Don't forget, you will earn 5 points for completing three of the five math problems." This limits the task, but the student is still doing some of it. Over time this amount can be increased. A response–cost system for continuing to refuse to complete the task may be used when the student contin-

52

Student: Ryan		Date: January 24–28, 2011			
Goal: 25 Points to get 10 minutes of computer time					
Passes can be used to: work on writing and math assignments in special folder during free writing time or small-group math.					

Daily Passes Each pass not used = 5 pts/day	**Monday** ☐ Earned reward	**Tuesday** ☐ Earned reward	**Wednesday** ☐ Earned reward	**Thursday** ☐ Earned reward	**Friday** ☐ Earned reward
Points Earned	IIII II	II	IIII	IIII	IIII
Points Removed	0	−5	0	0	0
Pass #1	X	X	X	X	X
Pass #2	X	X	+5	+5	+5
Pass #3	+5	X	+5	+5	+5
Pts Rolled Over = 8 **Cumulative Points:**	Total = 20	22−5 =17	Total = 32−25 for reward = 7	22	36−25 for reward = 11

Student Signature _____

Teacher Signature _____

FIGURE 3.6. Example of pass system.

ues to refuse (e.g., "If you don't complete three math problems, you will lose 5 points. It's your choice").

A system for reinforcing the student for using the passes also needs to be in place (e.g., the teacher uses verbal praise: "Thank you for using your pass"). Additionally, a system for reinforcing incremental increases in completing the unpreferred activity or task needs to be in place. For instance, each time the student chooses to complete the task rather than use a pass, he or she receives verbal praise in combination with a point that is linked to a reward for earning a certain number of points (e.g., every 25 points the student earns 5 minutes of free time). Another strategy is to reward the student for having passes left at the end of the day (e.g., student earns 5 points for each pass not used because he or she chose to complete the task). Lastly, a bit of compromise may be necessary initially to support incremental increases in completion behaviors (e.g., instead of having a student complete an entire worksheet, he or she completes half). Consider the following example: If a student becomes upset and slams down his book every time he is asked to read out loud, the teacher may initially precorrect him before asking him to read by saying, "I am going to ask you to read today. I will ask you to read only one sentence. You can choose to use a pass or to read. Remember, you get points for choosing to read." Over time, as the student experiences success with reading and begins to feel more comfortable reading out loud, the number of sentences he or she reads can be increased. Overall, the student is still reading more than before. The removal of points should be used only when the student continues to adamantly refuse to complete any portion of the task. Furthermore, if the student loses points after using all passes and continues to refuse to complete a portion of a task, consider that the reward earned by gaining a certain number of points may not be sufficiently reinforcing for that student.

To ensure that both the teacher and student understand the design of the pass system, have them both review the procedures for when a pass can be used and when it cannot, what will happen when a pass is used, what is the minimum that the student must do to have successfully completed a task to earn points, and under what circumstances points will be removed. Ultimately, going through this review process will increase the likelihood of success. As an indication of this shared understanding, the teacher and student can sign the tracking form. A Tier 2 team can arrange for this system to be taught to, and monitored for, small groups of students in need of this additional support toward increasing their completion of activities.

Choosing a Pass Rubric

Student Supports Targeted:	☐ Adult attention	☐ Academic support	☑ Teaching social behavior
	☐ Peer attention	☐ Support with organizing	☐ Cognitive coping
	☑ Avoid aversive activity	☑ Choices	☐ Problem solving
	☐ Avoid aversive social interaction	☑ Reinforce replacement behavior	☐ Home–school communication

Allowing Students to Take a Break to Avoid an Activity or Social Interaction

Another effective strategy for students in need of Tier 2 supports for externalizing behavior that is maintained by avoidance of an activity or social interaction is to establish a place in which the student can "take a break" and to teach a system for doing so. The space can be easily set up in a classroom or outside the classroom. For instance, a teacher may create a corner area in the classroom reserved for taking a break or relaxing by placing a bean bag, pillows, or simply a chair in that space.

Taking a Break Rubric

Student Supports Targeted:	☐ Adult attention	☐ Academic support	☑ Teaching social behavior
	☐ Peer attention	☐ Support with organizing	☐ Cognitive coping
	☑ Avoid aversive activity	☑ Choices	☐ Problem solving
	☑ Avoid aversive social interaction	☑ Reinforce replacement behavior	☐ Home–school communication

TAKING A BREAK

Allowing students to take a break to calm down as a Tier 2 intervention can be an effective approach for students for whom the antecedent is an aversive activity or social interaction. Students who benefit from this support are those who become angry or explosive when they are given negative feedback by adults or peers, when asked to do something they dislike, and/or when uncomfortable with a social situation. To implement the intervention, the student must first be taught the replacement behavior of calmly removing him- or herself from the situation to the area designated as the break spot and how to reenter (see Figure 3.3 for teaching social behavior). As Tier 2 teams identify students who would benefit from this type of support, they need to consider the following points to maximize the effectiveness of the intervention:

1. Give the student something to say when he or she needs to take a break (e.g., "I would like to take a break") and have him or her practice using this statement and going to the break area when he or she is *not* upset.

2. Determine the length of the break. For instance, a timer could be placed at the break site, and the student could be trained to set the timer to indicate when to return from the break (3–5 minutes). Or, the student could be told to come back after he or she feels calm.

3. Determine what the student should do while taking a break. Ideally, the student is also receiving additional supports in social skills training such as anger control and problem solving. The break area may house an anger thermometer, a poster of problem-solving steps, or other prompts for the skills the student is working toward acquiring during these social skills training sessions. The student can practice breathing or complete a problem-solving form to support him or her in the calming down process and allow the student to successfully return to the classroom.

4. Determine how the student will reenter the classroom (or situation). It is helpful to give the student a statement or procedure for returning that he or she practices when not upset. For example, the student may be taught to state, "I am ready to return," followed by his or her reentering the group. When he or she returns, the student should be quickly engaged by the teacher or another adult.

5. It is important to ensure that the student is reinforced for taking a break rather than becoming upset and disrupting the classroom or situation. The teacher could thank the student for making a good choice by choosing to take a break.

6. Determine how to effectively reengage the student in an activity or social interaction in a way that is positive and successful. By doing so, the student will be less likely to become upset and take a break in the future.

7. Last, the Tier 2 team should develop a method for tracking the frequency and the purposes for which a student is choosing to take breaks. This important information will guide how additional supports, such as teaching prosocial skills or reinforcing incremental increases in engaging in unpreferred activities or social interaction, can be layered to fully support the student.

Behavioral Contracting with Goal Setting

Behavioral contracts are written documents that specify the relationship between student behavior and the associated consequence. In other words, the contract defines the expected behavior and the outcome associated with engaging or not engaging in that behavior. Use of behavioral contracts has been shown to increase student productivity and assignment completion (Kelley & Stokes, 1984; White-Blackburn, Semb, & Semb, 1977), improve grades (Williams & Anandam, 1973), and increase student self-control (Drabman, Spitalnik, & O'Leary, 1973).

We have placed this practice under effective interventions for students with escape-maintained behaviors. However, behavior contracting can be effective for students with externalizing problems across the board. One way to increase the likelihood that this strategy is effective is to match the form of reinforcement, or what the student is working toward, with what tends to maintain the student's problem behavior. For instance, if a student exhibits behaviors that are thought to be attention maintained, have the reward for meeting the behavioral contract goal be a social reinforcer (e.g., time with favorite teacher, choosing a friend with whom to play a game). If a student's behavior is thought to be maintained by a desire to avoid a task or social situation, have the reward link to avoiding an unpreferred activity or social interaction (e.g., receives a pass on homework, receives free time instead of going to gym class). For students with escape-maintained behavior problems, it is a good idea to include a clause in the contract stating that they will be responsible for the task they were trying to avoid (e.g., "If your work is not completed at school, you will take it home to finish").

Tier 2 teams can use a general format for developing effective behavioral contracts with students. First, identify the behavior that the student needs to increase in order to be successful at school (e.g., homework completion, being respectful to people and materials, arriving at school on time, asking permission to leave desk). Then involve the student in determining a reasonable goal for decreasing the problem behavior and increasing the appropriate behavior. To do so, identify the frequency of the problem behavior, then come up with a number that reflects a gradual change that is manageable for the student. This goal can change to higher or lower depending on the behavior over time. Develop a list of reinforcers for daily success as well as additional reinforcers for goals met for the entire week. It is important to allow multiple opportunities for success. If only a weekly goal is established and the student determines early in the week that there is no possibility of achieving that goal, he or she may feel like there is no reason to continue trying. For instance, if a goal of arriving on time every day of the week is the only goal, and the student comes in late Monday morning, he or she has no incentive to try to come in on time the rest of the week. However, if a daily goal is set and a more reasonable weekly goal (e.g., for a chronically late student to arrive at school on time 3 out of 5 days) is determined, the student will remain committed and motivated to reach the goal.

Several components of the intervention must be in place for it to be successful. First, to support the likelihood that the student exhibits the behaviors targeted to be increased, take the time to review and teach the expected behaviors to him or her (see Figure 3.3). Second, involve the student in the creation of the contract to engage him or her and increase commitment to following through. Third, ensure that the goals are manageable and that the student has multiple opportunities to meet these goals. Fourth, develop a list of reinforcers with the student. If the reward for meeting a goal is not reinforcing to the student, the plan will not work. Fifth, it is a great idea to involve the student's parents or caregivers, when possible, in creating and signing the contract. This involvement can facilitate and increase important home–school communication. Sixth, the teacher or other adult in the school must follow through with the contract and reinforce the student appropriately. The contract should be signed by all parties, indicating that everyone agrees to its terms and conditions. Type up the contract and give a copy to everyone involved. Once implemented, if the contract is not effective in increasing the identified behaviors, revisit it to make sure that the student understands the behavioral expectations, the terms of the contract, and that the reinforcers are, in fact, effectively motivating and reinforcing to the student. Also, make sure that the goals being set are reasonable, indicating incremental or gradual increases in behavior. Form 3.5 in the Appendix provides a template for creating a behavioral contract.

Effective Practices for Supporting Students in Learning and Using Prosocial Behaviors

Students with externalizing behavior problems often react to problems in ineffective ways. They may lack the skills and/or misperceive or have ineffective cognitive coping strategies that lead them to use aggression or destructive behaviors when confronted with a problem. Tier 2 teams looking to support students with externalizing behavior problems can use

> To increase the likelihood that a Tier 2 support is effective, match the reinforcer or the reward that a student is working toward with what maintains the student's problem behavior.

group-based social skills training to help students learn more appropriate cognitive and social problem-solving strategies. A number of established social skills training curricula can be used to support students. We recommend that Tier 2 teams select a comprehensive social–emotional curriculum with evidence to support its effectiveness in teaching students prosocial behaviors. The following sections provide a review of some of the key topics for training when working with students displaying externalizing behaviors (see Chorpita & Daleiden, 2009, for a review of evidence-based treatment procedures for a range of externalizing problems in children).

Group-Based Skills Rubric

Student Supports Targeted:	☑ Adult attention	☐ Academic support	☑ Teaching social behavior
	☑ Peer attention	☐ Support with organizing	☑ Cognitive coping
	☐ Avoid aversive activity	☐ Choices	☑ Problem solving
	☐ Avoid aversive social interaction	☑ Reinforce replacement behavior	☐ Home–school communication

When identifying students for Tier 2 social skills group training, it is important to consider the fit in a group context. The strategies described here are meant to be preventive in that they intervene with students who would benefit from supports and who can effectively engage in groups. Students who need more intensive supports or who are not appropriate for group-based interventions because their behaviors are too severe or disruptive are unlikely to benefit from the supports outlined below when delivered in a group format.

Furthermore, when holding group meetings with students who have externalizing problems, it is important to provide structure and a system for reinforcing appropriate behavior and discouraging inappropriate behavior. Aggregating groups of students who display externalizing problems without adequate structure and use of behavior management strategies can actually increase problem behaviors. This phenomenon is referred to as *deviancy training* (Dishion, McCord, & Poulin, 1999; Reinke & Walker, 2006): Students learn new misbehaviors by interacting with one another in a group setting where behavior problems and deviant discussions are reinforced by others in the group. Using effective behavior management strategies, group rules, and a structure for each group can help to prevent this problem. However, it is always something that needs to be considered and monitored when bringing groups of students together who display externalizing behavior problems.

Anger Control Training

Students who use aggressive behavior tend to become more hostile and use less adaptive behaviors as they become more physiologically aroused and engage in more automatic, rather than deliberate, information processing (Lochman, Barry, & Pardini, 2003). In other words,

> **Aggregating groups of students who display externalizing problems without adequate structure and behavior management has the potential to *increase* their problem behaviors. This is something that needs to be considered and monitored when bringing groups of students together.**

these students are more likely to perceive the intentions of others as hostile, causing them to feel angry, which increases the likelihood that they will use fewer verbal solutions and more direct-action solutions involving physical aggression. Working with students to identify when they are feeling angry and providing them with strategies to control angry behaviors are effective strategies for Tier 2 interventions with students who have externalizing problems. Strategies for teaching self-control include working with students to identify the physiological indications that they are feeling angry (e.g., muscles feel tight, heart is beating fast), practices that can help the student to calm down (e.g., distracting him- or herself, positive self-talk, relaxation strategies), and helping the student to understand the perspectives and emotions of others. These skills are best generalized when teachers and parents are involved and are provided with ideas for supporting and reinforcing the new practices in the classroom and at home.

Cognitive Reframing

Some students who display aggressive or impulsive behaviors are more likely to have cognitive difficulties with social problem solving (Asarnow & Callan, 1985). These students may perceive social situations in hostile terms, have fewer prosocial ways for solving interpersonal conflict, and anticipate fewer negative consequences for being aggressive (Dodge & Price, 1994). Therefore, supporting students in thinking about a situation differently and helping them identify more effective coping thoughts is an effective Tier 2 strategy for students with externalizing behavior problems.

Helping students understand how the way they think about a situation affects how they feel—which, in turn, affects how they behave—is a crucial insight for interrupting aggressive and destructive behaviors (Bandura, 1986). When students experience negative emotions, such as anger or frustration, often there are underlying thoughts that accompany or precede the emotion that can reinforce, intensify, or even cause the emotion. Research indicates that students whose cognitions or "self-talk" is more negative get angry more easily than those who have more positive self-talk (Webster-Stratton, 2010). Teaching students to identify these negative thoughts and to substitute them with positive thoughts can reduce problem behaviors. Strategies for teaching this skill include having students list the negative thoughts they had, how each thought made them feel, and then change it into a positive coping thought. Next, role-play scenarios in which a problem occurs that may upset a student and have him or her say positive coping thoughts out loud, or model the use of positive self-talk during a difficult scenario. As with the other strategies for students displaying externalizing behavior problems, this strategy is most effective when taught, modeled, and practiced within the group as well as practiced outside the group. Therefore, including teachers and parents is important for generalization and maintenance.

Social Problem Solving

Students may display externalizing behavior problems either because they have not been taught more appropriate ways to problem-solve or because their inappropriate strategies have been inadvertently reinforced by parents, teachers, or peer responses. Consequently, explicitly teaching students to think of more prosocial solutions to their problems and to evaluate which solutions are better choices and more likely to lead to better outcomes is an effective Tier 2 intervention. Research evaluating the use of problem solving with students has shown improvement in social skills and cooperation strategies for resolving conflict (Webster-Stratton & Hammond, 1997). Generalization and maintenance of positive outcomes are enhanced when the training includes strategies to integrate the skills into the classroom environment and to support partnerships with parents (Lochman & Curry, 1986; Webster-Stratton & Hammond, 1997).

Research suggests that the problem-solving process can be divided into at least six steps (D'Zurilla & Goldfried, 1971). These steps can be presented as the following questions (see Webster-Stratton, 2010):

1. What is the problem? (Define problem.)
2. What is a solution? What are some more solutions? (Brainstorm.)
3. What are the consequences? (What will happen if I choose a solution?)
4. What is the best solution or choice? (Which choice will be safe and effective?)
5. Am I using my plan? (Did I go about it correctly?)
6. How did I do? (Did it work?)

There is a host of methods and strategies that can be used to teach each of these problem-solving skills. For instance, group leaders can use games, puppets, and hypothetical problem situations to teach, model, and practice effective problem solving. The intermediary goal is for students to stop themselves before acting and to come up with as many solutions as possible; the overall goal is that students can identify and use appropriate behaviors for solving problems. To support generalization of these skills, teachers and parents should be informed of the skills and given specific ways to encourage and reinforce the behaviors when they are displayed in the classroom and at home.

Effective Practices for Supporting Students with Organizational Problems

Many students struggle with organization-related issues, particularly those with externalizing problems. Research has found that children with attention-deficit/hyperactivity disorder (ADHD), in particular, have significant needs in this area and can self-report these needs (Zentall, Harper, & Stormont-Spurgin, 1993). Several strategies for supporting children with organizational difficulties have been recommended; these are categorized into *object organizational* and *time planning organizational needs* (Stormont-Spurgin, 1997; Stormont, 2007). Tier 2 teams can support students with externalizing problems who struggle because of organizational problems by providing them with materials and teaching them practical organizational strategies. The following sections provide a brief overview of effective organizational practices.

Organizational Supports Rubric

Student Supports Targeted:	☑ Adult attention ☐ Peer attention ☐ Avoid aversive activity ☐ Avoid aversive social interaction	☐ Academic support ☑ Support with organizing ☐ Choices ☑ Reinforce replacement behavior	☑ Teaching social behavior ☐ Cognitive coping ☐ Problem solving ☑ Home–school communication

Object Organization

Many children who are inattentive and poorly organized report losing things at school and completing their homework but losing it before they can turn it in (Zentall et al., 1993). Tier 2 teams can work to support students by teaching them routines for homework completion, including recording necessary information, bringing home necessary materials, and partnering with parents to identify a location and home routine for homework completion. Additionally, having a system for getting the homework back to school and a place to put the homework when arriving in the classroom can be helpful. Providing students with a system that uses labels, colored folders, index cards, and highlighters to organize homework and materials is an effective practice that can be used as Tier 2 supports for students struggling with organization. It is important to teach children where to put things that they will use every day and how to organize these items inside their desk or locker. For example, teachers could provide a special basket labeled "Keep at school" and teach the routine of where to place the basket for rapid retrieval. Additionally, students can be taught to use checklists to support their efforts in taking things home and bringing things back to school. Index cards with pictures of a home and a school, with places to write down things to be transported, could provide support for these children.

Time Planning Organization

Effective Tier 2 supports for children struggling with organization can support homework completion by allowing children to begin their homework in class. After children have completed part of their homework, have them estimate how long it will take them to finish. Then have them write the time on a sticky note and place this on the homework. Using a bright colored sticky note and the letters TAM (time at home) = 10 min may add some novelty that children like. Use of this note will help family members know how long the homework is likely to take to complete. Children with ADHD have difficulty with time estimation, so this exercise can support them in this area as well as with overall homework completion. Further, graphic organizers can be used to help children plan out their thoughts and have a concrete representation as they work to add details. To support students with larger long-term projects (e.g., book reports), help them break down each step using task analysis, identifying one step to complete each day (e.g., "Today choose two books you like"). After they have completed the project, show students and their parents how the larger task was broken down into steps to support success.

Homework Clubs

Tier 2 teams can establish homework clubs to support homework completion and academic competence for struggling students. These clubs can meet during the school day or after school to support students struggling with organizational issues, time management, and academic completion. Students who struggle organizationally could be paired with a peer who excels in this area in an effort to support improvement in homework completion. Individuals or student pairs should receive reinforcement for reaching goals. Additionally, parents can be given tips for facilitating their child's success in completing homework on a regular basis (e.g., devoting time and space for homework without distraction, looking over student work, signing off on planners, and helping the student return the homework by ensuring that it gets into a backpack).

All of the practices and strategies outlined above are enhanced by including parents or caregivers in the process. Further, the more people who know about the new behaviors a student is learning, including caregivers and teachers, the more likely these behaviors will be used and reinforced across multiple contexts. Additionally, combining several strategies to create a comprehensive but feasible Tier 2 intervention that targets multiple risk factors for students with externalizing problems will produce optimal results. The following section discusses strategies for including families, followed by a review of comprehensive evidence-based interventions that can be used with students who exhibit externalizing behavior problems.

Partnering with Parents/Caregivers

As noted in Chapter 2, the importance of involving families in supporting students cannot be understated. Research supports that when schools and families work together, students tend to succeed not just in school, but throughout life (Henderson & Berla, 1994). The following are just a few ideas for involving families to support students with externalizing problems in need of Tier 2 supports:

1. Send home notes that highlight the plan to support the student with learning new behaviors and tips for how the parents can support these behaviors at home.
2. Make phone calls home to share when the student is successful at school or does something well.
3. Arrange a meeting with parents/caregivers to review the student's progress, emphasizing positive attributes and success stories.
4. Make home visits to meet with the family and develop shared goals and plans to help support the student at home and school.
5. Develop a home–school communication system (e.g., daily behavior card, notebook with written notes).
6. Arrange parent education or parent behavior management groups to support parents in the use of effective behavior management practices, academic supports at home, and encouraging social and problem-solving skills outside school.

> **Any Tier 2 support should include some strategy to involve the parents as active partners.**

Any Tier 2 support should include some strategy to involve the parents/caregivers as active partners. Although this can be challenging in some cases, it is essential to include families—or else the impact of the intervention may be minimized.

REVIEW OF EVIDENCE-BASED PROGRAMS FOR INTERVENING IN EXTERNALIZING BEHAVIOR PROBLEMS

There are several programs available to schools that are based on sound theory, utilize the practices reviewed above, and have research supporting their efficacy with students who display externalizing behavior problems. This review is not exhaustive by any means, and additional programs can be found by reviewing prominent clearinghouses (e.g., Blueprints for Violence Prevention: *www.colorado.edu/cspv/blueprints/index.html*; What Works Clearinghouse: *ies.ed.gov/ncee/wwc*). The following sections provide a brief description of comprehensive Tier 2 interventions and information on where to find them. Figure 3.7 provides a rubric of the student supports targeted by each intervention.

Supports Provided:	Behavior Education Plan	Check & Connect	Coping Power	First Step to Success	Incredible Years	Strong Kids
Adult Attention	✓	✓	✓	✓	✓	✓
Peer Attention			✓	✓	✓	✓
Avoid Aversive Activity						
Avoid Aversive Social Interaction						
Academic Support						
Support with Organizing			✓			
Provide Choices						
Reinforce Replacement Behavior	✓	✓	✓	✓	✓	✓
Teach Social Behavior	✓	✓	✓	✓	✓	✓
Teach Cognitive Coping Strategies			✓		✓	✓
Teach Problem Solving		✓	✓		✓	✓
Home–School Communication	✓	✓		✓		
Parent Training			✓	✓	✓	

FIGURE 3.7. Summary of student supports targeted by highlighted interventions.

Behavior Education Plan

The Behavior Education Plan (Crone, Horner, & Hawken, 2004; Hawken, Pettersson, Mootz, & Anderson, 2005) is a Tier 2 intervention that provides daily support and monitoring for students at risk of developing serious behavior problems. It is based on a daily check-in/check-out system that provides students with immediate feedback on their behavior using teacher ratings on a daily progress report (DPR) and increased positive adult attention. Expectations for student behavior are identified and students are given both immediate (daily) reinforcement and delayed reinforcement for meeting behavioral expectations. Home–school communication is emphasized by sending the DPR home each day to be signed and returned. The core components of the intervention include (1) clearly defined behavioral expectations, (2) explicit instruction in social behaviors, (3) increased positive reinforcement for meeting expectations, (4) contingent consequences for problem behavior, (5) increased positive contact with an adult at school, (6) opportunities for self-management, and (7) home–school communication. Research indicates that this intervention is effective in supporting students with externalizing problems maintained by attention (Mitchell et al., 2011). This intervention is less effective in supporting students with escape-maintained problem behaviors (Clare, 2011).

Check and Connect School Engagement Program

The Check and Connect program (see Christenson et al., 2008) was developed to support students at high risk for school failure. The "check" component is designed to facilitate the continuous assessment of student levels of engagement with school and to guide intervention. Adult monitors gather information on indicators of attendance (tardy to school, skipping classes, absenteeism), social behavior performance (out-of-school suspension, ODRs, in-school suspension), and academic performance. The "connect" component connects students to intervention. Monitors routinely interact with students at school. Conversations cover the student's progress in school, the relationship between school completion and the "check" indicators of engagement, the importance of staying in school, and the use of problem-solving steps to resolve conflict and cope with life's challenges. The repeated conversations provide a regular opportunity for monitors to share information and reinforce skills that students need to actively promote their own connection with school. Studies with elementary-age students indicate increased school engagement (increased attendance and decreased tardiness) among identified students (Lehr, Sinclair, & Christenson, 2004).

Coping Power

The Coping Power Program (Lochman, Wells, & Lenhart, 2008) is a group-based preventive intervention delivered to at-risk children in the late elementary school years (grades 3–5). Coping Power is based on an empirical model of risk factors for externalizing behavior problems, and it addresses key factors, including social competence, self-regulation, and positive parental involvement. The program is designed to be implemented by trained leaders with five to seven children in a group format. The program lasts 15–18 months in its full form and incorporates both child and parent groups. Session topics in the child groups include goal setting, anger management, perspective taking, understanding and identifying emotions, relaxation training, social-cognitive problem solving, coping with peer pressure, and using positive peer networks. Coping Power parent group sessions teach social learning techniques such as giving effective instructions, rewarding and attending to appropriate child behaviors, establishing effective rules in the home, and applying effective consequences for negative child behaviors. Parents also learn how to manage child behavior outside the home, effective communication skills, and strategies to support the skills their children learn in the child groups. Coping Power has been shown to decrease delinquency and substance use as well as behavior problems at school (see Lochman, Boxmeyer, Powell, Barry, & Pardini, 2009).

First Step to Success

First Step to Success (Walker et al., 1997) is a preventive intervention for students with externalizing problems that can be used as a Tier 2 intervention for students in PreK to second grade. A trained consultant works with both the teachers (using CLASS) and parents (using HomeBase) to implement the First Step to Success program. During the CLASS portion of the program, the consultant works with the teacher and the student. The student is taught appropriate replacement behaviors and rewarded for using these behaviors appropriately and consistently, while teachers observe and learn the techniques and skills necessary to implement the program. Throughout the day, the student receives feedback about his or her behavior from the consultant using a red/green card (i.e., when not meeting expectations the card is turned to red). The student accrues points toward his or her behavioral goal. If the student reaches the daily goal, he or she gets to choose an activity or reward for the whole class. Parents receive feedback about their child's daily progress. Once the classroom teacher feels comfortable in taking responsibility for implementing the CLASS portion, the consultant begins working with the student's parents to enable them to implement the HomeBase component of the program. During the HomeBase phase, the consultant meets the student's parents for approximately 45 minutes per week for 6 weeks to teach them skills to enhance their child's adjustment. Research indicates that students receiving the program show a reduction in aggressive behavior and increased academic engagement (Walker et al., 2009).

Incredible Years Small Group Dinosaur School Program

Incredible Years Small Group Dinosaur School Program (Webster-Stratton et al., 2001) was developed to support children in preschool and early elementary grades who are exhibiting early conduct problems. The program is delivered by trained group leaders in 2-hour weekly small-group sessions with approximately six children. This 22-week program consists of a series of DVD programs (over 180 vignettes) that teach children appropriate classroom behavior, problem-solving strategies, social skills, feelings literacy, and emotion self-regulation skills. Ideally, it is offered in conjunction with the 2-hour weekly Incredible Years Parent Group sessions. The child program consists of seven main components: (1) introduction and rules, (2) empathy and emotion, (3) problem solving, (4) anger control, (5) friendship skills, (6) communication skills, and (7) school skills. Research indicates that the program increases student use of prosocial skills, improves social competence, and decreases aggressive behavior (Webster-Stratton & Hammond, 1997).

Strong Kids

The Strong Kids programs (Merrell, Whitcom, & Parisi, 2009; Merrell, Parisi, & Whitcom, 2007; Merrell, Carrizales, Feuerborn, Gueldner, & Tran, 2007) are brief social and emotional learning curricula designed for teaching social and emotional skills, promoting resilience, strengthening assets, and increasing the coping skills of students. There is a Strong Start for PreK and one for use with students in grades K–2. Strong Kids is designed for students in grades 3–5. Session topics are designed to be developmentally appropriate and include identifying and understanding emotions, social skills, cognitive reframing, relaxation strategies, and problem-solving strategies. The sessions can be delivered to small groups of students in need of Tier 2 supports. Several studies have been conducted to evaluate the impact of the Strong Kids programs. In general, these studies have reported positive results, showing that exposure to these social–emotional learning programs produces significant increases in knowledge of social–emotional concepts and coping skills. In some cases, decreases in problem symptoms have been noted as well as increases in social–emotional competence (see Merrell, 2010, for a review).

USE OF DATA TO INFORM INTERVENTION AND MONITOR PROGRESS

Once evidence-based interventions are implemented, student progress should be monitored frequently to determine the following: (1) Is the intervention effective, meaning, does the student exhibit improvement on key indicators? (2) Is the intervention being implemented as intended? On occasion, when an intervention appears to be ineffective based on student data, it is because the intervention was not implemented with a high level of fidelity. Therefore, gathering data to show that the intervention is being implemented as intended is an important part of progress monitoring. Chapter 7 further underscores the importance of implementation fidelity and provides examples of how teams can assess overall fidelity as well as fidelity to specific interventions.

Many students who receive Tier 2 interventions that are implemented with integrity will benefit, but not all. The goal of the Tier 2 intervention is to produce a discrepancy between baseline and postintervention levels of student performance (i.e., postintervention data showing an increase in prosocial behaviors). If this discrepancy does not occur, then the student may need more intensive supports, such as a Tier 3 intervention or evaluation for eligibility for special education services (Gresham, 2005). There are several ways to monitor progress of students on Tier 2 interventions for externalizing problems. In fact, the same data used to identify students for Tier 2 interventions can be used to track their progress (i.e., ODRs, behavioral rating scales). In addition, many of the Tier 2 interventions described in this chapter use a daily behavior card or some form of behavior monitoring system. These are data that can be tracked, graphed, and analyzed on a weekly basis to determine whether the intervention should be continued, modified, or faded. Regardless of how progress is monitored for Tier 2 interventions, data collection on implementation and student progress must be systematic. As discussed in Chapter 1, at the start of the intervention Tier 2 teams should identify the source of data to be used to monitor progress, those who will collect and summarize the data, how often the data will be reviewed, and what the goals are for determining if the intervention needs to be continued as is, modified, faded, or if the student needs additional supports.

SUMMARY

This chapter provides a review of evidence-based practices that can be used as Tier 2 supports for students with externalizing problems. Additionally, an overview of methods for identifying students needing these additional supports is included, as well as strategies for systematically monitoring student outcomes to determine if the intervention is effective, needs modification or fading, or if more individualized supports are needed. Lastly, several comprehensive evidence-based programs recommended for use by schools to support students with externalizing problems were reviewed. This chapter concludes with a list of additional resources to support Tier 2 intervention development.

ADDITIONAL RESOURCES

Christenson, S. L., et al. (2008). *Check & connect: A comprehensive student engagement intervention manual.* Available from *checkandconnect.org/.*

Crone, D. A., & Horner, R. H. (2003). *Building positive behavior support systems in schools: Functional behavioral assessment.* New York: Guilford Press.

Crone, D. A., Horner, R. H., & Hawken, L. S. (2004). *Responding to problem behavior in schools: The behavior education program.* New York: Guilford Press.

Hawken, L. S., Pettersson, H., Mootz, J., & Anderson, C. (2005). *The behavior education program: A check-in, check-out intervention for students at risk.* New York: Guilford Press.

Lochman, J., Wells, K., & Lenhart, S. (2008). *Coping power: Child facilitators guide.* New York: Oxford University Press.

Merrell, K. W. (2008). *Behavioral, social, and emotional assessment of children and adolescents* (3rd ed.). New York: Routledge/Taylor & Francis.

Merrell, K. W., Carrizales, D., Feuerborn, L., Gueldner, B. A., & Tran, O. K. (2007). *Strong Kids— 3–5: A social and emotional learning curriculum.* Baltimore: Brookes.

Merrell, K. W., & Gueldner, B. A. (2010). *Social and emotional learning in the classroom: Promoting mental health and academic success.* New York: Guilford Press.

Merrell, K. W., Parisi, D., & Whitcomb, S. A. (2007). *Strong Start—Grades K–2: A social and emotional learning curriculum*. Baltimore: Brookes.

Merrell, K. W., Whitcomb, S. A., & Parisi, D. A. (2009). *Strong Start—Pre–K: A social and emotional learning curriculum*. Baltimore: Brookes.

O'Neil, R. E., Horner, R. H., Albin, R. W., Sprague, J. R., Storey, K., & Newton, J. S. (1997). *Functional assessment and program development of problem behavior: A practical handbook*. (2nd ed.). Pacific Grove, CA: Brooks/Cole.

Rathvon, N. (2008). *Effective school interventions* (2nd ed). New York: Guilford Press.

Reinke, W. M., Herman, K. C., & Sprick, R. (2011). *Motivational interviewing for effective classroom management: The classroom check-up*. New York: Guilford Press.

Webster-Stratton, C. (2005). *Dina dinosaur child training program*. Seattle, WA: Incredible Years.

Webster-Stratton, C. (2005). *The Incredible Years: A trouble-shooting guide for parents of children ages 3–8*. Toronto: Umbrella Press.

Webster-Stratton, C. (2010). *How to promote children's social and emotional competence*. London: Chapman.

Walker, H., Stiller, B., Golly, A., Kavanagh, K., Severson, H., & Feil, D. (1997). *First step to success*. Longmont, CO: Sopris West.

CHAPTER 4

Tier 2 Interventions
for Internalizing Behavior Problems

Internalizing symptoms and disorders are some of the most prevalent emotional and behavioral problems experienced by youth. A recent national survey found anxiety disorders to be the most common mental disorder among youth (31.9%) and also to have one of the earliest median ages of onset (6 years) (Merikangas et al., 2010). Mood disorders, such as depression, were nearly as common (14.3%) as behavior disorders in youth. The number of youth who experience internalizing symptoms that cause impairment but who do not meet criteria for having a disorder, of course, far exceeds these numbers. Prior research has shown that depressive symptoms in youth that are not severe enough to meet diagnostic criteria have a comparable negative impact on youth functioning (Lewinsohn et al., 2003).

Unfortunately, only a very small percentage of youth who experience internalizing distress receive needed services or supports. Depression and anxiety symptoms in youth often go unnoticed, and most youngsters (up to 80%) do not receive any services for their symptoms (Beardslee, Keller, Lavori, Staley, & Sacks, 1993; Keller, Lavori, Beardslee, Wunder, & Ryan, 1991; Lewinsohn, Rohde, & Seeley, 1998; Miller, DuPaul, & Lutz, 2002). Students with untreated or undertreated mental health needs experience poor academic and social outcomes in the future, including lowered rates of current and future employment and increased likelihood of involvement in the criminal justice, adult mental health, welfare, and/or public health systems (Lewinsohn, Rohde, Seeley, Klein, & Gotlib, 2003; Pfeiffer & Reddy, 1998). Thus, effective school-based preventive supports and interventions could fill a critical void for the legion of children in the nation's schools who are impacted by internalizing symptoms and disorders.

Schools are optimal places for supporting children with internalizing problems. First, many of the experiences that engender fear, apprehension, and sadness in children occur at school. Unsuccessful or damaging peer interactions, poor academic skills and outcomes, and performance worries are common sources of anxiety and depression in children. Recent research suggests that these experiences may contribute to the development and maintenance of internalizing symptoms in children (see Herman, Reinke, Parkin, Traylor, & Agarwal, 2009). Thus, creating supports to mitigate these effects could lower children's symptoms and lessen the likelihood of life-course persistent internalizing problems. Second, schools are social laboratories where children spend a great deal of their lives; this factor gives intervention teams plenty of opportunities to structure their experiences in ways that other settings may not allow.

In this chapter, in addition to depressive symptoms, we focus on generalized anxiety and social phobias, rather than the more specific anxiety disorders (PTSD, obsessive–compulsive disorder [OCD], specific phobias, panic disorder). Because generalized and social anxiety symptoms are among the most common symptoms experienced by children at risk for any anxiety order, interventions that alleviate these symptoms provide key leverage in reducing children's risk for all anxiety disorders. Moreover, precise intervention protocols have been developed to support children who meet diagnostic criteria for the more specific anxiety disorders, and these should be consulted by professionals attempting to treat these conditions. The focus of this chapter is to provide efficient supports in a school setting for children showing early internalizing symptoms.

> **Many of the experiences that engender fear, apprehension, and sadness in children occur at school.**

THEORETICAL FOUNDATIONS FOR INTERVENING IN THE PROBLEM

Our approach to providing supports to elementary-age students with internalizing symptoms is guided by an integrated social-cognitive and behavior analytic perspective. Social-cognitive theory (Bandura, 1986) suggests that interpersonal contexts contribute to the development of internalizing symptoms in youth. In particular, maladaptive coping responses (e.g., avoidance of feared social situations and negative self-dialogue) are modeled and selectively reinforced by repeated encounters with the social environment. A behavior analytic perspective adds the notion that behavior is functional, and interventions are most likely to be effective when they address these functions. It is important to note that comprehensive biopsychosocial models indicate that various genetic and biological factors contribute to children's risk for developing internalizing problems (see Cicchetti & Toth, 1998). In this chapter, though, our focus is on identifying malleable risk factors that can be manipulated in a school environment to reduce children's symptoms and risk for ongoing internalizing distress.

Assumptions

Our model is guided by several key assumptions (see Table 4.1). First, a fundamental assumption of a tiered approach to internalizing interventions, now supported by abundant research, is that internalizing disorders can be prevented. When children showing early symptoms are identified and given adequate supports in school and home environments,

TABLE 4.1. Key Assumptions Guiding Interventions for Internalizing Behavior Problems

1. Internalizing symptoms and disorders can be prevented.

2. Internalizing symptoms are functional.

3. Internalizing symptoms can be described and understood as composed of three intertwined components of a child's experience: feelings/physiology, thoughts, and behaviors.

4. Children learn effective coping thoughts and behaviors through both explicit instruction and natural encounters with the environment.

5. Most elementary-age children do not yet have the cognitive capacity to fully benefit from cognitive-behavioral interventions that work so well with adolescents and adults.

6. Many of the environments and interventions known to be effective in deterring disruptive behaviors can also be helpful for children at risk for internalizing disorders.

studies have shown that effective interventions can lower symptoms and reduce the likelihood of future anxiety and depressive disorders (National Research Council and Institute of Medicine, 2009).

A second key assumption is that internalizing symptoms, like externalizing behavior problems, are functional. Although some internalizing symptoms (e.g., whining and reassurance seeking) are maintained by adult attention, one hallmark of both depressive and anxious behaviors is that they are commonly maintained by escape from or avoidance of unpleasant situations or feared stimuli. To be effective, Tier 2 supports must address the possibility that internalizing behaviors persist because of escape functions.

A third assumption in line with the social-cognitive perspective is that internalizing symptoms can be described and understood as composed of three intertwined components of a child's experience: feelings/physiology, thoughts, and behaviors. This framework implies that, in addition to external consequences, internalizing symptoms are maintained by negative feedback loops across these three domains. Likewise, adaptive functioning is created and maintained by positive feedback loops among these experiences.

A fourth assumption is that children learn effective coping thoughts and behaviors both through explicit instruction and also through natural encounters with the environment. Thus, efficient and effective supports to prevent internalizing symptoms in youth need to capitalize on the situations and experiences that occur in the natural environment to embed these opportunities in the daily experiences of all youth and reserving the more intensive, individualized interventions for students who do not fully benefit from these experiences.

Internalizing disorders can be prevented.

A fifth assumption is that most elementary-age children do not yet have the cognitive capacity to fully benefit from the cognitive-behavioral interventions that work so well with adolescents and adults unless they receive environmental supports from adults to reinforce, prompt, and practice the skills. Although these skills are critical for the independent coping and social problem solving that characterize adaptive adult functioning, children are newly developing these skills and learning to use them as part of their coping repertoire during the elementary years. For these skills to become automatic coping styles, children need to see them modeled, practiced, prompted, and reinforced repeatedly during early and middle childhood.

A sixth and final assumption is that many of the environments and interventions known to be effective in deterring disruptive behaviors can also be helpful for children at risk for internalizing disorders. For instance, although PBIS was originally developed to reduce disruptive behavior problems in schools, a recent study suggested that students with internalizing problems also benefited from strong SW-PBIS supports (Lane, Wehby, Robertson, & Rogers, 2007). Likewise, recent evidence is showing that parent and teacher behavior management interventions originally developed to treat conduct problems have positive collateral effects on child internalizing symptoms (Webster-Stratton & Herman, 2008; Herman, Borden, Reinke, & Webster-Stratton, 2011). Abundant research has now shown that many of the same risk factors for the exacerbation of conduct problems are risk factors for the worsening of internalizing symptoms; thus interventions to reduce these risks may alleviate multiple symptoms in children (see Herman, Reinke, Stormont, Puri, & Agarwal, 2010).

A key implication of these assumptions is that schools can efficiently provide supports for students at risk for anxiety and depression, just as many schools currently do for children with disruptive behaviors. The principles that guide Tier 1 and 2 supports are similar for both internalizing and externalizing problems. Clear expectations, consistent and predictable consequences, high rates of explicit praise and positive attention, and warm interactions with adults all provide the context for lessening children's risk for internalizing distress. Still, some children will not be fully responsive to these universal supports and will exhibit higher levels of internalizing symptoms.

> **Many of the environments and interventions known to be effective in deterring disruptive behaviors can also be helpful for children at risk for internalizing disorders.**

Intervention Principles

We have developed seven principles based on these assumptions to guide support teams in constructing effective behavior support interventions for children showing early internalizing symptoms (see Table 4.2). The first three of these principles are focused on what children with internalizing symptoms need: new experiences, encouragement and rewards, and structured and predictable environments. These principles are contrasted with prevailing views—those that are more appropriate for adults or adolescents with these types of symptoms—to ensure that behavior support teams are mindful of these distinctions. In other words, the first three principles suggest that supports for young children will be ineffective if they simply offer new explanations or ways of thinking, without environmental supports, to these children.

The next four principles focus on the characteristics of the interventions for youth exhibiting early internalizing symptoms. These principles make clear that effective supports are ecological, attentive to child strengths and resources, monitored and revised as needed, and team-based with multiple adults being involved at school and home.

These principles provide a flexible yet structured framework for guiding behavior support teams in designing support plans that are more likely to be helpful to children across a

TABLE 4.2. Intervention Principles for Developing Tier 2 Supports for Internalizing Behavior Problems

Children with internalizing symptoms need

1. New experiences, not just explanations. They need opportunities to practice new skills and receive feedback about them in their natural environments. Interventions are active, with the goal of remediating skill and performance deficits. Interventions can directly teach children the skills necessary to attain a high rate of social rewards in multiple systems and settings.

2. To be encouraged and rewarded for being active and taking risks. Only by interacting with the social environment in new ways will the child have the opportunity to unlearn past misrules and replace them with more positive consequences and expectations.

3. Predictable and structured environments, not just new ways of thinking. Young children develop positive attributions about themselves, their future, and their world by experiencing social and academic successes and by learning that their actions have predictable consequences in school and at home.

Effective supports for children with internalizing symptoms

4. Consider the multiple systems that may influence these symptoms, including schools, families, neighborhoods, care delivery systems, public policies, and their interactions.

5. Are guided by an assessment of all assets and problem areas of the child and the family, the settings of the assets and problem areas, and the role of significant others (peers, teachers, parents, siblings) in maintaining the assets and the problem behaviors.

6. Require continuous monitoring and flexibility.

7. Include primary caregivers, teachers, and other caring adults as models and coaches whenever possible.

> **Interventions for young children with internalizing symptoms will be ineffective if they simply offer new explanations or ways of thinking to these children without environmental supports.**

multitude of school environments while attending to child and family characteristics. These principles are intended to be used as a checklist by support teams during and after the design of Tier 2 interventions to encourage reflection on whether or not their support plans are attentive to these areas of concern.

Framework for Environmental Supports

Consistent with these principles, Figure 4.1 depicts our environmental supports framework for intervening in youth internalizing symptoms. The circles in Figure 4.1 highlight the intrapersonal context of internalizing symptoms; that is, the thoughts, feelings, and behaviors that are commonly experienced by youth with these symptoms and that can be the targets of interventions. The circle on the right in Figure 4.1 lists the feelings associated with internalizing symptoms. In addition to a high level of negative affect (e.g., apprehension, tension) and physiological hyperarousal, youth with anxiety symptoms often report feelings of helplessness. A distinguishing characteristic of youth who are depressed is that they are likely to experience feelings of hopelessness on top of a sense of helplessness. Children who

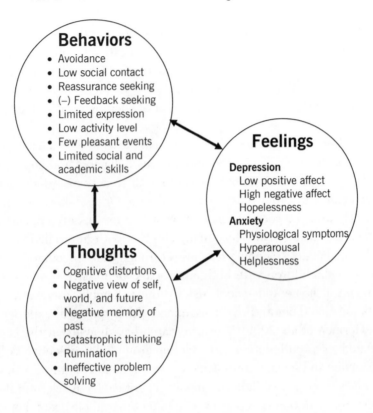

FIGURE 4.1. Thoughts, feelings, and behaviors associated with internalizing symptoms.

experience both anxiety and depressive symptoms report high levels of negative affect relative to higher-functioning peers; those who are depressed typically experience lower levels of positive affect even compared to children who have problems with anxiety.

From a social-cognitive perspective, the most proximal intrapersonal factors that maintain and exacerbate these internalized feelings are maladaptive thoughts and behaviors. Anxiety and depression are associated with an assortment of cognitive distortions and ineffective cognitive coping responses. Youth who are anxious tend to have a hypersensitivity to internal stimuli and overestimate risks associated with their well-being or that of others. They misinterpret bodily sensations and exaggerate perceived negative social consequences. Youth with depressive symptoms commonly develop negative perceptions of themselves, the world, and their future. Research has shown that these maladaptive cognitive processes and structures do not become fully crystallized until late childhood, making the elementary school years an optimal time to intervene and attempt to disrupt or alter these processes.

In response to maladaptive cognitions, children engage in predictable problematic behaviors. The most common and understandable behavior for a child who fears an external (social) or internal stimuli is to avoid it. Unfortunately, avoidance engenders more fear and negative cognitions, which in turn increases the likelihood that avoidance will persist as a coping strategy. Young children will also engage in reassurance seeking from adults in their environment to confirm that they are safe. If adults consistently comply with these requests, unfortunately children internalize the message that they are unable to cope with life challenges themselves. Some children also elicit negative feedback from their caregivers to confirm their negative self-perceptions. Youth who become increasingly depressed may come to avoid nearly all activities, including formerly pleasurable ones, decreasing the likelihood of experiencing any positive emotions or of eliciting positive feedback from their environment.

How do children develop these ineffective cognitive and behavior responses? One well-established mechanism: Depressed and anxious behaviors and coping responses are modeled by adult caregivers. Up to 80% of youth with anxiety disorders have one or more parents with an anxiety disorder (Last, Hersen, Kazdin, Orvaschel, & Perrin, 1991; Rosenbaum et al., 1992), and the social transmission of risk for anxiety appears to be at least as strong as genetic transmission. Thus, many children with internalizing symptoms have simply never learned effective coping responses through their encounters with the natural environment. Second, children with both anxiety and depressive symptoms often experience environments at home and school that are unpredictable, especially with regard to adults' expectations for them and the consequences that they will experience from their behavior (see Herman et al., 2009). Third, research has shown that the cognitive misappraisals associated with youth depression are often grounded in objective skill deficits, particularly in academic and social realms (Cole & Turner, 1993). That is, youth who are prone to view themselves in a negative light commonly get critical feedback from their social and/or academic environment that they are less competent than their peers. Fourth, because of their low rate of social and pleasurable behaviors, youth who are depressed often experience very low levels of positive reinforcement to counter their negative life experiences.

Each of these hypothesized mechanisms suggests potential supports that can be put in place to reduce these symptoms (see Figures 4.2 and 4.3). First, adults in school environments can intentionally model and reinforce effective coping behaviors and thoughts. The key is to make these modeling efforts explicit, especially since internal coping responses can only be observed by others if they are spoken or demonstrated in some way. In addition, effective coping responses can be explicitly taught either through direct instruction in small-group settings or through active modeling (incidental learning) throughout the day. Second, consistent, predictable environments at home and school can mitigate some of the distress experienced by these children.

> **Cognitive misappraisals associated with youth depression are often grounded in objective skill deficits, particularly in academic and social realms.**

Effective behavior management (clear expectations, consistent consequences, higher rates of positive than negative interactions) in all school settings fits with this necessary support. Aiding parents in developing effective parenting skills at home can further strengthen the child's comfort by building predictability throughout the day. Third, children showing early signs of anxiety or depression should be assessed for real social or academic skill deficits and be provided with the needed supports to remediate any observed problems in these domains. Fourth, children need to experience rich amounts of positive reinforcement for engaging in any desired behaviors, including the in-between steps toward the ultimate behavior objectives.

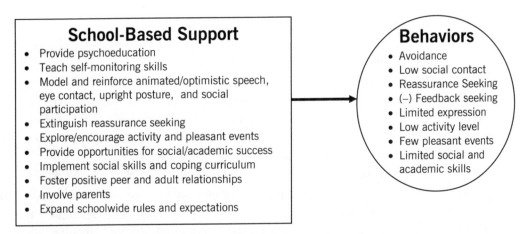

FIGURE 4.2. School-based leverage points to reduce depressive and anxious behaviors.

HOW TO IDENTIFY CHILDREN WITH INTERNALIZING BEHAVIOR PROBLEMS

Children with internalizing symptoms often go undetected. Sometimes the anxious, compliant behaviors exhibited by children who experience only internalizing problems are well received by teachers and other school adults who are overwhelmed with the overt challenges presented by children with externalizing problems. At the same time, a large number of children with internalizing symptoms simultaneously present with externalizing behavior problems. These children's internalizing symptoms are also often missed by school professionals because they draw less attention than their more striking behavior problems.

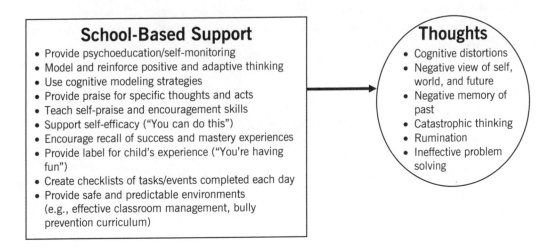

FIGURE 4.3. School-based leverage points to reduce depressive and anxious thoughts.

Thus, a key first step in creating an effective system for identifying youth with internalizing symptoms is to educate staff and professionals in schools about these issues and about the common symptoms associated with depression and anxiety.

The gold standard method for assessing children for internalizing distress is self-report. Even children as young as 6 years of age can accurately report on their internalizing symptoms (Ialongo, Edelsohn, & Kellam, 2001). Unfortunately, it is not practical to routinely ask all students to complete objective measures of depressive or anxious symptoms, and probably would be met with a fair amount of parent resistance if it were.

Instead, a tiered approach to assessment is the most viable model in schools. At the first level, teachers who have been trained to identify internalizing symptoms can be asked to nominate a subset of students who may be experiencing these symptoms. Then teachers can be asked to complete a rating scale on each nominated student. Students meeting a minimum threshold of symptoms can then be further evaluated with self-report, parent report, and/or school-based observations of the concerning symptoms.

Once a subset of youth who is showing early signs of anxiety or depression is identified (e.g., those with T-scores of 60–69 on objective measures of these symptoms), then Tier 2 supports can be planned and delivered. Much like the Tier 2 supports currently delivered to students with disruptive behaviors, the supports for these students at this level need to be efficient and delivered in group formats rather than individually tailored. Intensive individual supports are reserved for those students who show clinical levels of these symptoms (e.g., T-scores of 70 or greater) or who have not responded to the Tier 2 supports.

A prerequisite for a tiered approach is that support teams need to be very explicit about the observable behaviors that are of concern and tie their identification and monitoring system to these behaviors. Common tangible indicators of internalizing distress in elementary-age children include schoolwide absences and tardiness (Seagull & Weinshank, 1984), visits to the school nurse (Schneider, Friedman, & Fisher, 1995), somatic complaints reported to teachers or other school personnel (Schneider et al., 1995), social withdrawal, infrequent work completion, excessive reassurance seeking, crying or pouting or whining, negative self-statements, irritability, and low academic skills and performance (Patterson & Capaldi, 1990). Any of these behaviors, when present, may serve as objective targets of intervention that can be monitored over time.

Measures

The measures described in Chapter 3 for creating a multiple-gating system for externalizing problems are also applicable for creating such systems for internalizing problems. The *Systematic Screening for Behavior Disorders* (SSBD) rating system (Walker & Severson, 1992), *Social Skills Improvement System* (SISS; Gresham & Elliott, 2007), and the *Behavior Assessment System for Children–2* (BASC-2; Reynolds & Kamphaus, 2004) are all equally relevant for screening internalizing problems and can be used in similar ways as described in Chapter 3. In addition to using the multiple-informant protocols for these tools, support teams may wish to use more construct-specific child-report measures such as *Children's Depression Inventory* (Kovacs, 1991), Internalizing *Symptoms Scale for Children* (Merrell & Walters, 1998), or the *Multidimensional Anxiety Scale for Children* (MASC; March, Parker, Sullivan, Stallings, & Connor, 1997).

Additional Considerations

Because externalizing and internalizing symptoms commonly co-occur, school personnel should screen all children identified as having disruptive behaviors (including those with ADHD diagnoses) for internalizing symptoms. Likewise, all children with internalizing problems should be further screened for academic and social skill deficits, and vice versa.

REVIEW OF EVIDENCE-BASED PROGRAMS FOR INTERVENING IN INTERNALIZING BEHAVIOR PROBLEMS

Several professional review groups have created criteria for determining the quality and quantity of evidence to support particular interventions for youth. One group, Division 53 of the American Psychological Association, has created three categories or levels for defining evidence-based programs (EBPs). By their definition, designation as a *well-established* EBP requires that an intervention has shown itself to be more effective than an active placebo in two or more independent randomized trials. Interventions are deemed *probably efficacious* if they have been shown to be more effective than a wait-list control condition in two or more studies. Finally, interventions are rated as *possibly efficacious* if one strong study has found it to be effective.

Evidence-Based Programs for Child Anxiety

Using these criteria, the Division 53 Review Group rated three programs or practices as *probably efficacious* for the treatment of generalized anxiety in youth: individual or group cognitive-behavioral therapy (CBT), with or without parent involvement, and Coping Cat, a specific intervention for youth anxiety. *Possibly efficacious* interventions included variations of these primary ones, such as interventions that simultaneously targeted parental anxiety or coping or that included parental groups, family CBT, or Internet delivery. Three interventions were rated as *probably efficacious* for social phobia: Coping Cat, family-focused individual CBT, and social effectiveness training. We highlight Coping Cat as an exemplar of a specific intervention for child anxiety, given its strong research base and that all of the effective programs identified by this review group are grounded in the same cognitive-behavioral framework as Coping Cat. Additionally, the manuals and materials to support Coping Cat intervention implementation are easily accessible.

Coping Cat

Coping Cat was developed by Philip Kendall at Temple University (Kendall, Furr, & Podell, 2010). Kendall and colleagues have reported several randomized clinical trials that have evaluated the effects of Coping Cat in treating children as young as 7 years old who have generalized anxiety and/or social phobia disorders. These studies all found positive effects for individually or group-delivered Coping Cat for child anxiety symptoms and further reported that effects persisted (in one study, gains were maintained over 7 years).

The main components of Coping Cat include psychoeducation, cognitive restructuring, graded exposure, relaxation skills, and relapse prevention. Skills are taught principally through modeling and role plays. The first half of the intervention focuses on helping children develop a FEAR plan. FEAR is an acronym for guiding each step of the plan. *Feeling frightened* teaches essential self-monitoring and relaxation skills whereby the child is aided in becoming more aware of triggers for anxiety and alternate coping responses. *Expecting bad things to happen* refers to efforts to help the child become more aware of his or her distorted and problematic expectations and beliefs that worsen their anxiety. Over time, the child is taught methods for changing these cognitions into more adaptive ones. *Attitudes and actions* focuses on teaching the child effective problem-solving skills. Finally, *results and rewards* provides the child with reinforcement for brave behaviors that counter his or her avoidance coping strategies. The skills that are developed during the first half of the intervention prepare the child for the exposure assignments over the second half. The child and interventionist develop a hierarchy of fears and then practice approaching these fears in a graded manner, using both covert and in vivo procedures. In clinical settings, the intervention is typically delivered over 16 weeks, and parents are invited to attend several sessions.

> **Coping Cat is an exemplar of a specific intervention for child anxiety.**

Implementation of the program is supported by a treatment manual and participant workgroups that can be purchased through Workbook Publishing (*www.workbookpublishing.com*). Additionally, video-based examples of each of the core therapeutic interventions are also available for purchase.

School-Based Preventive Cognitive-Behavioral Therapy for Anxiety

Several other programs that parallel many of the same skills and therapeutic strategies found in Coping Cat have been applied in preventive contexts. Most notably, Barrett (2004) and Pahl and Barrett (2010) created a series of FRIENDS programs—various adaptations of Coping Cat delivered in a variety of clinical and school contexts, with and without family involvement. The program has been successfully delivered as a group preventive intervention in schools, and benefits have been found to persist for 6 years or longer. Intervention materials are available through Australian Academic Press (*www.friendsinfo.net*).

Ginsburg (2009) has also conducted small trials in schools and with families. In one excellent example, she created an eight-session preventive intervention for children not yet diagnosed with an anxiety disorder, but with one or more parents who had been. The intervention begins with two parent-only sessions in which parents are given psychoeducation about anxiety. The remaining sessions are delivered with parent and child together. Parents are encouraged to reinforce the target skills throughout the week. Initial evidence found this intervention to prevent anxiety in offspring of anxious parents.

Evidence-Based Programs for Child Depression

Group CBT with or without a parent component was deemed to be a *well-established* intervention for children with depression. *Probably efficacious* interventions included school-based group CBT, the Penn Prevention Program, self-control training, and behavior therapy. Unfortunately, very few of these interventions have been conducted with elementary-age children, so established interventions for this age group are sparse. Indicated prevention services (e.g., group training in social skills or cognitive restructuring, parenting classes) would be offered to children exhibiting early signs of depression. Examples of successful indicated prevention approaches include group-delivered coping skills training for adolescents (Clarke et al., 1995; Stark, Rouse, & Kurowski, 1994) and family training (see Muñoz, Le, Clarke, & Taycox, 2002).

Kevin Stark's Taking ACTION program and his recently developed ACTION program for girls have been implemented with children as young as 8 years old, and existing studies suggest positive effects on child depression. The core components of these interventions include mood monitoring, activating coping skills, problem solving, and cognitive restructuring. Intervention materials for these programs are available through Workbook Publishing (*www.workbookpublishing.com*).

REVIEW OF EVIDENCE-BASED PRACTICES FOR INTERVENING IN INTERNALIZING BEHAVIOR PROBLEMS

One way to summarize evidence-based practices for internalizing symptoms is to compile all available evidence-based programs (such as those we have just described) and then tally the number of times a given practice appears in each of the programs. The more often a practice appears, the more likely it is to be a key component of the programs' effects. Chorpita and Daleiden (2009) have done this, reviewing all literature regarding evidence-based practices for youth. They reviewed 615 treatment protocols from 322 randomized clinical trials and identified overlapping methods for each of the major child mental health syndromes. For all evidence-based anxiety interventions, the single most common component was exposure to the anxiety-provoking stimulus. Additional elements included relaxation training, cognitive coping, modeling, and psychoeducation for the child. For depression-focused interventions, the most common components included cognitive restructuring, child psychoeducation, activity scheduling, self-monitoring, problem solving, goal setting, and social skills training. Notably, the elements differed somewhat based on the target population. For depression interventions developed for African American youth, only two prominent components emerged: cognitive restructuring and communications skills. For Hispanic youth, the list of components paralleled those collapsed across child ethnicity, but with a stronger emphasis on parent involvement (e.g., parent psychoeducation and coping).

Taken together, some general implications can be derived from these data. First, evidence-based interventions for virtually any type of internalizing distress typically include a psychoeducational component for the child and some attention to cognitive coping strategies. Second, exposure strategies are nearly always a component of evidence-based interventions for anxiety. Third, depression-specific interventions typically include some attention to social problem-solving skills (including social or communication skills) and may vary slightly depending on the ethnicity of the target population.

Unfortunately, one limitation of this type of review is that it is largely based on interventions delivered in clinic settings to children with identified disorders. Thus, school-based interventions for children presenting with symptoms, but not disorders, may require some modification. Second, clinic-based interventions have tended to be dominated by traditional views of child psychopathology, which in general have represented downward extensions of interventions for adults. Thus, the interventions summarized by Chorpita and Daleiden tend to overemphasize within-child coping responses to the neglect of the broader ecological environment that is needed to support and retain acquisition of taught skills, especially

> **For all evidence-based anxiety interventions the single most common component is exposure to the anxiety-provoking stimulus.**

for young children. With these caveats in mind, though, the lessons from this large review suggest some markers for practices that should be considered when designing Tier 2 supports in school settings.

PUTTING IT ALL TOGETHER: STRATEGIES FOR BUILDING TIER 2 SUPPORTS FOR INTERNALIZING BEHAVIOR PROBLEMS

Building on the growing evidence base for practices and programs that support children experiencing internalizing distress as well as the effective Tier 2 delivery systems commonly used to support children with externalizing problems, we review several strategies and practices for designing effective behavior supports for children showing early symptoms of anxiety or depression. A basic premise is that Tier 2 supports must be delivered efficiently and pragmatically rather than intensively, as occurs when children experience severe emotional distress or disorders. Thus, the specific strategies described below are best delivered in small groups or using an efficient delivery mechanism such as that offered by the Behavior Education Program (Hawken, Adolphson, MacLeod, Schumann, 2009). Moreover, to be effective, all of these strategies must reflect incorporation of the key principles described earlier in this chapter. Below we describe several fundamental strategies that commonly appear in evidence-based practices for youth with internalizing problems that can be easily incorporated into group instruction or behavior support planning.

Daily Behavior Cards Modified for Internalizing Symptoms

The daily behavior card systems described in Chapter 3 can also be used with minimal modifications for youth with internalizing symptoms. The card can include different behavior targets that match the common behavior problems of children experiencing internalizing distress. For instance, the behavior targets on the daily rating form could be things such as *be positive, be brave,* and *participate* (see Figure 4.4 for an example). Of course, teams

Student: Jennifer | Date: February 18, 2011

☺ 3 = Great | Goal: 80% of points
☺ 2 = OK | Points Earned:
☹ 1 = Needs work | Goal Met? Y or N If yes, reward earned? Animal Game

Goals & Expectations	Subject Reading	Subject Spelling	Subject RTI	Subject Math	Subject Lunch	Subject Special	Subject Computer	Total Points
Goal 1: Be Positive 1. Say and do positive things 2. Say positive things about self	3	2	3	1	3	3	2	17
Goal 2: Be Brave 1. Show strong body/strong voice 2. Try new things	3	2	3	3	3	3	2	19
Goal 3: Participate 1. In class 2. With friends	3	2	3	3	3	3	2	19
Total Points Earned	55					% Earned Today: 55/63 = 87%		
Total Points Possible	63							

FIGURE 4.4. Daily behavior card targeting internalizing symptoms.

Parent Signature _____

would need to follow the guidelines described in Chapter 3 for explicitly teaching the child these expectations and the rules of reinforcement.

Psychoeducation

As noted above, nearly all effective interventions for child internalizing symptoms include a psychoeducational component. In our view, psychoeducation is most likely to be helpful for young children if parents and teachers are also given access to this same educational content. This access can be accomplished most efficiently if parents and/or teachers are present in the same session as when the information is shared with the child. The rationale is provided by one of the assumptions of our model: that young children typically do not have the cognitive capacity to use and generalize the informational knowledge provided without environmental supports. A second rationale for providing joint psychoeducation content to parents is that often children with internalizing symptoms live in households where one or more caregivers has similar symptoms. Thus, by providing psychoeducation to both the child and parent, support teams are potentially providing parents with access to needed information that can help them manage their own symptoms.

Psychoeducation about internalizing problems can be accomplished in a single individual, group, or family meeting and can be supplemented with written literature. The content of the session involves teaching the parent and child about the social-cognitive model of depression and/or anxiety (the manuals for Coping Cat, FRIENDS, and Taking ACTION provide excellent examples). Typically, interventionists draw the three circles representing thoughts, feelings, and behaviors on a sheet of paper and define the terms as in Figure 4.1. For instance, a school-based interventionist might say, "Feelings are the emotions we experience, and we usually use a single word to describe them, such as *happy, sad,* or *mad.*" Rather than simply presenting information didactically, interventionists need to engage the participants in the conversation. So here they might ask for other examples of feeling words. Feeling charts that show children's facial expressions with feelings labeled beneath are also useful in this regard. We have had success in creating our own feeling charts using pictures of pets (see Figure 4.5 for an example) or allowing children to draw facial expressions on blank ovals depicting various feeling states.

Next, the interventionist defines thoughts. An example is presented below:

"Thoughts are the stream of words and images that go through our mind much like a message board in Times Square. Our thoughts are always with us, and it is sometimes hard to become aware of them because they feel so automatic. Thoughts are best considered as complete sentences. So right now I'm thinking, 'I'm enjoying talking with you. You seem to be listening and understanding things.' We also know that thoughts and feelings are connected. When you feel something, you are more likely to have thoughts that go along with those feelings. So when you are happy, what are some thoughts that might be going through your head? [Responses] And when you are sad? [Responses]"

Happy

Sad

Relaxed

Worried

Alert

Tired

FIGURE 4.5. Recognizing feelings.

Again the interventionist might ask the child to come up with examples of thoughts, given scenarios matched to the child's experiences. For instance, if a child likes to play soccer, the interventionist might ask him or her to picture scoring the winning goal in a game and then ask him or her what feelings that would produce and also what thoughts would go along with those feelings.

Finally, the interventionist defines behaviors:

"Behaviors are the things we do. They are different than thoughts because thoughts are private events and behaviors are public, which means we can see them. We can't see thoughts. You have to tell us about them. But we can see behaviors. So what are some behaviors that go along with being happy? [Responses] What do you do when you are happy? [Responses] What are behaviors that go along with being sad? [Responses]"

Once the participants have a common understanding of the terms, the next step is to highlight how all of these experiences are interrelated. To illustrate how thoughts, feelings, and behaviors are connected, it is helpful to discuss the positive and negative cycles that they can engender. It is best to think of examples that are related to what you know about the child with whom you are working as you create your cycle examples. An example is presented below:

"Because thoughts, feelings, and behaviors are so interconnected, it is easy for us to get into positive and negative cycles where each builds off the others. First, let's think of a negative cycle. Let's say one morning you get up late for school (*points to behaviors on the handout*). You feel tired (*points to feelings*) and tell yourself, 'I want to sleep in' (*points to thoughts*). Your mom knocks on your door and tells you to get up. You just moan [behavior]. You think, 'Why doesn't she leave me alone? It's not fair' [thought]. Finally, you crawl out of bed and you feel irritated [feeling]. Your mom asks you about what you need for the day, and you say, 'Just leave me alone, I don't want to go to school' [behavior]. Then you get into an argument with your mom about school [behavior]. You think, 'What a hassle. Everyone's on my case. No one likes me' [thought], which makes you feel down [feeling]. Finally, you walk out the door, but you miss the bus [behavior] so your mom has to drive you to school. You know this is a problem because this will make her late to work [thought]. You feel guilty [feeling] and think, 'Boy what a screw-up I am' [thought]. You walk into your first class late [behavior]. You try not to make eye contact with anyone [behavior] and you have the thought, 'Everyone thinks I'm lazy' [thought], which makes you feel sad and lonely [behavior]. You sit quietly the rest of the class [behavior] and find yourself worrying about your grades and how far behind you are in class [thought]. So you can see how a cycle that started with one event, waking up late, spiraled out of control and kept getting worse by the things you were thinking and doing, so that by the time you reached school you were feeling sad, guilty, and lonely. Now let's imagine a positive cycle."

Next, the interventionist would repeat the cycle except this time replacing positive thoughts and behaviors that build on each other so that by the time the student reaches class, he or she is feeling relaxed and ready to learn.

Finally, it is helpful to ask how a child could turn a negative cycle into a positive cycle. An interventionist might ask, "Of these three parts of our lives, which one do you think is the hardest to change directly?" The answer is that feelings are the hardest to change directly because we do not have a feeling switch that we can automatically use to shift our moods. Instead, we can change our mood by either changing our thoughts or our behavior. This is a central premise of all cognitive and behavioral coping skills that we want children and adults to understand: To manage their mood, they need to learn effective coping thoughts or behaviors. All of the interventions and supports follow from this basic premise. With this premise as a foundation, the child and parent have a common framework for thinking about effective coping strategies.

When anxiety is a prominent symptom, it is important to discuss the common physiological responses associated with anxiety, such as rapid heart rate, sweaty palms, rapid breathing, shortness of breath, and shakiness. These physiological responses are discussed as part of the feeling domain of experience, and the interconnectedness of thoughts and behaviors with these experiences is emphasized.

Self-Monitoring

Self-monitoring is nearly always a component of interventions for internalizing problems. An assumption of a social-cognitive approach to mood and anxiety management is that children must learn to monitor their feelings as a signal to prompt effective coping. Monitoring often also includes awareness of thoughts and behaviors that are tied to their emotions. More generally, Tier 2 supports include a monitoring system for tracking child behaviors, as observed by teachers throughout the day, as a form of feedback to improve those behaviors by using them as targets to supplement, prompt, and teach self-monitoring skills.

Monitoring mood is a fairly complex skill that requires language for labeling emotions, self-reflection and awareness, and an ability not only to differentiate feeling states from one another, but also ultimately to gauge the intensity of each feeling state. Children are typically not able to do all of these things, even with training and support, until late childhood. So mood monitoring systems for young children might simply start with three or four emotions (happy, sad, mad, and tired) and not focus on intensity at all. One simple strategy for young children is to have them create a watch using construction paper with an hour hand that can be rotated and three feelings marked on the watch face (see Friedberg & McClure, 2002, for other examples). An adult can prompt the child throughout the day to check his or her mood and to move the feeling hand to match it. As with all the strategies discussed in this section, elementary-age children need environmental supports to ensure that they develop these skills and generalize them to real-world settings. The Emotion Coaching section discussed later provides one type of support that can create incidental learning opportunities to supplement explicit instruction for learning to self-monitor.

For older children, more complex forms can be used that include scaling dimensions such as depicted in Figure 4.6 (see Form 4.1 in the Appendix for a blank version). Even more complex forms for cognitively sophisticated children might include multiple feeling states and intensity levels. The child can be asked to complete the form throughout the day or simply to give an overall score at the end of each day to track feelings and thoughts and the behaviors related to them.

If scaling is used, children need to be assisted in understanding how to differentiate the intensity of feelings. One strategy is to give children lots of examples of using anchors and intensity on other domains that are more tangible than feeling states, such as temperature, speed, and height. So children could be asked to think about the hottest day they ever remember and to mark it on a temperature scale. Then they could be asked about the coldest day, which could be marked on the opposite end of the scale. Next, they could be asked about today's temperature, and then they could be helped ito mark it on the scale and determine if it is closer to the coldest or hottest day. Next, they could be asked about the day before, and so on. Once it is clear that the child understands scaling after providing several examples like this, the feeling scale can be introduced and anchors can be established in a similar way. For example:

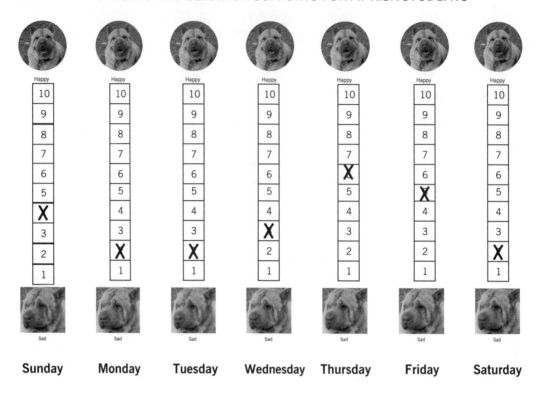

Sunday   Monday   Tuesday   Wednesday   Thursday   Friday   Saturday

Positive thoughts or activities that made me happy: <u>Playing soccer with my brother after school,</u> <u>when my mom said she was proud of me, getting a good grade on my spelling test Thursday,</u> <u>when I earned my reward for being brave, meeting with Ms. Jenkins to go over my day, thinking</u> <u>that I'm happy for trying hard.</u>

Negative thoughts or activities that made me sad: <u>Playing by myself on the weekend, getting</u> <u>to school late on Monday, sitting by myself at lunch. When the teacher called on me and I</u> <u>didn't know the answer, thinking that I'm not as smart as other kids, hearing my mom and dad</u> <u>arguing, thinking that no one likes me.</u>

FIGURE 4.6. Sample mood monitoring form with scaling on two dimensions.

"What is the happiest you ever felt?" (Write down the example by the 10.)

"The saddest?" (Write down the example as a 1.)

"How are you feeling right now?" (Choose a number from 1 to 10.)

> **As with all the strategies, elementary-age children need environmental supports to ensure that they develop these skills and generalize them to real-world settings.**

Teaching Adaptive Thinking Skills

Helping students develop adaptive thinking is often a key component of changing internalizing behaviors. For older children, self-monitoring naturally leads into efforts to build more constructive thinking processes. Two primary methods for teaching adaptive thinking skills are simply to develop and prompt targeted coping thoughts or to use more active cognitive restructuring methods. The former method is more appropriate for young children. The latter method requires cognitive sophistication to be able to monitor one's thoughts and feelings on a moment-to-moment basis and then to challenge and change unconstructive thoughts in the moment. Again, these methods will not be successful if children are simply taught the skills and expected to apply them, on their own, in their natural environments. Children need adult support to learn to use these coping strategies outside of training sessions.

Planting positive thoughts is as simple as creating a list of adaptive coping thoughts that professionals would like the child to learn. This list can be created in collaboration with the child and parent. Positive coping thoughts include statements such as "I can do this—I'm doing the best I can" as well as self-reward statements (e.g., "I'm proud of myself") and challenge coping statements (e.g., "I am going to try this because I know it is good for me"). Professionals can also plant coping questions that are designed to elicit coping thoughts: for example, "What's the worst that could happen?", "Is anyone going to remember this 100 years from now?", or "Is this helpful for me to be thinking about right now?" After creating a list of coping statements and/or questions, the next goal is get the child to review the list regularly throughout the day. The list can be written on an index card that the child pulls out and reads several times a day. Teachers or parents can help by prompting use of the card (see Form 4.2 in the Appendix for an example).

As children get older (10 and above), they are more likely to be able to use active coping and problem-solving methods. One well-established method for helping older children and adolescents to change maladaptive thinking is the ABC (DE) method associated with rational emotive therapy. Figure 4.7 contains an example of a more advanced form for helping children develop this skill (see Form 4.3 in the Appendix for a blank version). Children are assisted in learning to use this form with specific examples of times they have had strong negative feelings. The first step is for the child to complete step C and write down the consequences or "creepy feelings" that they experienced. The reason it is important to start here is because children are most aware of their feelings, and it is this part of the experience that prompts use of the form. For example, a child might notice that he or she is feeling anxious, with a racing heart, as a first step that prompts him or her to pull out the form.

Any Event or Situation

Teacher said that we will have to give a speech about our science projects

Just the Facts

(1) What happened just before I started feeling upset?

(2) Who? What? Where? When?

Beliefs or Thoughts

How much do you believe each belief? Rate 0–100 before and after Disputing.

	Before	After
I'm going to say something stupid and people will think I'm stupid	90	40
Everyone will see how nervous I am and think that I'm a baby	80	40
My science project is dumb	100	10

The Prime Suspect

(1) What went through my mind about A that caused C ?
(2) Why does that bother me?
(3) If my belief is true, so what?
(4) What does it say about me?
(5) What is the worst part of it?
(6) Are these thoughts enough to make me feel this bad?
  ✓ Watch for "should" "must" "never" "always" "awful"
  ✓ Think of thoughts in complete sentences

Creepy Feelings

Scared and worried and sad

The Clues

(1) What am or was I feeling?
(2) What's the strongest feeling?

  ✓ Use single words to identify my feelings.

Start Here

Disprove/Dispute/Debate

It's okay to make mistakes. Everyone does.
Everyone gets nervous. It just means we want to do our best.
The more that I give speeches the better I will become.
My science project was good. My teacher gave it a good grade and said it was clever.
No one will remember this speech next year.

Questioning

(1) What's the proof?
(2) Are there other ways of thinking about it?
(3) What would an optimist think?
(4) What would I tell a close friend in the same situation?
(5) How does it help/hurt me to think this way?
(6) How will I feel about this in a week/month/year/decade?
(7) What's the worst that could happen? How would I cope?
(8) Practice my positive thoughts.

Evaluate

Still a little worried because I want to do well. But also a little excited. I don't feel sad about it anymore.

Evaluate/Exonerate

(1) How do I feel now?
(2) Did I exonerate myself?
(3) If I don't feel better, find new arguments in D.

FIGURE 4.7. Example of a completed thought detective form.

Next, children are asked to write down what happened just prior to the start of the negative feelings (step A). Here they document a factual depiction of events that transpired right before they started feeling anxious, sad, or angry (e.g., by answering who, what, where, when). Continuing the example, the child might write, "I was sitting in class when my teacher said that tomorrow we will be giving speeches about our science projects in front of the whole class."

Next, the child is asked to consider what he or she was thinking about the event that was leading them to feel the negative feelings (step B). The child in this example might write, "Oh, no, I hate giving speeches! People will think I'm stupid. People will see I'm nervous and think I'm a baby. Besides, my science project was stupid and everyone knows it."

These first three steps (A–C) are essentially components of an advanced self-monitoring system as described earlier. Several weeks could be spent helping a child or group of children learn to use these first three steps simply to become more aware of their feelings, thoughts, and common triggers.

After these self-monitoring skills are established, the final task is to help the child learn new adaptive thoughts to counter the negative thoughts and beliefs that exacerbate or maintain the negative emotions. At step D, the child is taught to actively *dispute* the irrational beliefs identified in step B. Several skills here may be helpful in disputing those beliefs, and some are listed in the margin of the handout. These include asking questions to challenge the beliefs: "What's the proof? What would an optimist think? What's the worst that could happen? Do I have other evidence?" The child is encouraged to write adaptive thoughts to dispute the maladaptive ones. The child in this example might write, "I can survive this. It's just one speech. Each time I give a speech I will become better at it. One hundred years from now, no one will remember the speech I give. My teacher actually liked my science project and thought it was clever."

As a final step (E), the child is asked to Evaluate the effects of the new belief. If the new belief was effective, the child should experience a new positive emotion or at least a significantly less intense negative emotion. If not, the child goes back to an earlier step, either identifying new maladaptive thoughts that were unconsidered before or a new coping thought, until a new effect is achieved.

Building Effective Social Skills

Many students with internalizing symptoms lack effective social skills and will continue to experience negative thoughts and feelings if they are not helped to develop these skills. Consistent with the social-cognitive model, positive new behaviors and success in the social domain can elicit both positive thoughts and feelings in young children. There are many ways to support children in developing these skills. Many specific curricula have been developed to teach children effective social skills, and these can be delivered in group settings (see examples in Chapter 3). Alternately, interventionists can identify the specific skill deficits and create lessons that help the child learn the targeted skills, as described in Chapter 3. Regardless of the approach, successful social skills development requires opportunities to practice the target skill in role plays and real-world settings, receive positive feedback and achieve successive approximations toward the targeted behavior, and then plan actively to generalize learned skills across school and home settings.

For young children, one simple and efficient method for building social competence is through peer-mediated learning strategies (Fantuzzo, Manz, Atkins, & Meyers, 2005). In this approach, withdrawn children or those with lower social skills are paired with higher-functioning peers during social times of the day, in as limited as 15-minute sessions. The teacher sets up the interactions to be successful and gives children targeted activities to complete during their time together.

Social and Emotional Learning Interventions

Social and emotional learning (SEL) interventions have become increasingly popular in recent years to address the growing mental health problems of students in schools. SEL refers to "a process through which we learn to recognize and manage emotions, care about others, make good decisions, behave ethically and responsibly, develop positive relationships, and avoid negative behaviors" (Zins, Bloodworth, Weissberg, & Walber, 2004, p. 4). Growing research supports the application of these methods in schools and their positive impact on student behaviors (see Merrell & Gueldner, 2010). In the following sections we outline how to teach and support SEL skills.

Explicit Instruction

Several programs have been developed to provide explicit instruction in core SEL skills. Most programs are delivered in the classroom setting by teachers or school counselors in brief sessions spread out over the school year. Although these programs are commonly used as a universal support available to all students, they can also be used in small groups for more targeted and intensive training with students who are unresponsive to classwide supports. Some familiar programs include promoting alternative thinking strategies (PATHS; Kusche & Greenberg, 1994), Second Step (Committee for Children, 1988), and I Can Problem Solve (Shure, 1992). Merrell and Gueldner's (2010) recent book on the topic describes all of these programs.

We focus on the Strong Kids Curriculum Series (see Merrell & Gueldner, 2010) as an exemplar of this category of support for three reasons: (1) it is relatively inexpensive and easily accessible; (2) it has been delivered in small-group contexts and shown to impact students in need of Tier 2 supports; and (3) separate books are available to target students across PreK through 12th grade. The curriculum ranges from 10 to 12 sessions across the various grade levels and can be delivered by classroom teachers or other school personnel. Strong Kids focuses on building student competencies, assets, and coping skills so as to promote wellness and prevent future psychological problems, including internalizing distress. See the Strong Kids website for more information (www.strongkids.uoregon.edu).

Explicit instruction of SEL skills need not be tied to a specific curriculum, though; teachers have opportunities throughout the day to incorporate SEL instruction into their daily routines. For instance, teachers can initiate and facilitate discussions about SEL topics such as what makes a good friend or teammate, how to respond to bullying or peer pressure, and how to overcome peer rejection, or include these as topics for writing assignments. An effective and efficient method for starting these conversations is to select books for classroom reading that have SEL themes and to discuss these themes using group facilitation methods. The key facilitation skills for effective instruction of SEL skills, whether delivered through a curriculum or through classroom assignments, include guided questions, reflection, modeling, and role playing.

Social and Emotion Coaching

Beyond explicit instruction, social and emotion coaching can occur throughout the school day in brief interactions between students and school personnel. These types of interactions, especially when they involve real-life situations in typical life settings (e.g., conflict over sharing toys, problem solving social isolation on the playground), serve as great opportunities for students to learn, retain, and repeat the skills. The benefit of real-time coaching is that the skills become linked to the very situations for which we want students to be able to generate adaptive responses. Thus, coached skills are more likely to be generalized and maintained than if they are only presented through classroom discussions and practice.

Parents and teachers can be trained to be effective social and emotion coaches for all children, especially for those showing early signs of internalizing problems. Coaching involves helping children become more aware of their feelings and possible coping responses during the natural occurrence of social situations. John Gottman's (1997) approach to social and emotion coaching breaks the coaching task into several core skill areas. First, adults need to be able to perceive and recognize child emotional states and approach dynamic emotional states as an opportunity for instruction. Next, they have to be able to listen empathically and give the child language with which to label and understand his or her emotional states. Finally, effective coaches are able to provide structure, including setting limits as needed, while helping guide the child through the problem-solving process.

Coaching is a critical skill targeted in Carolyn Webster-Stratton's (1999) well-established Incredible Years (IY) series. Both the IY Parent and Teacher Training programs focus on equipping adults with effective coaching skills. According to the social-cognitive framework that guides this program, children learn to be socially and emotionally competent by observing adults, especially teachers and parents, who model appropriate social interactions, self-regulation, positive emotional expressions, and coping responses. In turn, children are likely to emit these behaviors and repeat them if adults give them positive attention when they occur. The three primary categories of coaching include emotion coaching, social skills coaching, and problem-solving coaching. The key coaching strategies of each category can be broken down into explicit instruction, descriptive commenting, prompting, redirecting, monitoring/feedback/reinforcement, and teaching and modeling social problem solving (see Table 4.3).

Coaching involves helping children become more aware of their feelings and possible coping responses during the natural occurrence of social situations.

In addition to the explicit instruction strategies discussed earlier, in the IY model, a foundation for

TABLE 4.3. Core Coaching Skills and Specific Coaching Strategies

Social and emotion coaches need to be able to

1. Perceive and recognize child emotional states.
2. Approach dynamic emotional states as an opportunity for instruction.
3. Listen empathically.
4. Provide the child with language to label and understand his or her emotional states.
5. Provide structure while guiding the child through the problem-solving process.

Specific coaching strategies:

1. Explicit instruction
2. Descriptive commenting
3. Prompting (verbal, physical), scaffolding, creating opportunities for success
4. Redirecting, distracting, and positive predictions
5. Monitoring and providing ongoing feedback and reinforcement
6. Teaching and modeling social problem-solving steps through guided questions

being an effective emotion coach is the ability to use descriptive commenting as social encounters unfold. Descriptive commenting is the equivalent of reflective listening skills in counseling, except what is being reflected is a description of the child's behavior. The adult simply maintains an ongoing monologue using nondirective phrases to describe a child's behavior as he or she is completing a task or engaging in social interactions. Much like a sports commentary given by a play-by-play announcer, the goal is to describe what is occurring without asking questions or making judgments. The content of the comments can include academic, emotion, or social language that adults want the child to learn. "Juan is thinking really hard about where he wants to put that yellow Lego. Hmm. He's putting it on top of the blue circle. He's trying really hard to get it to stay. He's sticking with it. How patient. He did it! That feels good to keep trying and work things out." In this example, the teacher is using language to highlight academic words (shapes, colors, direction) and also describing emotion words while praising the child's perseverance. The value of this type of coaching is that it provides children with language to understand their own behavior and experience using real-time descriptors that are more likely to be retained because they are immediately connected to exhibited behaviors.

Prompting, a third critical skill for effective SEL coaching, refers to teacher assistance in providing explicit cues or direct instruction for how to respond and behave in real-time circumstances. A prerequisite for prompting is scaffolding. That is, teachers have to be mindful of the different aspects and steps involved in acquiring any social or emotional skill and be able to assess each child's position in the process of independently using the skill. Consider the skill of responding calmly to peer intrusion. First, a student needs to be aware of how he or she is impacted by the behavior. Next the student needs to stay calm and consider options for responding. He or she then needs to be able to generate a range of possible responses and select the one with the greatest probability of success. Because effective solutions often require verbal responses, the child then needs to be able to generate words in a way that accurately conveys his or her feelings or wishes. Finally, the child needs to be able to tolerate whatever response the peer provides and then seek further solutions as needed. Most early-elementary-age children cannot master all of these steps. As such, teachers need to monitor

Descriptive commenting provides children with language to understand their own behavior and experiences using real-time descriptors that are more likely to be retained because they are immediately connected to exhibited behaviors.

which step a child needs assistance with and then provide the necessary supports for the child to be successful. Children early in the learning stages may need practice and prompts to take deep breaths and stay calm. Other students will need prompts to help them generate solutions ("What solutions might we try?") or be given explicit solutions to enact ("Why don't you tell Charley how that made you feel"). Effective prompts may also be physical (gestures, pointing to picture cues, blocking, or guiding). For instance, younger children just learning to take turns may need verbal prompts ("It's Sophia's turn—give the toy to her") as well as physical prompts such as guiding their hands to deliver the toy.

Consider another example of trying to coach the valuable skill of complimenting others. To become an independent complimenter, children need to acquire several critical skills: They must notice the behavior of others, deem it to be positive/desirable, access language to describe the behavior, and then produce language in positive terms to convey the compliment. Students early in this learning sequence will need very specific prompts to notice the behavior ("Oh, look, Alex is sharing with you—that is so nice") and to produce a positive response ("Say, 'Thank you, Alex.'"). Older children who have already practiced noticing positive/desirable behaviors and producing language may simply need to be prompted with a question ("What would be nice to say to Alex right now?") or a visual reminder (pointing at a compliment chart in the room).

Another element of effective prompting and scaffolding involves creating opportunities for success. Effective coaches monitor the frustration level of students as they are navigating the steps of learning a new skill. This monitoring allows them to intervene, prompt, and support the child to preclude overwhelming him or her. In addition to prompting behaviors, teachers can create mini-success experiences along the way. For instance, a teacher who is helping students persist in solving a difficult puzzle might lay two linked pieces near each other, prompt the student to notice the pieces, and assist him or her (if needed) to put them together. The idea is to strike a balance between success and challenging experiences that are not overly frustrating.

Redirecting is a fourth key skill used in coaching. Redirecting helps distract the student from negative perceptions or events so that he or she can more effectively solve a problem. One example of redirecting that provides classwide learning opportunities is to elicit the assistance of peers in solving social problems. Teachers can elicit the help of others, particularly neutral classroom peers, to prompt and redirect. One successful strategy, when one or more students experience conflict, is for the teacher to invite another student to help generate solutions. This method distracts the student(s) from the immediate tension and focuses attention on a new student and on solutions. It can also be helpful to discuss a stu-

> **Effective coaches need to combine coping responses with any negative emotions that they describe.**

dent with others present as a redirection and subtly prompt for desired behavior (e.g., "I think he's just thinking about it" or "So you think he should apologize"). Finally, it can be useful to make positive predictions that the desired behavior will occur (e.g., "He will calm himself down," "He will think of a solution," "He will make a good decision," "He will share soon"). It is important to distinguish positive predictions from reinforcing a behavior before it occurs. Sometimes adults will compliment or praise children for doing something they have not yet done in hopes of prompting the behavior (e.g., "Thank you for throwing that in the garbage" before the student actually does it). The problem here is that the child has learned that he or she will receive praise and attention for *not* complying. With positive prediction, the attention is minimal and the praise is withheld until after the behavior occurs.

Another key aspect of effective coaching involves monitoring and providing ongoing feedback and positive attention. Coaching does not end with solution generation. Students need to be monitored and given ongoing feedback and reinforcement (when warranted) for their performance. The teacher needs to check the follow-through of the skill to ensure that students are completing the solution in a successful way. If not, the teacher can prompt the solution or guide the child through the process. Providing positive attentive and specific praise while selectively ignoring minor misbehaviors help reinforce skill acquisition.

Teaching and Modeling Social Problem Solving

Social problem solving brings together all of these skills. As school personnel attempt to coach students through social problems, it is helpful for them to be mindful of the problem-solving steps and then explicitly teach students these steps: (1) define the problem, (2) brainstorm possible solutions, (3) select one solution, (4) plan to implement the solution, (5) evaluate the effect of the solution, and (6) repeat steps as needed. When problems arise, the teacher then can prompt each of these steps through questions:

"What's the problem?"
"What solutions have you tried?"
"What other solutions could you try?" (Invite others to contribute to brainstorming.)
"Which solution do you want to try?"

Or a more specific prompt that includes a suggestion for a solution can be given, for example, "Try asking for help." For more complicated solutions, the coach might say, "Let's come up with a plan for when, where, and how you will do this." To complete the process, the coach asks, "How will you know if this worked?"

The same skills can be used to assist children in acquiring social problem-solving skills. Consider how a teacher might use the skills described above to prompt a withdrawn child to participate socially. "Misha is playing with the dry erase board. I wonder if Kendra might like to play with her. Misha asks Kendra if she would like to play. Success! Great job listening and sharing, Misha. Kendra is having fun. I love how the two of you are playing and getting along." Here the teacher uses descriptive commenting, verbal prompts, and explicit praise to support the children in overcoming a social problem.

Effective social and emotion coaches are mindful of the behavior targets for children who are struggling to learn these skills, and they use language specific to those targets to systematically prompt and reinforce occurrences of those behaviors. A common behavior target for children who are irritable and easily frustrated (common symptoms of childhood depression) is patience. A social and emotion coach would label the desired behavior (patience or waiting), and then use the label and positive praise whenever the child displays patience. Additionally, an emotion coach might refer to the goal as using

> **Coaches intentionally associate social and emotion skills with strength and power to highlight how these skills are truly courageous and to counter prevailing cultural teachings about strength and power involving conflict and fighting.**

"patience muscles": "Great job using your patience muscles." Coaches intentionally associate social and emotion skills with strength and power to highlight how these skills are truly courageous and to counter prevailing cultural teachings about strength and power involving conflict and fighting.

Because perseverance is a common behavior target for children with emotional and behavior problems, IY gives special attention to improving this skill for children. Examples include:

"You're sticking with it."
"You're trying really hard."
"You're giving it your all."

An important point is that effective coaches need to combine coping responses with any negative emotions that they describe. Only highlighting the negative emotion (e.g., "You're feeling frustrated") will intensify this feeling for the child if the adult does not assist with finding a solution or note the positive ways the child is already coping. For instance, after articulating that a child is frustrated, the adult may add, "But you are staying calm, and you're taking your time and reminding yourself that you can do this." An adult can also prompt a child to use effective coping responses. For example, an adult could say, "Remember to ask for help if you need it."

A Final Point Regarding Social and Emotional Learning

Although social and emotion coaching is a useful strategy, it is important to remember that it is only one component of a child support plan. As Merrell and Gueldner (2010) noted, SEL should not be a "stand-alone effort in promoting children's resiliency, mental health, and academic success" (p.11). Rather it is most likely to be effective when embedded within a mosaic of environmental and educational supports. By itself, SEL is unlikely to be sufficient support for children showing early signs of internalizing problems.

Exposure and Other Strategies for Escape-Motivated Behaviors

One of the great challenges in intervening with children who have internalizing distress is that often these behaviors are learned and maintained through escape or avoidance. Although analyses of the function of behavior is commonly reserved for Tier 3 supports, at least some attention must be given to function considerations at Tier 2, else the intervention will likely fail or even exacerbate the problem. All of the strategies for managing escape-motivated behaviors that were described in Chapter 3 are also relevant for managing these behaviors when they are observed in children with internalizing symptoms.

As noted earlier in the chapter, a hallmark of nearly all effective anxiety interventions is exposure. So one check of whether a Tier 2 support is adequately addressing the avoidance function of anxiety is to assess whether exposure strategies are incorporated into the plan. This can be accomplished through group intervention practices and should also be supported with generalization strategies.

Social avoidance or escape, work avoidance, and activity avoidance are common examples of escape-maintained behaviors used by children with internalizing problems. Children who show early signs of depression, for instance, may commonly limit their social interactions and their activities. In so doing, they also limit their opportunities for positive reinforcement, pleasurable activities, and for learning new social skills across development. In turn, this limitation makes it likely that their avoidance will continue, if not worsen. Thus, effective Tier 2 supports need to provide students with opportunities to engage in successful social interactions and fun events.

Most exposure interventions are based on the systematic desensitization method. With children who are anxious, it is helpful to create a hierarchy of fears related to events or activities that create only mild fear to those that create intense fear for the child. Sometimes hierarchy lists are created around a specific fear; other times the list is simply the range of fears a child might have (riding elevators, sleeping in the dark, etc.). Then the child, with support from adults, is prompted to encounter each of the fears on the list, progressing from the lowest to the highest feared item. For each step, the child is prompted to give self-praise and to reward him- or herself. The idea is that the child is learning both to approach the feared situation and to experience mastery over it. In turn, the child develops more confidence to approach more feared situations, and so on. A sample completed fear hierarchy form is given in Figure 4.8 (see Form 4.4 in the Appendix for a blank version). In this example, the child listed several fears and chose to focus on overcoming one of them: "being in groups of kids." In the

> All of the strategies for managing escape-motivated behaviors described in Chapter 3 are also relevant for managing these behaviors when they are observed in children with internalizing symptoms.

lower half of the form, the interventionist helped the child develop a list of feared activities within this broad area, starting with the least-fear-provoking item (saying "Hi" to a kid in the hall) and progressing to the most fear-provoking (attending a sleepover at someone else's

One Step at a Time

What fears do you want to overcome?

Sleep alone in the dark, being in groups of kids, talking in class

Choose one to start with:

Being in groups of kids

Write down steps that you can take to reach the top of the ladder:

Most Feared

Step 10: Going to a sleepover at someone else's house

Step 9: Visiting another kid's house

Step 8: Having a friend for a sleepover

Step 7: Having two or more friends visit my house

Step 6: Having one friend visit my house

Step 5: Asking a group of kids if I can play with them

Step 4: Asking a kid I don't know well to play

Step 3: Asking my friend to play with me

Step 2: Saying "Hi" to an adult in the hall

Step 1: Saying "Hi" to a kid in the hall

Least Feared

FIGURE 4.8. Example of a completed fear hierarchy form.

house). After constructing this list, the team would work with the parent and child as the child tried each of these feared activities, one by one, until the child reported reduced fear at each step. For depressed children, a similar approach can be used to shape successive approximations to desired behavior and activity levels.

Relaxation Training

As noted by Chorpita and Daleiden's (2009) review, relaxation training is a common component of effective interventions for youth with anxiety problems. It often goes along with exposure training so that children are equipped with tools to calm themselves during stressful exposure experiences. Used alone, it is not an effective treatment for youth depression. Several protocols for conducting relaxation training with youth have been developed; all involve activities, guided thinking, and/or deep breathing exercises designed to activate the parasympathetic nervous system (slowing breath, heart rate, and blood pressure) and in turn the relaxation response. Such protocols are widely available, so we do not describe them in depth here (see treatment manuals for Coping Cat, FRIENDS, or Taking ACTION for examples).

Effective Behavior Management across Settings

Ensuring predictable environments helps children learn the relationship between their actions and consequences. Building this understanding serves as the foundation for children to develop perceptions of control—that is, the belief that they can achieve desired outcomes in their lives. Feelings of helplessness are common symptoms for children who have internalizing problems. Thus, a key step for these children is to replace these feelings with beliefs about self-efficacy and influence.

Recent evidence suggests that interventions that improve parent and teacher behavior management help decrease students' internalizing symptoms (Webster-Stratton & Herman, 2008). These programs typically focus on similar principles: increasing positive interactions and noncontingent attention, use of behavior-specific praise, clear expectations, predictable consequences, and explicit reprimands that are used infrequently, relative to positive attention.

USE OF DATA
TO INFORM INTERVENTION AND MONITOR PROGRESS

Use of data for progress monitoring depends on the behavior targeted. Using the daily behavior report system, progress can be monitored using the number of successful days or periods within a day. For children with discrete, observable, and frequent behaviors that commonly go along with internalizing symptoms (e.g., absences, visits to school nurse, somatic complaints, reassurance seeking), teams can create incident report checklists for team members and school personnel to complete on a daily basis to document changes in these behaviors.

If school teams elect to use child self-report to monitor internalizing states, several good measures can be used and repeatedly administered on a weekly basis to monitor improvements. These measures might include self-reported cognitive, affective, and behavioral symptoms captured by instruments such as the Children's Depression Inventory (Kovacs, 1991) or the Internalizing Symptoms Scale for Children (Merrell & Walters, 1998).

CULTURAL CONSIDERATIONS

School intervention teams need to extend their vision and theories beyond the school to include the broader sociostructural systems that influence children. Such systems that are known to profoundly influence child development and, potentially, responsiveness to intervention include sociodemographic characteristics of the child, family, peers, and school personnel, as well as neighborhoods, public policies, and media. Staying mindful of the cultural influences on child systems is consistent with an ecological perspective. Cultural factors clearly influence changing rates of youth emotional problems, and many of these factors lie external to the child, family, or school. Factors that may have influenced the growing rates of youth depression in this country include increasing urbanization, greater geographic mobility, loss of meaningful social relations and attachments, changes in family structure, alterations in gender roles, and expanding work and family roles for women (see Klerman & Weissman, 1989). Without considering these variables, prevention strategies could inadvertently perpetuate the very social structures that contribute to the rising rates of internalizing distress in children.

SUMMARY

In this chapter we reviewed principles, practices, and programs relevant for creating effective Tier 2 supports for children with internalizing symptoms. Many of these principles and practices parallel the supports described in Chapter 3. Internalizing and externalizing symptoms share many common antecedents, and thus effective supports to ameliorate these symptoms are often similar. In particular, providing effective, nurturing, and predictable environments is helpful for all children. With students who have internalizing symptoms it is especially important to watch for academic and/or social skills deficits that often precipitate such symptoms and for the avoidance coping strategies that often maintain them. A key challenge is for school teams to create surveillance systems that are sensitive to detecting children with these problems, given how often they go unnoticed. Once teams are successful in identifying children who are showing early signs of these problems, they are pleasantly surprised to learn that they already have the requisite skills and support plans for meeting the needs of these children.

ADDITIONAL RESOURCES

Barrett, P. (2004). *FRIENDS for Life program: Group leader's workbook for children* (4th ed.). Brisbane, Queensland: Australian Academic Press.

Friedber, R. D., & McClure, J. M. (2002). *Clinical practice of cognitive therapy with children and adolescents*. New York: Guilford Press.

Gottman, J. (1997). *The heart of parenting: Raising an emotionally intelligent child*. New York: Simon & Schuster.

Kendall, P. C., & Hedtke, K. A. (2006). *Cognitive behavior therapy for anxious children: Therapist manual* (3rd ed.). Ardmore, PA: Workbook.

Merrell, K. W. (2008). *Behavioral, social, and emotional assessment of children and adolescents* (3rd ed.). New York: Routledge/Taylor & Francis.

Merrell, K. W. (2008). *Helping students overcome depression and anxiety* (2nd ed.). New York: Guilford Press.

Merrell, K. W., Carrizales, D., Feuerborn, L., Gueldner, B. A., & Tran, O. K. (2007). *Strong Kids—3–5: A social and emotional learning curriculum*. Baltimore: Brookes.

Merrell, K. W., & Gueldner, B. A. (2010). *Social and emotional learning in the classroom: Promoting mental health and academic success*. New York: Guilford Press.

Merrell, K. W., Parisi, D., & Whitcomb, S. A. (2007). *Strong Start—Grades K–2: A social and emotional learning curriculum*. Baltimore: Brookes.

Merrell, K. W., Whitcomb, S. A., & Parisi, D. A. (2009). *Strong Start—Pre–K: A social and emotional learning curriculum*. Baltimore: Brookes.

Rapee, R. M., Wignall, A., Spence, S. H., Cobham, V., & Lyneham, H. (2008). *Helping your anxious child* (2nd ed.). Oakland, CA: New Harbinger Press.

Stark, K., Simpson, J., Schnoebelen, S. Hargrave, J., Glenn, R., & Molnar, J. (2006). *Therapists' manual for ACTION*. Broadmore, PA: Workbook.

Webster-Stratton, C. (1999). *How to promote children's social and emotional competence*. Thousand Oaks, CA: Sage.

CHAPTER 5

Tier 2 Interventions
for Reading Difficulties

Reading is perhaps one of the most difficult and complicated subjects to teach and, not surprisingly, one in which students struggle the most. According to the National Association of Educational Progress (2009) data, 34% of fourth-grade students and 26% of twelfth-grade students are below basic in reading. Long-term outcomes for students who are nonreaders at fourth grade are dismal; many of these students end up dropping out of school or incarcerated. According to the National Institute of Child Health and Human Development (NICHD) (*www.nichd.nih.gov*):

- Children who fail in reading in grade 1 are very likely to fail in reading (and in all academic areas) in grades 4, 8, and 12.
- From 10–15% of all students with reading problems drop out of high school.
- Only 2% of reading-impaired students complete 4 years of college.
- About 50% of adolescents and young adults with criminal records have reading difficulties.
- About 50% of young people with a history of substance abuse have reading problems.

These are sobering statistics in light of the complicated nature of teaching reading.

Due to the large number of students who struggle in reading, professionals who support students within general education or special education will invariably have students with reading difficulties. As described in Chapter 1, many of these students who are struggling in reading are in general education and are likely to be characterized as Tier 2 students. A smaller number also characterized as Tier 2 may be receiving special education services in the form of speech/language services or services in an academic area

> Reading is perhaps one of the most difficult and complicated subjects to teach—and one in which students struggle the most.

other than reading. These Tier 2 students are those who teachers or schools might think of as "slipping through the cracks" or "students in the gray area." Teachers face many issues as they determine how to intervene with these struggling Tier 2 readers. Teachers may feel underprepared to address students' learning needs in reading because they feel that they did not receive adequate preparation in their teacher training programs. Furthermore, identifying students' specific difficulties and where intervention should be targeted is a complicated process that involves (1) choosing interventions that are evidence-based and can be implemented in either a small-group or whole-class setting, while keeping training needs and intervention costs reasonable; and (2) meeting the needs of struggling readers while maintaining quality instruction for other students in the class. Maintaining a balance between these competing needs is a continual challenge.

How do teachers navigate these issues? First of all, teachers need to continually update their skills through professional development and by accessing resources for evidence-based practice. This chapter provides many ideas for reading interventions that can be utilized for hard-to-reach or hard-to-teach students, as well as resources that teachers can access for continued professional development of evidence-based practices. Second, this chapter includes a discussion of how to make decisions about when and in what areas we should intervene for students struggling in reading. More specifically, identification of particular students and their specific needs is addressed. Third, because of concern about the amount of time it takes to learn how to implement evidence-based interventions and the costs of the training and materials, this chapter primarily discusses interventions for students in Tier 2 that are manualized or scripted and low or free of cost. In addition, many of the interventions discussed in this chapter can be used with larger groups (10–12 students) or modified in structure and intensity to meet the needs of groups of three to five students. Fourth, meeting the needs of all students in the class—those who have the most significant needs, those who are struggling slightly or are falling further and further behind, and those who are average or above average—puts continual pressure on teachers. This chapter presents structures and strategies that are applicable to an entire class, whereas others are intended or can be modified for a smaller group of Tier 2 students during guided reading or intervention time. Prior to providing an overview of these interventions, it is important to gain a better understanding of what constitutes an evidence-based intervention and what the research suggests as key areas of focus in reading interventions. In addition, criteria for how to identify these students and how to assess intervention effectiveness are discussed.

RESEARCH SUPPORT OF TIER 2 INTERVENTIONS FOR READING DIFFICULTIES

There is much discussion these days about what constitutes evidence-based practice. Most recently, a distinction has been made regarding the difference between *evidence-based practices* and *research-based practices* in the area of academics. The National Center on Response to Intervention (*rti4success.org*) recently posted a guidance document on RTI titled "Essential Components of RTI: A Closer Look at Response to Intervention" (National

Center on Response to Intervention, 2010). In the document, the authors describe evidence-based interventions or curricula as interventions that have been rigorously studied and have data that demonstrate their effectiveness, whereas research-based interventions or curricula incorporate fea-

> **Most recently, a distinction has been made regarding the difference between *evidence-based* practices and *research-based* practices in the area of academics.**

tures that have been researched, but have not been specifically researched and validated as a whole. A good example of a research-based curricula might be a published reading curriculum that emphasizes activities that are evidence-based (e.g., repeated reading, specific comprehension instruction), but the curriculum has not been researched as a whole to determine its effects on the reading achievement of students.

Many of the interventions described in this chapter are evidence-based, meaning that the research utilized a control group, included a sufficient sample size, was replicated in a variety of settings, and was published in peer-reviewed journals. Also, in some cases, examples are given of activities or curricula that are research-based. Either way, the level of support for the practice is specified. It is important to provide this information because teachers sometimes receive mixed messages about the evidence that supports a practice. For instance, at one conference the presenter says that a practice is research-based and then at the next conference, the presenter says that a practice is supported by research studies. According to our explanation above, the former example describes research-based support and the latter represents evidence-based support, which is a stronger source of validation. The information in this chapter is as explicit as possible regarding the nature of research support for practices and interventions.

In the area of reading, the primary research that has guided instruction is the report of the National Reading Panel (NRP; National Institute of Child Health and Human Development, 2000). Members of the panel reviewed, synthesized, and summarized the research findings in reading over 100,000 studies (NICHD, 2001) and determined that there were five critical areas that should be the focus of reading instruction: phonemic awareness, phonics, fluency, vocabulary, and comprehension. These areas, subsequently known as the "big five" areas of reading, have provided the founda-

> **In the area of reading, the primary research that has guided instruction is the report of the National Reading Panel (NICHD, 2000).**

tion for curricula and interventions in reading since the time the report was published. Each of these areas is summarized in the following sections.

Phonemic Awareness

Phonemic awareness addresses prereading skills at the individual sound level and is the ability to "detect, identify, and manipulate phonemes in spoken words" (Honig, Diamond, & Gutlohn, 2008, p. 116). *Phonemes* are the smallest units of sound that make up the spoken language. Students gradually learn to combine or blend these sound units into words as their phonemic awareness becomes more sophisticated. Why is it important to focus on teaching phonemic awareness? The assumption is that if students can hear and blend sounds, and also break words apart into individual sounds, they will be one step closer to mastering the alphabetic principle, which means connecting sounds to letters and knowing that letters represent sounds (Snow, Burns, & Griffin, 1998). Phonemic awareness is a good predictor of later reading ability (Bishop, 2003; Ehri, Nunes, & Willows, 2001) and is best taught by teachers who understand the structure of language and can model phonemic awareness activities effectively (Moats, 2000). Research presented in the NRP report (2000) indicates that no more than one or two phonemic awareness skills should be taught at a time. These skills might include practice activities with sounds such as blending (a teacher draws out all the sounds in a word [*mmmm-aaaaaaaa-nnnn*] and then asks the student what word was said) or segmenting, wherein the teacher says a word and then the student says all the sounds that he or she heard. More than 52 studies reviewed as part of the NRP report indicated that there are significant benefits associated with phonemic awareness practice, particularly when combined with an introduction to letter names (Vaughn & Linan-Thompson, 2004). This topic leads naturally to the next primary area for intervention—phonics.

Phonics

Phonics is an instructional method that explicitly teaches the relationships between letters and sounds in a systematic way (Honig et al., 2008). Phonics instruction is for beginning readers as well as for older readers who are struggling (NICHD, 2000). The NRP report indicated that students who receive systematic and explicit phonics instruction had stronger reading achievement than students who received nonexplicit or no phonics instruction. At this point, it is important to more clearly define the terms *explicit* and *systematic*. Systematic teaching of letter–sound relationships involves teaching and building on previously learned skills in a logical sequence (NICHD, 2000). Explicit instruction involves direct and specific modeling of skills to be taught, with clear, overt teaching methods (Carnine, Silbert, Kame'enui, & Tarver, 2010). A good example of phonics skills taught in an explicit and systematic manner would be the introduction of letters and sounds of the alphabet. While a likely assumption might be that letters and sounds should be taught in alphabetical order, it is actually more effective for students to learn letter–sound relationships in a way that incorporates the following guidelines (Honig et al., 2008):

> **At this point, it is important to more clearly define the terms *explicit* and *systematic*.**

- Introduce the most common sound for a letter first (/k/ for the letter *c*).
- Introduce high-utility letters/sounds early—those that students can begin to use to read and sound out words. For instance, introducing *a, m, t, s, i,* and *f* in the first few weeks of teaching allows students to begin to make small words such as *mat, it, fit,* and others right away.
- Introduce letters that use continuous sounds (e.g., /mmmmm/, /ssssssss/) prior to introducing those that have stop sounds (e.g., /p/ and /t/). This allows for an easier blending of sounds into words early on.

- Separate the teaching of letters that are similar in sound or shape (for instance *h/n*, *e/i*) to maximize the chance that students will learn those letters and sounds.

Once students have mastered some letter–sound correspondences, work immediately begins on combining sounds into the simplest word types (consonant–vowel–consonant [CVC] words such as *cat* and *mop*) and decoding simple word types. Carnine et al. (2010) provide an overview of the potential sequence of the first lessons in phonemic awareness and phonics instruction. Students' ability to master these letter–sound correspondences that lead to efficient decoding of words provides the building block to the next important reading area in the big five: fluency.

Fluency

Although some would say that *fluency* means fast reading, it is important to understand that fluency is actually comprised of multiple skills, including accuracy, rapid decoding, and reading with expression and phrasing—sometimes called prosody (Honig et al., 2008). In their seminal article on fluency, LaBerge and Samuels (1974) described students' automaticity with words as they begin to quickly recognize and name sounds, word parts, and words. As students become more automatic with their reading of text, their rate and accuracy improve, which leads to more "energy" to devote to reading with expression (prosody) and understanding what they read (comprehension). Many studies have reported the strong relationship between reading fluency and reading comprehension (e.g., NICHD, 2000; Samuels, 1988; Torgeson & Hudson, 2006).

The strongest intervention support in the area of fluency is to provide opportunities for repeated reading (Therrien, 2004; Samuels, 1997; Dowhower, 1987; Chard, Vaughn, & Tyler, 2002). Variations on repeated reading might include student–adult reading, choral reading with an adult and other students, tape or computer-assisted reading, partner reading, and Readers' Theatre (NICHD, 2001). More details about these approaches can be found in the section on evidence-based practices later in the chapter. Key features of fluency instruction include (1) level of the passage (should be at an independent level if students are working with partners), (2) length of the passage (between 100 and 250 words for repeated reading), aspects to focus on (e.g., paying attention to fluency cues such as punctuation marks), and number of times practiced (three to four times is sufficient in repeated reading) (NICHD, 2000). One of the unique and somewhat controversial findings of the NRP in the area of fluency was that there is no evidence to support silent reading with minimal or no guidance. Although encouraging and promoting wide reading of a variety of texts are important, for students who are struggling, class time might be better spent focused specific instruction of skills rather than independent, silent reading from which these students might not profit.

Once students are becoming more adept in the area of fluency, the focus turns to our ultimate reason for reading: comprehending text. However, prior to introducing comprehension strategies, it is important that students understand important vocabulary words and their meanings.

Vocabulary

"Vocabulary is the knowledge of words and word meanings" (Honig et al., 2008, p. 407). Vocabulary is more than just reciting or copying definitions; it is an understanding of words, their meanings, and how they fit in the context of the story. Direct teaching of vocabulary is important, as most students enter school with far less vocabulary knowledge than what they need (Carnine et al., 2010). In the document *Put Reading First* (NICHD, 2001), the authors discuss both oral vocabulary and reading vocabulary, with *oral vocabulary* referring to words we use in speaking and recognize in listening and *reading vocabulary* referring to the printed word. Carnine and his colleagues suggest the use of three methods for teaching vocabulary words: the use of modeling, synonyms, and definitions. For words that can be modeled (e.g., the word *above*), the teacher models the word—in this case, using gesture—and then shows examples and nonexamples (e.g., "My hand is above my head," "My hand is above the desk," "Now, is my hand above, or not above, the table?"). At times, a word cannot be modeled, but a synonym for a word that the students already know can be used. For example, if students already know the meaning of the word *large*, they can be taught the word *gigantic* by explaining that "Gigantic means really, really *large*." Then they would practice examples and nonexamples of the word *gigantic*, provided by the teacher, and students could provide examples, too. Finally, for some words, students may need to be given definitions. It is important to clearly operationalize word meanings by providing the definition together with examples and nonexamples. If students are given the definition "An *exit* is a door that leads out of a building," for example, students might then point to the exit sign above their classroom door in confusion. If the definition is refined to say "An *exit* is a door that leads out of a room or a building," it is a closer match to readily available examples.

The final step in reading, or the major outcome, is comprehension, described as constructing meaning from text (Vaughn & Linan-Thompson, 2004). When students can understand and interact with text, they have reached a major milestone in their reading timeline.

Comprehension

In their review of the extant literature, the NRP (NICHD, 2000) discusses comprehension as "the reason for reading" (p. 41, *Put Reading First*). The RAND Reading Study Group (RRSG, 2002) discusses comprehension as gaining meaning while interacting with written language. RRSG also discusses three key components associated with comprehension: setting a purpose for reading, applying a range of processes depending on the purpose for reading (e.g., scanning when reading the newspaper), and identifying the consequences or outcomes of reading (e.g., improved comprehension or engagement with text). Comprehension is made more difficult for students who are struggling because it involves accessing background knowledge,

> **The final step in reading, or the major outcome, is comprehension.**

monitoring one's own comprehension, making inferences, and understanding context and pragmatics. Comprehension questions are explicit and literal or implicit and inferential (Vaughn & Linan-Thompson, 2004); students can be directly taught these types of questions and the information to look for to help answer each type.

The NRP report provides a summary of some of the most important comprehension strategies to teach (e.g., prediction and brainstorming), and more detail is provided regarding these in the intervention section. Most important, comprehension strategies must be taught using a standard routine that facilitates learning. For example, a standard routine for teaching that also adheres to a research-based process for introducing content (direct instruction; Carnine et al., 2010) is to (1) provide a rationale and evidence for the effectiveness of the strategy; (2) model the strategy by thinking aloud; (3) provide supported practice and feedback; (4) provide opportunities for independent practice; and (5) revisit to maintain learning and generalize it to other settings.

The research in these five primary areas of reading has guided researchers, publishers, assessment companies, and teachers, and all of these stakeholders have impacted what happens with students. It is critically important that we identify the correct students to bring in to Tier 2 intervention, with a focus on trying not to over- or underidentify. Next we examine some ways in which we identify students who might be struggling.

IDENTIFICATION AND SELECTION CRITERIA

In Tier 2 in an RTI model, schools primarily use some type of schoolwide screening or benchmarking data as the criteria to identify students who need additional reading support. This screening or benchmarking is normally conducted three times per year, and best practice is to use a reliable and valid measure, or set of measures, that is given to all students. Schools may also use a standardized reading test that is given in the district, but often these tests are not administered three times per year. One system of data collection that is commonly used in RTI models is some form of curriculum-based measurement (CBM). CBMs are short-duration, efficient-to-administer measures whose results serve as indicators of academic proficiency (Deno, 1985). In reading, these measures include 1-minute measures of oral reading, letter–sound naming, and phoneme segmentation, among others. Although these measures are not meant to provide specific information on *what* to teach, they do provide a reliable and valid indication of *when* to make a change in teaching. Schools use systems of CBM to screen or benchmark all students on common measures three times per year, as an efficient way to collect data on who is doing well and who is not. The best analogy for how we use CBM for screening is that we are screening for academic "health" problems similar to how physicians screen for health problems when individuals go in for a checkup. At the doctor's office, short tests are adminis-

> **In Tier 2 in an RTI model, schools primarily use some type of schoolwide screening or benchmarking data as the criteria to identify students who need additional reading support.**

tered (taking patient's temperature or blood pressure), and the results serve as indicators of overall health.

Following administration of either CBMs or some other type of standardized measure, data are examined and compared to norms to determine which students might be placed in Tier 1 (not at risk at this time), Tier 2 (at risk for academic failure), or Tier 3 (very at risk for academic failure). These CBM data are used as the primary criteria because of their technical adequacy, but they may also be used in addition to other standardized data sources that the school collects to make final decisions about student

> Although these measures are not meant to provide specific information on *what* to teach, they do provide a reliable and valid indication of *when* to make a change in teaching.

placement in a tier. Following identification through use of benchmarking data, students in Tiers 2 or 3 can either begin intervention immediately or may go through a period of weekly data collection using CBMs to monitor progress and either confirm or disconfirm placement in a tiered level. For instance, if a student was initially identified as Tier 2 following benchmarking, the student's classroom teacher might give that student a 1-minute CBM each week and graph the data for 4 weeks. After 4 weeks of data collection, if all 4 data points are below the long-term goal line (based on national norms), Tier 2 status is confirmed and the student begins Tier 2 intervention. If all data points are above the long-term goal line, the

> The best analogy for how we use CBM for screening is that we are screening for academic "health" problems similar to how physicians screen for health problems when individuals get a checkup.

student's status might be disconfirmed, and he or she might not be placed in Tier 2 intervention. If the data points are both above and below the goal line, progress monitoring might continue until a determination can be made. Much more detail on specific decision-making rules for data on students in Tier 2 can be found in a document authored by Dexter and Hughes (2008) at *www.rtinetwork.*

org/learn/research/making-decisions-about-adequate-progress-in-tier-2. A sample graph depicting this process can be seen in Figure 5.1, an example of a reading progress monitoring graph.

After a determination is made that an intervention or an intervention change is needed, the next step is to use diagnostic data to determine in which area the intervention or intervention change should be implemented. For instance, teachers might give students some type of miscue analysis such as a running record or a qualitative reading inventory. For either of these, students read a story or passage out loud and answer comprehension questions about it as the teacher monitors and records the types of errors made. Errors are then categorized and the teacher makes a determination about what type of intervention is needed based on the number and types of errors. Another diagnostic tool might be a checklist of words that contains a particular pattern (e.g., words with a silent *e* on the end) to determine whether a student is struggling with this skill. Once a determination is made regarding *where* (in what reading skill area) an intervention or change is needed, the next step is to determine which intervention should be implemented and for how long each day or each week.

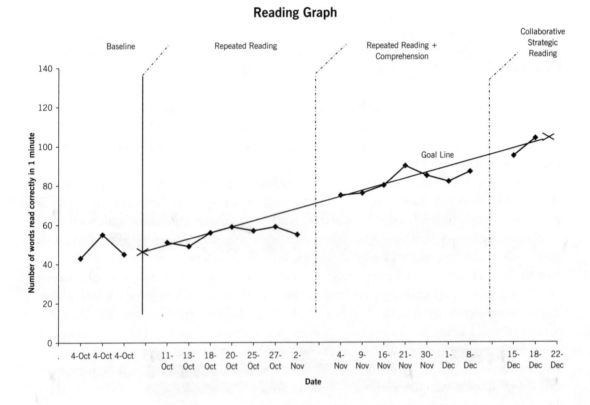

FIGURE 5.1. Example of a progress monitoring graph.

KEY EVIDENCE-BASED PRACTICES

Understanding *what* should be included in Tier 2 interventions is critical, but understanding *how* to teach those skills is equally as important. The most effective way to teach reading skills is to proceed in a systematic and explicit manner (Carnine et al., 2010; Gersten, Compton, et al., 2009). This is emphasized as the *only* recommendation supported by strong evidence in the U.S. Department of Education practice guide on assisting students struggling with reading as part of RTI (Gersten, Compton, et al., 2009). As previously stated, *systematic* means a logical sequence wherein skills build on one another and instruction is *explicit* in that multiple examples are provided and teaching is overt.

As teachers and other professionals determine which interventions to put into place for Tier 2 students who are struggling with reading, the first consideration should not be *what to do* in Tier 2, but *what might not be happening* in Tier 1 that should be happening. If a school has a large number of students in Tier 2 or Tier 3, putting on intervention "Band-Aids" by developing and delivering interventions to all of these students is not going to get to the root of the problem. In fact, it could be that the core curriculum is failing the students—possibly for a variety of reasons. It could be that the core curriculum is not evidence-based or does

> **Understanding *what* should be included in Tier 2 intervention is critical, but understanding *how* to teach those skills is equally as important.**

not focus on evidence-based components such as the big five areas of reading highlighted in the NRP report (NICHD, 2000). It could be that the program is of high quality, but implementation fidelity is not adequate. Schools need to access fidelity checklists that come with the curriculum or develop their own (i.e., see Figure 5.2). Fidelity of implementation can be checked on a regular basis for either core instruction or Tier 2 or 3 interventions and can be assessed through self-checks, colleague checks, or administrator checks.

Once it is determined that core reading instruction is being effectively implemented, then professionals will have more confidence that the students identified as needing Tier 2 supports are truly in need of that level of intervention. Tier 2 instruction is generally characterized as instruction that would be delivered to approximately 15% of students (Torgesen, 2002) and is designed as supplemental reading instruction. Denton and Vaughn (2010) discuss the importance of Tier 2 interventions as a way to close the gap between at-risk readers and their average-performing peers. To close this gap, Denton and Vaughn suggest that Tier 2 instruction needs to be both "highly effective and efficient" (p. 476). Vaughn, Wanzek, Woodruff, and Linan-Thompson (2007) discuss characteristics of each tier of instruction and describe Tier 2 interventions as those that take place in small groups (one to five student–teacher ratio maximum) for a minimum of 20 minutes per day, are provided by personnel trained to provide intervention, and include progress monitoring at least twice per month. In addition, the program and instruction would consist of an evidence-based reading program with additional opportunities to practice learned skills. Gersten et al. (2008) describe Tier 2 intervention as supplemental to general classroom instruction and delivered in small groups, with instruction focused on building foundational reading skills. While these essential elements of Tier 2 should be maintained to the greatest extent possible, it is important to recognize that some buildings will have many more students in Tiers 2 and 3 than can be taught in groups of three to five by interventionists. In reality, some buildings may have 10–12 students in Tier 2, and, in these cases, teachers should plan accordingly for intervention implementation with these larger groups. Although the interventions suggested below are supported by research, in many cases, the research is conducted with very small groups of students. If these interventions are to be extended to larger groups, the teacher needs to be prepared to utilize an intervention that is less teacher-directed and that can work effectively with larger groups. Continued progress monitoring of these Tier 2 students is key in determining whether the intervention is effective for these students.

Although a comprehensive list of all potential Tier 2 interventions is beyond the scope of this chapter, the following sections describe key interventions in each of the big five areas of reading. These interventions are characterized as either standard treatment protocols or interventions using a problem-solving model. *Standard treatment protocols* are interven-

> **Gersten et al. (2008) describe Tier 2 intervention as supplemental to general classroom instruction and delivered in small groups, with instruction focused on building foundational reading skills.**

Teacher Name: Date: Observer:

On the Wall(s)
☐ Evident display of *weekly* information and activities
   ○ Target for comprehension strategy
   ○ Target for comprehension skill
   ○ Decoding/spelling focus
   ○ Vocabulary words (often in a pocket chart)
   ○ Graphic organizer for comprehension strategy

Evidence of Student Understanding
☐ Student explanation of theme and connection to content area
☐ Student explanation of comprehension strategy or skill
☐ Student's use of vocabulary in sentence or example
☐ Student understands purpose of reading or rereading
☐ Conversation about fluency

Observations during Instruction

Phonemic Awareness & Phonics (K–2)
☐ Phonemic awareness: Phonemic awareness is auditory and does not involve words in print (heaviest emphasis at K and 1)
   ○ Isolating and identifying sounds
   ○ Categorizing words with similar and dissimilar sounds (*mat, mug, sun*)
   ○ Deleting and adding sounds (delete /s/ from *smile* . . . *mile*)
   ○ Blending sounds into words (/b/ /i/ /g/ . . . *big*)
   ○ Segmenting (*fish* . . . /f/ /i/ /sh/)
   ○ Substitution (change /r/ in *run* to /s/ . . . *sun*).
☐ Phonics (K–2)
   ○ Connection between phonemic awareness and spelling (hear it, see it, write it)
   ○ Letter–sound cards posted
   ○ Letter–sound targets
   ○ Students can explain the phonics focus
☐ Word blending and word-building activities
☐ Active participation from students
   ○ Word/letter cards for response
   ○ Think, pair, share
   ○ Think, write, share
   ○ Signal or verbal cue

Vocabulary K–6
☐ Vocabulary word cards displayed
☐ Use of student-friendly vocabulary routine (define, example, ask)
☐ Meaningful definitions from students
☐ Students can distinguish between an example and a nonexample of the word
☐ Active participation from students

(cont.)

FIGURE 5.2. Example of a treatment fidelity checklist for a reading curriculum. Based on Walk Through Tool for *Treasures* Core Program (Macmillan/McGraw-Hill, 2005).

Observations during Instruction (continued)

Comprehension Strategy & Skill K–6
☐ Student explanation of strategy and skill
☐ Use of graphic organizers by teacher and students
☐ Use of retelling cards at K–2
☐ Student explanation of how strategy helps answer questions
☐ Text-to-self, text-to-text, and text-to-world connections
☐ Student can demonstrate application of strategy or skill
☐ Extended reading time in connected text
☐ Evidence of writing (or drawing at K–1) as a response to reading
☐ Active participation from students

Fluency (1–6)
☐ Explicit instruction using teaching charts (1–2) or transparencies (3–6)
☐ Paired/buddy reading in main selection or paired selection
☐ Weekly practice using leveled passages and fluency solutions compact disc
☐ Individuals or partners practicing timed readings—1 minute
☐ Active participation from students

Differentiated Instruction—Whole and Small-Group Instruction (K–6)
☐ Leveled practice materials in use
☐ Small groups reading main selection, paired selection, or leveled books
    ○ Sets the purpose (fluency, application of comprehension, practice new vocabulary)
    ○ Specific skill taught, retaught, or extended
    ○ Active student participation; each child is heard often
    ○ Corrective feedback is given
    ○ Teacher selects and modifies the use of support or removal of support for gradual release of responsibility
☐ Work station flip charts in use
☐ Students using independent time to practice and apply previously learned skills
☐ Treasures technology in use
☐ Evidence of writing as a response to reading (increases with grade level)
☐ Active participation from students

Assessment (K–6)
☐ Quick checks are used to determine flexible groupings and target instruction
☐ Weekly and unit assessments are used to assess basic skills
☐ Fluency assessments and diagnostic assessments are given frequently to select students in order to meet individual needs

FIGURE 5.2. *(cont.)*

tion packages or protocols that do not vary for different students in a group. In a standard treatment protocol approach, interventions are delivered for a fixed duration using a specific routine or set of directions (Fuchs & Fuchs, 2006; McMaster, Fuchs, Fuchs, & Compton, 2005; Vaughn, Linan-Thompson, & Hickman, 2003; Vellutino et al., 1996). Often it is easier to train staff on interventions that are standard treatment protocols, and it is also easier to check on fidelity, because the essential elements of the intervention are clearly laid out (Fuchs & Fuchs). When using a *problem-solving model* to develop interventions, teams of teachers engage in a six-step process for each student at each level of intervention: (1) determining what the problem is and how serious it is, (2) determining the causes of the problem, (3) designing and implementing an intervention, (4) monitoring progress on the effectiveness of the intervention, (5) making changes as needed based on the data, and (6) evaluating the effectiveness of the intervention as a whole and determining next steps (Marston, Muyskens, Lau, & Canter, 2003). Progress monitoring data guide decision making at each step of the process. So in a problem-solving model, there may be slightly different interventions occurring for students in a small group, or there may be a uniform structure that is followed during the intervention time, but content may vary by student.

> These interventions are characterized as either standard treatment protocols or interventions using a problem-solving model.

Next we discuss interventions within each area of reading discussed previously (phonemic awareness, phonics, fluency, vocabulary, and comprehension) that are evidence-based and fall into the category of standard treatment protocols or those developed using a problem-solving model. Although not a comprehensive list, these interventions, along with the resources provided at the end of the chapter, will give professionals some high-quality resources. If professionals are using a standard treatment protocol, the directions for implementation should be followed and fidelity checked on a frequent and scheduled basis. If a problem-solving model is used, then teachers should choose an instructional routine that is based on research and that we know promotes student learning. Carnine et al. (2010) provide guidance on a lesson structure that includes the following elements:

- Provide an objective for the lesson in concrete and measureable terms.
- Give students a rationale for the strategy that they will be taught.
- Introduce the strategy through modeling.
- Use the strategy with the students on a short piece of text (guided practice).
- Have the students repeat back the steps in the strategy.
- Have students work independently or in pairs to implement the strategy as they read some text.
- Teach for generalization.
- Teach for maintenance.

These elements can be utilized to develop the lesson plan, routine, or framework for teaching skills using a problem-solving model.

> **If a problem-solving model is used, then teachers should choose an instructional routine that is based on research and that is known to promote student learning.**

Next, we provide suggestions or examples of interventions in the big five areas of reading. These interventions were primarily chosen because of their strong evidence base, and most of the standard treatment protocols have been reviewed by the What Works Clearinghouse (WWC; *ies.ed.gov/ ncee/wwc*) and determined to have moderate to large effects for at least one area of reading. The WWC, funded by the U.S. Department of Education, provides rigorous reviews of interventions. The reports are posted on their website and effects for the programs are categorized from small to large. Those that are reviewed have significance, as the majority of programs do not have the rigorous study design (randomized controls) to meet criteria. So even when effects are small, the program has been supported by sufficient high-quality research up to that point to merit review by the WWC.

In addition, it should be noted that the standard treatment protocols described here can be used as supplemental programs for students who are struggling, but the listed programs are meant to be used with students who might be characterized as Tier 2—students who are *not* the lowest-performing readers in their class and who would benefit from additional supplemental support in a smaller-group setting with work on more specific skills. It is important to reiterate at this time that group size and teacher–student ratio have a large impact on effectiveness and use of an intervention. For instance, if a professional is implementing a very scripted program such as Corrective Reading (SRA/McGraw-Hill; *sraonline.com*) with a small group of four to five students, the intensity and teacher–student ratio might indicate that the intervention would be a good match for students in Tier 3. However, Corrective Reading can also be implemented in a whole-class format, and in this case, it might be an excellent choice if there is a larger (10–12) group of Tier 2 students.

Standard Treatment Protocols for Early Literacy

Ladders to Literacy

Ladders to Literacy (O'Connor, Notari-Syverson, & Vadasy, 2005) is an evidence-based program for kindergarten students that focuses on print awareness, phonological awareness, and oral language, with about 20 activities for each section. There is a single, low-cost manual that contains all of the components for the program. The teacher can implement the activities as part of normal classroom routines and most activities are designed for large groups. The WWC describes the evidence as moderate to large for alphabetics and comprehension and small for fluency. More details about this program can be found on the publisher's website: *www.brookespublishing.com*.

Road to the Code

Road to the Code (Blachman, Ball, Black, & Tangel, 2000) is an intervention for kindergarten and grade 1 students focused on teaching phonemic awareness and letter–sound correspondence. Lessons for the 11-week program are described in the single, low-cost manual. Each of the 44, 15- to 20-minute lessons focuses on three activities: Say It and Move It, where students segment words; Letter Name and Sound Instruction, with game-like activities that are focused on letters that can be used to make CVC words; and Phonological Awareness Practice, with activities such as sound categorization, rhyming, and modeling of segmenting. There is more than 10 years of evidence to support the activities that comprise the intervention, and each intervention component has been specifically studied (e.g., see Ball & Blachman, 1988, 1991; Blachman, Ball, Black, & Tangel, 1994). More details about the program can be found in a review on the Florida Center for Reading Research site (*fcrr. org*) and on the publisher's website: *www.pbrookes.com.*

Sound Partners

Sound Partners (Vadasy & Sanders, 2004) is a phonics-based tutoring program for students in grades K–3 with below-average reading skills that has been researched through 18 studies. Little training is required for tutors who implement the program, which can be implemented during an intervention time or in an after-school program. Instruction focuses on skills such as letter–sound correspondences, phoneme blending, reading high-frequency words, and applying learned skills to text. The WWC describes the evidence for this program as medium to large for alphabetics, fluency, and comprehension, and small for general reading achievement. More details can be found on the distributor's website: *www.sopris-learning.com.*

Earobics

Earobics (*earobics.com*) is a software program designed to provide supplemental instruction in language arts to students in PreK through grade 3. The program is split into versions for students in PreK–grade 1 and grades 2–3. There is a strong phonemic awareness and phonics emphasis, with the software supported by other materials such as level readers and word cards. The WWC describes the evidence to support Earobics as small for alphabetic and reading fluency. However, the small effects are due in part to the lack of studies that are randomized. There has been a total of 28 studies overall on this intervention, and the review on the Florida Center site characterizes the research base as strong (it should be noted that the Florida Center for Reading Research does not endorse these programs, but provides independent evaluations for their consumers).

Lindamood Phoneme Sequencing

Lindamood Phoneme Sequencing (LiPS), developed by Patricia and Phyllis Lindamood and published by Pro-Ed (*proedinc.com*), is designed for students in grades K–3 or for struggling readers. LiPS is a multisensory program in which students work on hearing, seeing, and feeling the speech sounds of English. The goal of the program is to build skills in fluency and spelling. The WWC describes the evidence as small for alphabetics and comprehension; 37 studies have been completed on the program, and the review on the Florida Center site characterizes the research base as strong.

Other programs in early literacy that have been reviewed by WWC and are described as having small effects on literacy components are listed in Table 5.1.

Standard Treatment Protocols: Multicomponent Interventions

Accelerated Reader

Accelerated Reader (developed by Judi and Terry Paul, *www.renlearn.com/ar/*) is a computerized supplementary reading program. Students read stories independently on the computer and then are quizzed on the stories. Teachers are also provided with suggestions on how to support students during guided independent reading. While the WWC does describe the effects for this program as medium to large for comprehension and small for reading fluency and general reading achievement, it should be noted that as mentioned before, in the research section under fluency, the NRP found that there was no evidence to confirm that time spent on silent reading with minimal guidance or feedback was valuable. So the continued feedback component of this program is critical.

Wilson Reading System and Fundations

Wilson Reading System and Fundations (developed by Barbara Wilson, *www.wilsonlanguage.com/w_wrs.htm*) are reading and writing curricula that teach all reading skills in the big five in a very explicit and systematic manner through lessons that are clearly scripted. Wilson is used for grades 2 and above and Fundations for grades K–3. Concepts are introduced in small increments and practiced to mastery. The WWC described the extent of the evidence to be small for alphabetics, fluency, and comprehension for Wilson's. Fundations has not been reviewed by WWC. The programs have also been reviewed by the Florida Center.

Read Naturally

Read Naturally (developed by Candyce Ihnot, *www.readnaturally.com*) is an intervention designed to improve reading fluency by listening to stories on CDs, reading books that accompany the stories, and systematically monitoring students (both self- and teacher monitoring). The program is intended for readers of any age. The WWC considers the evidence to be small for fluency and comprehension. The program has also been reviewed by the Florida Center. As with Accelerated Reader, considerations should be given to the amount of time that students read independently with minimal guidance or feedback.

TABLE 5.1. Other Standard Treatment Protocols Supported by Evidence and Reviewed on WWC (Not Discussed in Text)

Program	Website for more information	Skills addressed/grade level	Research support
Daisy Quest	Available from a wide range of software distributors	Software targeting phonological awareness (ages 3–7)	Small positive effects in alphabetics
Waterford Early Reading Program	*www.pearsondigital. com/waterford*	Software focusing on reading, writing, and typing (grades K–2)	Small positive effects in alphabetics and comprehension
Lexia Reading	*www.lexialearning. com*	Computerized program providing phonics instruction and independent practice in basic reading skills (PreK–adult)	Small positive effects for alphabetics, fluency, comprehension, and general reading achievement
Stepping Stones to Literacy	*www.sopriswest.com*	Program focusing on listening, print conventions, phonological and phonemic awareness, and rapid naming (PreK–grade 1)	Small effects for alphabetics
Little Books	*www.goodyyearbooks. com*	Designed for interactive book reading between parents and children or teachers and students (K level)	Small effects for general reading achievement
Fluency Formula	*www.scholastic.com/ fluency/formula*	Daily lessons that focus on building reading fluency through automatic word recognition, accurate decoding, and oral expression (grades 1–6)	Small effects for fluency and comprehension
Cooperative Integrated Reading and Composition (CIRC)	*www.successforall. net/ elementary/ readingwings.htm*	Story-related activities, direct instruction in reading comprehension, and integrated reading and language arts activities (grades 2–8)	Moderate-to-large effects for comprehension

Note. Information in this table is modified from information on these programs available from the U.S. Department of Education's What Works Clearinghouse (*ies.ed.gov/ncee/wwc/*). Refer to other sample programs in the text of the chapter.

Corrective Reading

Corrective Reading (distributed by SRA/McGraw-Hill, *www.mheonline.com*) is a systematic and explicit direct instruction program focused on building the decoding, fluency, and comprehension skills of students in third grade or higher. Reading Mastery is a similar program for grades K–5. Lessons are 45 minutes and can be taught four to five times per week. This would be an intervention that might be targeted toward some of the lowest Tier 2 students in a small group or some of the stronger Tier 2 students if there is a group larger than four or five. The WWC suggests that the evidence is small for alphabetics, fluency, and comprehension; the program is also reviewed by the Florida Center.

Peer-Assisted Learning Strategies

Peer-assisted learning strategies (PALS, developed by Lynn and Doug Fuchs and their colleagues from Vanderbilt, *kc.vanderbilt.edu/pals/*; also developed by Patricia Mathes, *soprislearning.com*) is a classwide peer tutoring program modeled after Greenwoods research in classwide peer tutoring (e.g., Delquadri, Greenwood, Stretton, & Hall, 1983).). PALS is available in both reading and mathematics. Although PALS is ideally used classwide as a supplement to core reading instruction, in some cases the program is being used with larger Tier 2 groups when teachers need a systematic set of activities that is part of a standard treatment protocol In the PALS reading program for students in grades 2 and above, students are taught to work together and provide feedback to one another as they participate in three activities: partner reading (modeled reading and rereading), paragraph shrinking (summarization and main idea practice), and prediction relay (prediction, summarization, and main idea practice). All activities occur in the context of story or passage reading from text that is at the independent level of the lowest reader in the pair. PALS for grades K and 1 in reading has specific student lesson sheets, and teachers also choose materials for partner reading. The WWC described the evidence as small for alphabetics, fluency, and comprehension, and the studies were combined across grades and programs (K-PALS, first grade PALS, and PALS for grades 2–6). Recently (in the last 5 years) a scale-up grant from the U.S. Department of Education was provided to examine the effects of PALS with much larger populations. Some brief detail and references can be found in the newsletter item by Kristen McMaster, one of the investigators on the project, at *www.teachingld.org/pdf/ NewTimes_ScalingUpPals2010.pdf*.

Collaborative Strategic Reading

Collaborative Strategic Reading (CSR; Klingner, Vaughn, Dimino, Schumm, & Bryant, 2001; *soprislearning.com*) is a reading comprehension intervention that provides essential comprehension strategies on which students work in cooperative groups or in pairs. The four activities the students participate in are Preview (predict and generate background knowledge); Click and Clunk (self-monitoring strategy to use during reading, including determining when comprehension is not happening [clunk] and using fix-up strategies to help things "click"); Get the Gist (students identify the main idea for portions of text as they read); and Wrap Up (students identify the most significant ideas in the entire passage they have read, including generating questions concerning what they've read). Direct evidence supports the use of CSR at the elementary level with fourth-grade students (Klingner, Vaughn, & Schumm, 1998; Klingner, Vaughn, Argüelles, Hughes, & Ahwee, 2004) and with bilingual students (Klingner & Vaughn, 2000).

Interventions Using a Problem-Solving Method

At times it may make more sense to implement an intervention that uses a problem-solving method. These times might occur when there is no money to purchase a standardized program, when the students in a Tier 2 group have very different needs, or when professionals want to build in some specific skill work that is covered too broadly in a standard treatment protocol. In these instances, professionals may prefer to choose an intervention that is evidence- or research-based. Following are some examples of interventions that are strongly supported by research. Many more activities in all areas are provided in resources such as the CORE reading sourcebook (Honig et al., 2008), in which lesson models are provided for many skills within each area of the big five. Other resources for lesson activities include the text *Research-Based Methods of Reading Instruction, Grades K–3* (Vaughn & Linan-Thompson, 2004) and the Florida Center for Reading Research website (*fcrr.org*), where activities in each area of the big five are separated by grade level and are presented, free of charge, in pdf format. *The Struggling Reader: Interventions That Work* (Cooper, Chard, & Kiger, 2006) is another example of an easy-to-read text that provides an intervention framework for each area of reading, mirroring steps in the problem-solving model, and also provides examples of what an intervention would look like when conducted with students.

Phonemic Awareness Activities

In the *Put Reading First* report (NICHD, 2001), several suggestions for activities to build phonemic awareness are discussed and examples are provided. Phonemic awareness activities might focus on phoneme isolation, identification, categorization, blending, segmentation, deletion, addition, or substitution. The NRP report (2000) suggests working on no more than one or two skills at a time. Students who are nonreaders may start with blending and segmentation, whereas students who are further along in their "sound work" may be working on more advanced skills such as addition or substitution.

Phonics Activities

One of the best ways to teach letter–sound relationships is in a logical sequence wherein each skill builds upon the next. These skills should be taught explicitly and in a predetermined order (Carnine et al., 2010). The use of decodable text is an excellent method to teach these skills in that decodable text is controlled so that skills that are introduced build upon one another. For instance, words that are introduced only contain letters to which students have been previously introduced. Blevins (2006) studied the use of decodable text and found that students who use it in their early reading instruction have a stronger foundation of reading skills going forward.

Repeated Reading

As mentioned in the section on fluency, repeated reading is one of the key activities that promotes fluency (Samuels, 1997; Chard et al., 2002). Generally, students read 100- to 250-word passages three to four times, trying to increase their score each time (Therrien, 2004). There are many variations of repeated reading, including partner reading, choral reading, Readers' Theatre, and reading with recordings. An overview of all of these methods is provided in a table on page 365 of the Honig et al. (2008) text. Readers' Theatre is an engaging way to practice text multiple times, with plays or text that include dialogue used to practice reading, rereading, listening, and in some cases, performing, while focusing on important elements of fluency, such as reading with expression and attending to punctuation cues.

> **Readers' Theatre is an engaging way to practice text multiple times, with plays or text that include dialogue used to practice reading, rereading, listening, and in some cases, performing, while focusing on important elements of fluency, such as reading with expression and attending to punctuation cues.**

Vocabulary Enrichment

The NRP report (NICHD, 2000) suggests that we teach students vocabulary words both through specific word instruction (providing modeling, synonyms, or definitions, as discussed earlier in this chapter) and through word-learning strategies. In the Put Reading First document (NICHD, 2001), suggestions include teaching specific words before reading, providing extended instruction that promotes active engagement with vocabulary (using new words and in different contexts), and planning for repeated exposure to vocabulary in many contexts, such as in other subject areas during the day.

Students also benefit from word-learning strategies that they can apply when they encounter words they don't know. Suggestions for word-learning strategies in the Put Reading First document include "teaching students: how to use dictionaries and other reference aids to learn word meanings and to deepen knowledge of word meanings; how to use information about word parts to figure out the meanings of words in text; and how to use context clues to determine word meanings" (NICHD, 2001, p. 32). This instruction might include using a thesaurus, creating a dictionary or bookmark of learned words, strengthening students' understanding of prefixes and suffixes, and teaching students to look for specific clues within the context that might aid with word meanings (e.g., is there a synonym or antonym in the sentence that might give a clue about the word meaning?).

Comprehension Strategies

The NRP report (NICHD, 2000) suggests that comprehension instruction focus on the following areas: monitoring comprehension, using graphic and semantic organizers, answering questions, generating questions, recognizing story structure, and summarizing. These strategies would be taught using a structure or framework that has essential teaching components, such as the framework introduced in the research section of this chapter. Teachers should explicitly guide students through each step of the strategy, modeling, providing guided practice, and having the students independently practice on text that is familiar to them. This teaching of the strategy would occur over time prior to students implementing the strategy on their own. There are many suggestions for comprehension activities in the Honig et al. CORE book (2008) and in the form of before, during, and after reading strategies in the Beers (2008) text, *When Kids Can't Read: What Teachers Can Do.*

USE OF DATA TO MONITOR PROGRESS
AND INFORM INTERVENTION

Once a student begins to receive Tier 2 interventions, the student's progress is monitored by using CBMs on a frequent basis. For many students, this is as often as weekly, or at least every other week. The student's teacher administers and scores a 1-minute reading measure and then plots the score on a graph that includes a goal line for comparison that represents the norm for that grade level for the next benchmarking point. The student's reading progress is then assessed after 4–6 data points have been collected. Examples of decision-making rules include the 4-point rule or the trend line rule (see *rti4success.org*). As mentioned previously, when using the 4-point rule, if the most recent 4 data points are below the goal line, an instructional change is implemented. If the most recent 4 points are above the goal line, the goal is raised. If points are both above and below the goal line, data collection is continued until a rule can be applied. The trend line rule is similar, except that after 6 data points are collected, the trend of the data is calculated and the trend line is then compared to the goal line. If

> Once a student begins to receive Tier 2 interventions, that student's progress is monitored by using CBMs on a frequent basis.

the trend line is less steep than the goal line, an instructional change is warranted. If the trend line is steeper than the goal line, the goal can be raised. If the trend line is parallel and close to the goal line, data collection is continued and no change is made.

If data indicate that an instructional change is needed, then the person responsible for intervention will need to administer a diagnostic test (or multiple diagnostics) to determine where intervention might be targeted. In addition to the aforementioned diagnostics such as running records and individual reading inventories, standardized diagnostics may be used, such as measures from the book *Assessing Reading: Multiple Measures* (Diamond & Thorsnes, 2008). Changes in instruction can be described either as *revolutionary* or *evo-*

lutionary. Evolutionary changes might be described as small tweaks or refinement in the current intervention/instruction combination; instruction evolves over time. Revolutionary changes are those that provide a significant modification to the current intervention or, in some cases, where the intervention is replaced. For instance, if a professional was using a repeated reading intervention but diagnostic information indicated that the student was also having difficulty with comprehension, an evolutionary change might include adding some comprehension activities each time the reading is completed. A revolutionary change might be to discontinue repeated reading using a problem-solving model and using a standard-treatment protocol such as the one described in *Collaborative Strategic Reading* (Klingner et al., 2001). The professional would use the results from the student's progress monitoring data as well as diagnostic data to determine the extent of the intervention, with very low, plateau-like data indicating the need for a more substantial change. See an example of a reading graph and changes in instruction in Figure 5.1.

> **Changes in instruction can be described either as *revolutionary or evolutionary.***

SUMMARY

As professionals consider how to instruct students who are in Tier 2, it is important to continue to attend to the evidence that supports interventions, while also considering the length of time, resources (including staff), and materials available for intervention. In buildings where screening or benchmarking data indicate that numerous students are at Tiers 2 and 3, it is critically important to examine core reading instruction to determine if it is meeting the needs of students in the school and if it is being implemented with fidelity.

> **Fidelity of intervention is of utmost importance.**

This chapter has provided suggestions for quality instructional routines when teaching Tier 2 students, methods to identify and track the progress of students who are in Tier 2, and examples of interventions that are either standard treatment protocols or developed using a problem-solving model. Fidelity of intervention is of utmost importance, and fidelity checklist samples are provided with many programs. Additional resources are provided in Table 5.2.

TABLE 5.2. Evidence-Based Intervention Resources in Reading

Websites	Articles, books, reports
Florida Center on Reading Research *fcrr.org* Reviews of programs, activities	Beers, K. (2002). *When kids can't read: What teachers can do.* Portsmouth, NH: Heinemann.
What Works Clearinghouse *wwc.ed.gov* Practice guides	Honig, B., Diamond, L., & Gutlohn, L. (2008). *Teaching reading sourcebook.* Berkeley, CA: Arena Press.
Bestevidence.org Program reviews	National Association of School Psychologists. (2010). *Interventions for achievement and behavior problems in a three-tier model including RTI.* Bethesda, MD: Author.
Interventioncentral.org Evidence-based interventions in reading, mathematics, and behavior	Haager, D., Klingner, J., & Vaughn, S. (2007). *Evidence-based reading practices for response to intervention.* Baltimore: Brookes.
Center on Instruction Evidence-based reading resources *www.center-on-instruction.org/index.cfm*	Haager, D., Dimino, J. A., & Windmeuller, M. P. (2007). *Interventions for reading success.* Baltimore: Brookes.
Doing What Works Takes research-based practices and makes them into practical tools to use in the classroom. *dww.ed.gov*	Vaughn, S., & Linan-Thompson, S. (2004). *Research based methods of reading instruction, grades K–3.* Alexandria, VA: Association for Supervision and Curriculum Development.
	Cooper, J. D., Chard, D. J., & Kiger, N. D. (2006). *Struggling readers—interventions that work.* New York: Scholastic.
	National Institute of Child Health and Human Development. (2001). *Put reading first: The research building blocks for teaching children to read.* Washington, DC: U.S. Government Printing Office.

CHAPTER 6

Tier 2 Interventions
for Mathematics Difficulties

Next to reading, the academic area where students struggle the most appears to be mathematics (Gersten, Beckmann, et al., 2009). Data from the National Assessment of Educational Progress (NAEP; 2009) indicate that only 39% of fourth-grade students are at or above a proficient level in mathematics, and that there was no change between 2007 and 2009. Results of international comparative studies on mathematics performance of students indicate that U.S. students are not comparing well to their international counterparts (National Mathematics Advisory Panel (NMP), 2008; Mullis, Martin, Gonzales, & Chrostowski, 2004). These data from national and international sources are concerning because students are not being prepared as adequately as they should to be successful in the world of work once they graduate. At an individual level, teachers worry that students may not be getting the basic skills to function at the next grade level or to support them as they move on to the next most difficult skill (e.g., having a strong foundation of skill in whole-number arithmetic before moving on to algorithms in algebra).

To some extent, mathematics curriculum development has followed the pattern of reading in the cycle of more constructivist or discovery approaches moving to direct instruction approaches and back again (Stein, Kinder, Zapp, & Feuerborn, 2010). As teachers work to do their best to implement curriculum with fidelity, they struggle with students for whom the curriculum may not be meeting their needs. The first step for a teacher would be to provide better differentiation of the material for students in the classroom—for instance, providing more modeling of skills for the entire class and being more systematic about introduction of skills. This differentiated instruction is the first step toward meeting the needs of students who are at-risk in mathematics. In their book on RTI in math, Riccomini and Witzel (2010) comment that meeting the needs of 80% (the standard in RTI if the core curriculum is working effectively) of students in a school is an ambitious goal that cannot be met if teachers are not differentiating instruction for students who need it and providing additional instructional supports in the general education classroom.

There are some key principles that are essential to the success of RTI in the area of mathematics. Newman-Gonchar, Clarke, and Gersten (2009) discuss these essential elements, including the use of evidence-based practices in classroom instruction; scheduled screening of all students; frequent progress monitoring of Tiers 2 and 3 students, using valid and reliable measures; use of preventive methods such as in-class support or tutoring that functions as a Tier 2 intervention; and use of diagnostics in mathematics to determine student strengths and weaknesses, leading to a better developed instructional plan.

Teachers struggle with what to do with students who are in the "gray" area (Tier 2), meaning those students who are not having sufficient academic problems in mathematics to qualify for special services, but whose needs do slow down the students in class and make basic assignments difficult, while also putting them at risk for greater failure on high-stakes assessments. Teachers need a variety of strategies to use with these students, as some need just a bit of differentiated instructional support to help get them back on track, while others need much more significant intervention. The next section provides theoretical foundations to help conceptualize the areas of mathematics in which students struggle, as well as what areas researchers believe are critical to focus on to build mathematics proficiency for Tier 2 students.

> **As teachers work to do their best to implement curriculum with fidelity, they struggle with students for whom the curriculum may not be meeting their needs.**

THEORETICAL FOUNDATIONS

Recently, many important reviews of the literature have provided information for education professionals regarding the specific skills on which teachers should focus in the area of mathematics. While professionals should consult the National Council of Teachers of Mathematics (NCTM) for important topics or standards that students should meet overall in mathematics as they progress through their academic careers (*nctm.org/standards*), the reports discussed here more specifically address teaching methods or programs that are supported by evidence that can help teachers help students reach these standards.

The National Mathematics Advisory Panel (2008) was established by former President George W. Bush in 2006 with a goal of identifying the best available scientific evidence to inform recommendations that would lead to better mathematics performance for American students. The panel reviewed over 16,000 research publications and policy reports and received public testimony from 110 individuals. The panel also reviewed commentary submitted by 160 organizations and analyzed survey results from 743 algebra teachers. The findings were synthesized and the most important ones were published in the report. The findings and recommendations of the NMP focused on several broad areas: curricular content, learning processes, teachers and teacher education, instructional practices, instructional materials, assessment, and research policies and mechanisms. Although all 45 recommendations cannot be adequately covered in this chapter, some of the recommendations that are relevant to a discussion of Tier 2 interventions for elementary-age students are especially pertinent:

- There should be a common goal and set of expectations to prepare students for algebra, and the critical foundations of algebra should be taught in a sequential order throughout the grades. "To prepare students for Algebra (considered a foundational skill), the curriculum must simultaneously develop conceptual understanding, computational fluency, and problem-solving skills" (p. xix).
- One goal should be proficiency with fractions.
- Fluency in basic facts, including properties, and with standard algorithms is important.
- Instruction that is completely teacher- or student-centered is not supported by research.
- Cooperative learning approaches are supported by research, including one such approach, team-assisted individualization (TAI).
- Using real-world contexts to introduce mathematical problems is important.
- Providing explicit instruction on both computation and word problems for students who are struggling has demonstrated consistently positive effects.
- Instructional software can be a valuable tool, although results vary by type of software.

A discussion of the potential interventions that might align with these key findings is provided in the interventions section later in this chapter. In addition, a quick overview of the recommendations that parents might implement can be found at *www2.ed.gov/about/bdscomm/list/mathpanel/parent_brochure.pdf.*

A second significant report that has been published recently is the practice guide on "Assisting Students Struggling with Mathematics: Response to Intervention (RTI) for Elementary and Middle Schools" (Gersten, Beckmann, et al., 2009). Similar to the NMP, the research and practitioners that were part of the panel that created the RTI practice guide evaluated studies addressing mathematics interventions and screening and progress monitoring measures. Following this review of the current literature, the panel proposed recommendations for either Tier 1 or Tiers 2 and 3 and rated the recommendations as low to strong, based on the strength of the research evidence. *Strong recommendations* have consistent and generalizable evidence that the practice produces better mathematics outcomes. *Moderate recommendations* are those for which we can assume strong causal conclusions, but perhaps they cannot be generalized because the interventions have not been widely replicated, for instance. *Recommendations with low ratings* still have reasonable research to support them, but not at the level of moderate or strong recommendations. Recommendations in the areas of the Tiers 2 and 3 interventions and their levels of support include the following (Gertsen, Beckmann, et al., 2009, p. 6):

> **Explicit instruction on both computation and word problems for students who are struggling has demonstrated consistently positive effects.**

- Instruction during the intervention should be explicit and systematic. This includes providing models of proficient problem solving, verbalization of thought processes, guided practice, corrective feedback, and frequent cumulative review. (Strong)
- Interventions should include instruction on solving word problems that is based on common underlying structures. (Strong)
- Intervention materials should include opportunities for students to work with visual representations of mathematical ideas, and interventionists should be proficient in the use of visual representations of mathematical ideas. (Moderate)
- Interventions at all grade levels should devote about 10 minutes in each session to building fluent retrieval of basic arithmetic facts. (Moderate)
- Instructional materials for students receiving interventions should focus intensely on in-depth treatment of whole numbers in kindergarten through grade 5 and on rational numbers in grades 4 through 8. These materials should be selected by committee. (Low)
- Monitor the progress of students receiving supplemental instruction and other students who are at risk. (Low)
- Include motivational strategies in Tier 2 and Tier 3 interventions. (Low)

We discuss more specific interventions that relate to these recommendations in the evidence-based practice section later in the chapter.

The Center on Instruction (*centeroninstruction.org*) published a document entitled "A Summary of Nine Key Studies: Multi-Tier Intervention and Response to Interventions for Students Struggling in Mathematics" (Newman-Gonchar et al., 2009). In particular, the studies selected for review in the document focus on Tier 2 interventions for students, so are directly related to the content of this chapter. From a large number of studies related to RTI and mathematics intervention, studies were reduced based on three additional criteria: (1) Each study had to include a screening process to identify students in need of intervention; (2) there had to be a Tier 2 intervention delivered; and (3) there had to be a procedure to monitor response to intervention (p. 11). In the report, Newman-Gonchar et al. summarize each article in an annotated bibliographic style, providing a brief overview of the methods and results. In their book on RTI and mathematics, Riccomini and Witzel (2010) aptly summarize the "overaching principles" that emerged from the Center on Instruction report on using an RTI framework in mathematics. These conclusions include:

> 1) increased instructional time and supports, 2) small group instruction, 3) explicit methods of instruction, 4) the use of concrete and pictorial representations, 5) strategy instruction for problem solving, 6) focusing on basic facts and word problems, 7) aligning instruction from Tier 1 with Tier 2 to maximize the effectiveness, and 8) screening and progress monitoring to focus instruction on deficit areas. (p. 7)

Finally, another report posted on the Center on Instruction site (*centeroninstruction. org*) and authored by Gersten et al. (2008) provides an overview of "Mathematics Instruction for Students with Learning Disabilities or Difficulty Learning Mathematics: A Synthesis of the Research." Their findings mirror many of those discussed so far. In order to enhance mathematics outcomes:

- Instruction should be explicit.
- Students should use verbalization before, during, and after problem solving.
- Visual representations should be utilized as an important enhancement when teaching mathematics concepts.
- Well-chosen examples that are sequenced and provide a range of illustrations should be selected.
- Providing strategy instruction and strategies that applied broadly to a range of problems is important.
- Providing data to teachers and students on mathematics performance and progress is beneficial.
- Cross-age peer tutoring seems to be more beneficial than within-class tutoring.

As we look across findings from the four reports, similarities can be noted, as can focus areas, which comprise the intervention section of this chapter:

- Intervention should be explicit and systematic.
- Practice on basic facts and basic algorithms is essential.
- Screening students and providing ongoing progress monitoring, using reliable and valid measures, are necessary.
- Visual representations should be used.
- Strategy instruction should be provided for problem solving.

Next we consider one aspect that the research has indicated is important as we begin intervention: a reliable and valid way to identify those students who might be in need of intervention.

IDENTIFICATION AND SELECTION CRITERIA

One of the key findings from the most recent research syntheses is that we need valid and reliable screening measures to help us determine who is struggling in mathematics. In mathematics, as in reading, teachers can administer standardized measures to all students in their class on a regular basis to determine which students might not be achieving as expected. Although a norm-referenced, standardized test that assesses multiple skills directly might provide the most detailed information about student performance, the time that it takes to administer such a test (a minimum of 20 minutes per student) makes it prohibitive for classroom teachers and interventionists. The best example of measures that can be administered frequently, are reliable and valid for determining proficiency in mathematics, but take only a few minutes to administer are CBMs. Initial development on these measures began in the mid-1970s at the University of Minnesota (e.g., see Deno,

2003), and development and refining has continued to the present. CBMs are short duration (most between 1 and 5 minutes) evaluations in both computation and applied concepts that provide an indicator of overall mathematics proficiency. Measures have been developed in early numeracy (e.g., see Lembke & Foegen, 2009; Clarke & Shinn, 2004; Chard et al., 2005), in elementary mathematics (e.g., see Fuchs, Hamlett, and Fuchs 1998, 1999), and at the secondary level in mathematics (e.g., see Foegen, 2000; Foegen, Olson, & Impecoven-Lind, 2008). In early numeracy, measures include 1-minute assessments of skill in numbers and operations such as number identification and quantity discrimination (e.g., "Name the larger number"). In elementary mathematics, measures include 2- to 7-minute assessments of mixed computation or concepts and applica-tions. At the secondary level, most of the work has been completed by Foegen and her col-leagues (cited above), with measures developed in the areas of estimation at the middle school level and algebra for middle school or early high school students.

> **One of the key findings from the most recent research syntheses is that we need valid and reliable screening measures to help us determine who is struggling in mathematics.**

Typically, teachers administer CBMs to all students in a class, grade, school, or district three times per year (this is called *screening* or *benchmarking*) and then use the benchmark levels associated with the set of measures to determine which students might be low achiev-ing compared to their peers and, in some cases, their peers around the nation. Alternatively, teachers could administer these measures and then identify students for intervention based on which students are in the lowest percentiles for their class or grade. To identify Tier 2 students, teachers would not be looking for the lowest student scores on the measures, but rather those students who are either just "off the target," meaning they are hovering just below where their average-achieving peers are, down to and including those students who are "just making it"—those who are at risk of slipping into Tier 3 or at risk of needing special education services. One example of a criterion that a school might use to identify Tier 2 students is to target those who test between the 11th and 25th percentiles as com-pared to national benchmarks. More detail about screening in mathematics as part of RTI can be found in the practice guide "Assisting Students Struggling with Mathematics in an RTI system," published by the U.S. Department of Education (Gersten, Beckmann, et al., 2009). In addition, as mentioned in Chapter 5, a great resource for identifying reliable and valid screening measures is on the National Center for RTI website (*rti4success.org*), which posts information on screening and progress monitoring tools that have been examined and verified by a technical review committee of experts in the field. Examples of measures listed that have been reviewed include those from AIMSweb.com, mCLASS mathematics (*wirelessgeneration.com*), and Monitoring Basic Skills Progress (MBSP; Fuchs et al., 1998, 1999; *proedinc.com*).

Although CBMs provide a reliable and valid tool for identifying students who might be at risk in mathematics, there may also be the need to verify or triangulate CBM results with other mathematics data sources. For instance, teachers or schools may list all students' scores from standardized mathematics measures side by side (on a spreadsheet) and then data from other measures (e.g., district-required standardized tests or state tests) are examined for students who fall in Tier 2 or 3 based upon CBM benchmarks. If there is a question about placement in Tier 2 or Tier 3 following CBM benchmarking, data on additional measures could be examined to confirm or disconfirm Tier 2 and 3 membership. For example, teachers might determine that to place a student in Tier 2 or Tier 3 intervention, the student has to be in the bottom percentage based on CBM benchmarks and also in the lowest percentile on at least one other standardized mathematics measure. In their practice guide on RTI in mathematics, Gersten, Beckmann, et al. (2009) discuss the need to be cautious about over- or underidentification when using CBM. For instance, the screening measures that a school uses may identify some students as in need of intervention, when really they are not (*false positives*), and other students will not be identified when they really should be (*false negatives*). This possibility of under- or overidentification of students in need of intervention argues for the use of more than one screening measure when there might be doubt about placement. Greater specificity in identification is also particularly important when schools have limited resources to serve large numbers of students that are identified with Tier 2 or Tier 3 concerns.

> **This possibility of under- or overidentification argues for the use of more than one screening measure when there might be doubt about placement.**

KEY EVIDENCE-BASED PRACTICES

In this section we provide examples of research- and evidence-based interventions (see RTI guidance document, *rti4success.org*, or Chapter 5 for a description of research- vs. evidence-based intervention) in the area of mathematics for students in Tier 2. Similar to RTI recommendations in reading, Tier 2 interventions in mathematics are those defined as supplemental to the core curriculum, provided in small groups, and with content that is more explicit and systematic in teaching particular skills than the mathematics teaching and content that the student normally receives (Fuchs, Fuchs, & Vaughn, 2008).

> **Interventions for Tier 2 students include both standard treatment protocols and interventions developed using a problem-solving model.**

Prior to beginning a discussion about interventions, it is important to once again (as in Chapter 5) refocus on what should be happening universally as part of core mathematics instruction. With differences in curriculum (either more teacher-directed or more student-centered) schools sometimes find it difficult to meet all students' needs. It is important that teachers implement the core curriculum with fidelity, checking themselves or having colleagues check, on a frequent basis. In addition, if students are not performing well on outcome measures, it would be important to conduct some frequent progress monitoring checks on all students to continue to monitor their success in the core curriculum. As mentioned before in the larger discussion on RTI, if the core curriculum, implemented with fidelity, is not meeting the needs of the majority of the students in the class, a district may need to revisit a change to the core or the addition of a supplemental program (see Riccomini & Witzel, 2010, for a larger discussion).

As discussed earlier in the chapter, there are key reports, articles, and books published in the last 3–4 years that give teachers much more guidance about what is evidence-based in mathematics intervention and, even more specifically, what is evidence-based for students in Tier 2. The recommendations with the strongest evidence include:

- Intervention that is explicit and systematic.
- Practice on basic facts and basic algorithms.
- Screening students and providing ongoing progress monitoring using reliable and valid measures.
- The use of visual representations.
- Strategy instruction for problem solving.

Interventions for Tier 2 students include both standard treatment protocols and interventions developed using a problem-solving model. As discussed in Chapter 5, a standard treatment protocol is an intervention that is delivered for a fixed duration, using a specific routine or set of directions, to a group of students with similar needs (Fuchs & Fuchs, 2006). *Standard* means a model of instruction that has been verified or approved by evidence. *Treatment* is the instruction that we're providing to the students, including both how we are teaching and what we are teaching. *Protocol* means a set of instructional routines and directions that does not vary. This notion of a standard treatment protocol comes from a medical model, with physicians prescribing or suggesting a treatment regimen (this is the protocol), such as walking 20 minutes each day at 4 miles per hour, that is supported by medical evidence for the particular condition with which the patient is faced. In the area of mathematics, a standard treatment protocol might supplement core mathematics instruction with an evidence-based program such as PALS (Fuchs, Fuchs, Yazdian, & Powell, 2002; Fuchs, Fuchs, & Karns, 2001), implementing the program three times per week for 30 minutes in addition to core instruction. This addition of an *intervention* for all students may not seem very Tier 2-ish, but in fact, bolstering core instruction is exactly what many schools need to do to reduce the number of Tier 2 students. Another example of a standard treatment protocol is the use of a tutoring routine (e.g., see Bryant, Bryant, Gersten, Scammacca, & Chavez, 2008; Fuchs, Fuchs, Finelli, Courey, & Hamlett, 2004) with a small group of students who need more assistance with problem solving. All students in Tier 2, whether part of a whole class or small-group supplement, continue to participate in frequent progress monitoring (as often as once per week) to assess the effects of the intervention.

Alternatively, some interventions are developed using a problem-solving method (also more thoroughly described in Chapter 5), wherein the teacher determines each student's needs through assessment (define the problem), implements an evidence-based intervention with fidelity, uses ongoing assessment data to determine the effectiveness of the intervention, and then either continues with the intervention or makes an instructional change (Tilly, 2002). For instance, after assessing students on diagnostic measures that include both computation and applied problems and having the students talk through the problems as they solve them (a form of online or "as they process" talk-aloud), the data show that two of the students in the group have deficits in basic multiplication facts, whereas the other three students have deficits in applied problems that deal with money. Although the teacher cannot teach a separate lesson to each student or even to each group, he or she can individualize instruction to meet each student's needs. For each tutoring session (30 minutes) the teacher does 10 minutes of basic fact work with the entire group, as this is supported by recent evidence (see research section above). Then, for the next 10 minutes, the teacher pairs the two students who need more multiplication fact work for a peer-tutoring activity for which they have received specific training, while he or she works with the other three students on money problems. Every other day, during this second 10 minutes, the "money group" works independently while the teacher works with the "multiplication group." Finally, for the last 10 minutes of the lesson, the students all work together again, playing a math game wherein they have to apply their knowledge in many areas, or they work on a word problem strategy that includes both multiplication and money. The students are given progress monitoring measures on a frequent basis to determine whether the current instruction is effective for each of them. Overall, it can be more complicated to set up an instructional time using the problem-solving method, but in some cases, the intervention provided is much more specifically tailored to students' needs.

Usually a standard treatment protocol is one packaged intervention that is delivered to a group of students with similar needs, whereas the problem-solving method tailors intervention to each individual. In some schools, the professionals working on RTI want more control of the intervention implementation, with the ability to easily check fidelity, which results in a standard treatment protocol. In other buildings, there is no money to purchase a packaged intervention and Tier 2 mathematics groups do not seem very homogeneous, so the staff chooses to use the problem-solving model. There are pros and cons of both, detailed more in Chapter 5 and in resources, like the guidance document from the National Center on Response to Intervention (*rti4success.org/pdf/rtiessentialcomponents_042710.pdf*).

We now discuss intervention options in some of the key areas noted in the reports discussed earlier in the research section (with the exception of screening and progress monitoring, which are addressed in the sections just prior to and following this), with examples provided.

Intervention That Is Explicit and Systematic

Providing explicit and systematic interventions is a clear recommendation in the literature (Gersten, Beckmann, et al., 2009; NMP, 2008) and was described as having strong evidence in the RTI math practice guide, with positive effects for both word problems and operations. Characteristics or components of explicit instruction (NMP) include providing:

- "Clear models for solving a problem type with an array of examples,
- Extensive practice in use of newly learned strategies or skills,
- Opportunities for students to think aloud, and
- Extensive feedback" (p. xxiii).

Although not all instruction for students needs to be explicit, the NMP recommends that some instruction for struggling students be delivered explicitly on a regular basis. Characteristics of systematic instruction include providing:

- Instruction that introduces math concepts in a logical sequence that promotes student learning of the concepts.
- Many applied examples for each problem.
- Consistent review of previously learned concepts.

Explicit and systematic instruction can perhaps be applied best through a structured lesson format, which includes the essential elements noted above. The literature on direct instruction of skills (see Carnine et al., 2010) provides the lesson characteristics or lesson framework that can best facilitate implementation of these explicit and systematic components. The lesson elements include (1) progress monitoring once per week or at least every other week; (2) a review of previously learned skills from the day before and a maintenance review of skills learned prior; (3) providing an objective and a rationale for the lesson; (4) opportunities to connect to mathematics vocabulary; (5) skill/concept development through modeling, guided practice, and independent practice; and (6) application to problems and/or real-world settings. A framework for how these elements fit into a lesson plan format is provided in Figure 6.1 (p. 134). A sample lesson in the area of early numeracy (quantity comparison) is provided in Figure 6.2 (pp. 135–137), and a sample worksheet that accompanies the lesson is provided in Figure 6.3 (p. 137).

Examples of standard treatment protocol programs that are evidence-based in mathematics and include systematic and explicit lesson plan frameworks are *Hot Math* and *PALS Math*. *Hot Math* (Fuchs, Fuchs, & Hollenbeck, 2007; Fuchs et al., 2004; Fuchs, Fuchs, Prentice, Burch, & Paulsen, 2002) is a structured intervention that can be used in Tier 1 (whole class) or Tier 2 (as tutoring) and that focuses on explicit instruction and self-regulation strategies. More detail on *Hot Math*, including examples, can be found in Riccomini and Witzel's (2010) book on RTI in mathematics; the contact for more information is *flora.murray@vanderbilt.edu*.

PALS Math (Fuchs, Fuchs, Yazdian et al., 2002; *www.kc.vanderbilt.kennedy/pals*) is an evidence-based, classwide tutoring method that has been researched with students at both elementary and secondary levels. There are separate manuals and materials for kindergarten, grade 1, and grades 2–6. In kindergarten, the focus of each 20- to 30-minute lesson is on number concepts, comparing numbers, and addition and subtraction concepts. At grade 1, the focus is on number concepts, comparing numbers, addition and subtraction (one- and two-digit), place value, and missing addends. In grades 2–6, computation concepts and application materials are provided by grade level. At all levels, coaches and players (the peer partners) are trained by the teacher to help each other work through problems, giving each other feedback along the way. The lesson routine is very structured and the activities are engaging.

> The literature on direct instruction of skills provides the lesson characteristics or lesson framework that can best facilitate implementation of these explicit and systematic components.

Next we discuss an area that was also clearly emphasized in the NMP report (2008) and in the RTI practice guide (Gersten, Beckmann, et al., 2009) as well as in the Newman-Gonchar et al. (2009) report on nine key studies for Tier 2 interventions: practice on basic facts or enhancement of basic facts fluency.

Instructional Activities	Teacher–Student Ratio	Time	Materials	Motivational Plan
Administer Progress Monitoring Probe Teacher administers one or more of the early numeracy probes to the student for 1 minute each.	1:1–5	3 min	Probes, pencil	Increasing score on probe; timed task
Review Teacher briefly reviews topic from previous session and presents two to three problems from the session and asks for the student to solve them.	1:1–5	3 min	Dry erase board or paper to practice problems, pencil	Success on a previously introduced topic
Lesson Objective and Rationale Teacher orally states the topic and purpose of the lesson and why the lesson is relevant to the student.	1:1–5	1 min	None	Establish relevance
Math Vocabulary 1. Teacher introduces or reviews math vocabulary needed for skill/concept development activities. 2. Teacher models examples and nonexamples. 3. Students generate examples and nonexamples.	1:1–5	5 min	None	Provide praise
Skill/Concept Development Teacher chooses from domains (number/operations, measurement, attributes/patterns, shapes, charts, and graphs) according to student needs and applies the instructional routine to the domain-specific activities. 1. Modeling 2. Guided practice 3. Independent practice	1:1–5	13 min	Writing material and writing utensil (e.g., paper, pencil, dry erase board, marker)	Teacher support
Problem Solving and Wrap-Up Teacher asks student to apply skill/concept knowledge to real-world context. Teacher should ask questions that elicit justification or reasoning for answers.	1:1–5	5 min	Writing material and writing utensil (e.g., paper, pencil, dry erase board, marker)	Opportunity for generalization

FIGURE 6.1. Lesson plan format in early mathematics.

Instructional Activities	Teacher–Student Ratio	Time	Materials	Motivational Plan
Administer Progress Monitoring Probe T: Administers early numeracy probe(s) to student, using standardized procedures. Score and graph following the lesson.	1:1–5	3 min	Probes, pencil	Increasing score on probe; Timed task
Review T: Yesterday we talked about comparing two groups of counters to see if the groups were equal. We used the plastic bears to compare two groups at a time. How did we decide if the groups were the same? [Looking to see if numbers are the same.] Were all of the groups the same size? S: (*Responds.*) T: Let's practice comparing some groups like we did yesterday. Here are two groups of bears (*demonstrates using two bears and three bears on overhead or in front of students*). Are these equal? S: (*Responds.*) T: Show four bears and four bears. Are these equal? S: (*Responds.*) T: Show five bears and six bears. Are these equal? S: (*Responds.*) T: So when we compare, how do we know if the groups are the same? [Should be the same number.] How do we know if they're different? [Counts each group and numbers are different.] Is it OK to count one group and then count on as we move to the next group? S: (*Responds.*)	1:1–5	3 min	Dry erase board or paper to practice problems, pencil	Success on a previously introduced topic
Lesson Objective and Rationale T: Today we are going to continue to compare two groups of objects. We're going to look at whether groups are equal, and we're also going to decide which group has more and which group has less. It's important to be able to compare two groups of items to know if they are equal, because it can help us get ready for addition and subtraction, and it helps us at home, too. If there are two piles of jelly beans laid out and you are going to pick one, which one will you pick? How will you know which one is bigger? S: (*Responds.*)	1:1–5	1 min	None	Establish relevance
Math Vocabulary T: Yesterday we compared groups (*writes the word* compare *on the board*). What does *compare* mean? [Solicits answers; looking for answers such as, see if they are the same or different, see which one is bigger, count them both.] S: (*Responds.*)	1:1–5	3 min	None	Provide praise

(cont.)

FIGURE 6.2. Sample lesson plan in early mathematics for kindergarten: Quantity comparison.

Instructional Activities	Teacher–Student Ratio	Time	Materials	Motivational Plan
Math Vocabulary (cont.) T: If I am only looking at one group, is that comparing? If I count both groups and then just go on to the next problem, is that comparing? If I count both groups and think about whether the numbers are the same or different, is that comparing? S: (*Responds.*) T: Who can think of another example of comparing? What would be an example of something that I would do if I was *not* comparing? S: (*Responds.*) T: We also used the word *equal* (*writes word on board*). What does that mean? [the same] S: (*Responds.*) T: If I have two bears and three bears, is that equal? Four bears and four bears? Five candies and three candies? Six students and five students? S: (*Responds.*) T: Who can think of another example of *equal*? What is an example of *not* equal? S: (*Responds.*) T: Today we're going to use two other words in our lesson—*more* and *less* [could modify to *greater than, less than*]. (*Writes words on the board.*) *More* means that this pile or group is bigger. Have two groups of students [two and three students] come up to the front. (*Orally counts the students.*) Three is more than two, so the group with three is bigger. That group has more students. (*Puts six and six groups of pennies on the table or overhead and orally counts the pennies in each group*.) Six and six are equal, so these groups are the same. One does not have more. One group does not have less. (*Continues with additional examples as necessary.*) Can you give me an example of a group that would have more or less? Show me two groups with counters and tell me more or less. [Have each student give at least one example.] S: (*Provides examples.*)				
Skill/Concept Development T: I just practiced modeling what *more* and *less* look like. First I count how many are in each group. What is important to remember while we're counting (*touches each object and says the next number*)? Next, I compare the two groups and I think about which number is bigger or if the two numbers are the same. Then I know if the groups are equal, or if one group is more or less. Now I'm going to put some counters up on the overhead, and I want you to make the same size groups on your desk. (*Puts up at least five examples, with two groups each less than 10. Gives a variety of examples with more, less, and equal*.) [Each time you put up an example, have the students model your example and then ask them which group is more, less, or if they are equal.]	1:1–5	8 min	Writing material and writing utensil (e.g., paper, pencil, dry erase board, marker)	Teacher support

(cont.)

FIGURE 6.2. *(cont.)*

Instructional Activities	Teacher–Student Ratio	Time	Materials	Motivational Plan
Skill/Concept Development (cont.) S: (*Models making groups and responds to prompt.*) T: Now you're going to decide which group is more, which is less, or if they are equal. [Reads the directions on the more/less/equal worksheet (Figure 6.3) to the students. Do #1 together. Monitors students as they complete the worksheet. Go through problems together as a group or correct later.]				
Problem Solving and Wrap-Up T: So if you're in P.E. and you need to divide into two equal groups, what can you do? S: (*Responds.*) T: How do you know that will work? How do you know if you have more french fries or less french fries than your friend at lunch? S: (*Responds.*) T: Why will it work to do what you said? S: (*Responds.*) T: What was one word that we learned about today? What does that mean? [Reviews all major objectives.]	1:1–5	2 min	Writing material and writing utensil (e.g., paper, pencil, dry erase board, marker)	Opportunity for generalization

FIGURE 6.2. *(cont.)*

Name: _____

Circle the group that is more. If they are the same, circle both groups.

1. ☺☺☺☺
   ☺☺☺

2. ☺☺
   ☺☺

3. ☺☺☺☺☺
   ☺☺☺☺☺☺

4. ☺☺☺
   ☺

Circle the group that is less. If they are the same, circle both groups.

5. ☺
   ☺☺

6. ☺☺☺☺☺
   ☺☺☺☺☺

7. ☺☺☺☺
   ☺☺

8. ☺☺☺☺
   ☺☺

FIGURE 6.3. More/less/equal worksheet to accompany lesson plan.

Practice on Basic Facts and Algorithms

The NMP (2008) suggests that automatic retrieval of basic mathematics facts is critical to students' success in mathematics. In the practice guide on RTI in mathematics, Gersten, Beckmann, et al. (2009) provide moderate support for this practice and recommend that interventions at all grade levels should devote about 10 minutes of each session to basic facts practice. Riccomini and Witzel (2010) provide guidelines for increasing basic facts proficiency, including a six-step, "direct instruction" sequence they cite (Stein, Kinder, Silbert, & Carnine, 2006), wherein professionals determine "(1) specific criterion for introducing new facts, (2) intensive practice on newly introduced facts, (3) systematic practice of previously learned facts, (4) adequate instructional time, (5) progress monitoring and record keeping, and (6) motivational procedures" (pp. 80–81). Many of these steps are included in the lesson plan format provided in Figure 6.1 and are detailed in the Riccomini and Witzel and in Stein et al. texts.

The RTI practice guide (Gersten, Beckmann, et al., 2009) provides suggestions on how to facilitate the practice of facts, including presenting facts in number families, and how to maintain facts by integrating previously learned facts into new learning. Gersten and his colleagues also suggest that one of the keys to later fluency with basic facts is early counting efficiency acquired, ideally, when students are in grades K–2. For instance, working on strategies such as counting up, counting back, and even one-to-one correspondence can be beneficial. Finally, the RTI practice guide suggests teaching about properties such as the commutative, distributive, and associative law, but then following up with basic fact practice. Examples of all properties are provided in the glossary of the practice guide (Gersten, Beckmann, et al., 2009) and are generally defined as follows:

- Commutative—two numbers added or multiplied together will provide the same answer when inverted ($2 \times 9 = 9 \times 2$ or $2 + 9 = 9 + 2$).
- Distributive—when a number is multiplied by an addition fact, one can break the addition fact into two separate numbers and multiply by each number ($7 \times (10 + 3) = 7 \times 10 + 7 \times 3$).
- Associative—an algorithm that has one number added or multiplied to the sum or product of two other numbers can be "regrouped" $(4 + 3) + 5 = 4 + (3 + 5)$ or $(4 \times 3) \times 5 = 4 \times (3 \times 5)$.

> **The NMP (2008) suggests that automatic retrieval of basic mathematics facts is critical to students' success in mathematics.**

How does knowledge of these strategies aid students? When students can think about calculation methods flexibly, it allows them to think about and solve problems in a variety of ways. For instance, in the problem $10 \times (7 + 3)$, it may be easier for students to think about what $10 \times 7 + 10 \times 3$ is, then to think about what $7 + 3$ equals, and then multiply by 10. If students already know the basic fact 10×10, then they would want to stay with the original equation. But one can see the flexibility in problem-solving methods.

With respect to standard treatment protocols, PALS (Fuchs, Fuchs, Yazdian, et al., 2002), discussed earlier, is an example of a program that focuses on basic math facts as one activity in the instructional routine.

The Use of Visual Representations

The use of visual representations was emphasized in all reports (NMP, Practice Guide, Center on Instruction reports) and has a moderate level of evidence, according to the RTI in mathematics practice guide (Gersten, Beckmann, et al., 2009). Examples of visual representations might include number lines, graphs, simple drawings of objects or tallies. As we think about how to scaffold learning for students, we often go back to that notion of introducing or understanding problems at the concrete, semiconcrete, and abstract levels (CSA; see Mercer & Mercer, 2005, for an extended discussion and many examples). The concrete level involves actual manipulation of objects and is an example of the use of visual representations. At the semiconcrete level, we transition to the use of illustrations instead of objects. At the abstract level, we use numerals only. At all points along the way, however, we are introducing numbers and equations as we use manipulatives or visuals, so that students see parallel examples. An example of the use of CSA might be using chips or erasers at the concrete level to model a multiplication problem, 3×2, demonstrated in Figure 6.4. At the semiconcrete level, we would remove the tokens and provide only pictures (like the smiley faces shown in the figure). Finally, at the abstract level, we would provide numbers only: 3×2.

1. "How many rows?"
2. "How many faces in each row?"
3. "How many in all?"

Concrete to Semiconcrete to Abstract (CSA)

—Concrete: manipulatives

—Semiconcrete: pictures

—Abstract: number symbols

FIGURE 6.4. Sample application of the CSA strategy for the problem 3×2.

In the early grades, foundational concepts of addition and subtraction can be taught using number lines, with a goal of having students create their own "mental" number line. Teaching counting up on, or counting down on, a number line to demonstrate addition and subtraction is an example of effective use. In addition, diagrams and pictorial representations can help students understand fractions and basic components of word problems as they encounter more difficult math concepts (Gersten, Beckmann, et al., 2009). Examples are provided in the RTI math practice guide.

> **As we think about how to scaffold learning for students, we often go back to that notion of introducing or understanding problems at the concrete, semiconcrete, and abstract levels.**

Strategy Instruction for Problem Solving

In the RTI math practice guide, instruction on math word problems using common structures was specified as having a strong level of evidence. Word problem solving seems to be one of the most difficult areas for students who struggle because of the reading and extra information involved (Riccomini & Witzel, 2010; Mercer & Mercer, 2005). There are several strategies that can assist with problem solving, including the aforementioned *Hot Math* program (Fuchs et al., 2007), a problem-solving strategy called *Pirate Math* (Fuchs, Fuchs, Powell, et al., 2008), and a program based on schema strategy instruction researched primarily by Jitendra and her colleagues (see Jitendra, 2007; Jitendra et al., 1998).

Pirate Math (Fuchs, Fuchs, Powell, et al., 2008) is described as a 16-week tutoring program, with 25- to 30-minute lessons implemented three times per week. Peer tutoring and teacher-directed activities are blended, and each lesson has five activities: (1) math fact flash cards, which includes teaching a count-up strategy; (2) word problem warm-up, wherein students revisit a problem from the previous lesson and use a think aloud activity to review; (3) the lesson, the primary portion of the session, wherein students learn to recognize a problem type, set up the correct number sentence, and solve the equation; (4) sorting cards, for which the students sort problems into problem types; and (5) pirate problems, for which students solve algebraic equations and word problems. Motivators (treasure coins) are provided throughout for good behavior and academic engagement. For more information on *Pirate Math*, contact *flora.murray@vanderbilt.edu*.

Schema-based problem solving is a well-researched practice wherein students learn to recognize problem types for word problems (change, group, compare), diagram the problem type, determine the math operation associated with the problem type, and compute the problem (Jitendra et al., 1998). Jitendra (2007) has a version of this strategy available as a teacher-directed intervention program (as noted, *Solving Math Word Problems*; *proedinc. com*). An example of two types of problems (compare and group) is provided in Figure 6.5. For each of these word problems, the student would read the word problem and determine the problem type, develop a diagram that illustrates the problem, write an equation, and solve the problem. Teacher-directed instruction is scaffolded throughout to facilitate learning of the strategy.

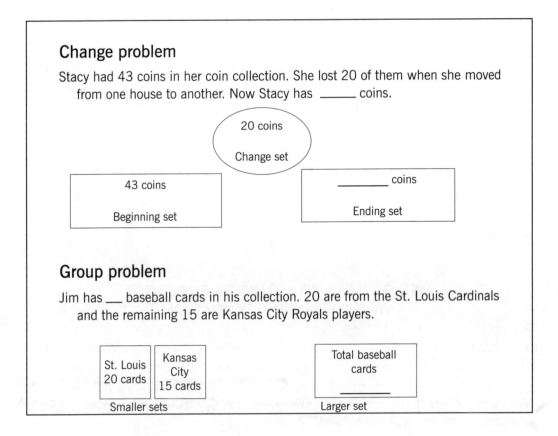

FIGURE 6.5. Example of schema-based strategy instruction.

We have discussed many single types of strategies; others combine elements of many different evidence-based practices into a multiple-strategy intervention.

Multiple-Strategy Interventions

Some strategies are constructed to incorporate many of the important elements described in the literature. For instance, the *PALS* strategy (Fuchs, Fuchs, Yazdian, & Powell, 2002) includes peer tutoring, visual representations, and basic facts practice. The only mathematics intervention program positively reviewed by the What Works Clearinghouse (others are reviewed, but they are mathematics curriculum programs) is *Accelerated Math* (*www. renlearn.com/am*). According to the description on the WWC site (*wwc.ed.gov*), this is a software program that can be used in addition to whole-class instruction and provides follow-up assignments and progress monitoring individualized by student. Students receive feedback about their performance and teachers can also receive class reports. This program was described as having medium to large effects for elementary students in general math achievement.

As with all interventions that are evidence- or research-based, the intervention is only as good as the way that it is implemented. As teachers work to meet the needs of all of their students, including those at Tier 2, preventive intervention may be provided to the whole class as part of differentiated instruction, or students may be pulled out of the classroom for tutoring sessions. Implementers should continue to examine fidelity checklists that accompany the programs they purchase, or they should develop their own if none is available. One could easily take the important elements or "big ideas" in the lesson plan provided in Figure 6.1, for instance and create a fidelity checklist modeled after the fidelity checklist in Figure 5.2.

Once high-quality interventions supported by research or evidence are chosen, the next and most important step is to continue to collect data on the effectiveness of the intervention with Tier 2 students.

USE OF DATA TO MONITOR PROGRESS AND INFORM INTERVENTION

Using data to monitor progress and inform intervention is an important area that was highlighted in many of the research reviews discussed earlier (NMP, 2008; Gersten, Beckmann, et al., 2009; Newman-Gonchar et al., 2009). Ongoing data collection that is valid and reliable is necessary to determine progress in mathematics over time, and diagnostic data can inform changes that may need to be made.

As detailed in Chapter 5, once students begins to receive Tier 2 intervention, those students are monitored using a reliable and valid progress measure on a frequent basis (CBM is the best example). For many students, this monitoring occurs as often as weekly or at least every other week. The interventionist or classroom teacher administers and scores a mathematics measure and then plots the score on a graph that includes a goal line for comparison, representing the norm for that grade level for the next benchmarking point. The measures in mathematics needed to monitor progress include those in the area of early numeracy (number identification, quantity discrimination, missing number, oral counting), computation, concepts and applications, estimation, and algebra. Several references for these measures can be found in the section on identification in this chapter; the best place to identify measures is the National Center on Response to Intervention website (*rti4success.org*), which provides a technical adequacy chart for both screening and progress monitoring measures. Most of these measures take between 1 and 8 minutes, and some in the later grades can be group administered, which adds to efficiency (see Foegen, Jiban, & Deno, 2007, for a comprehensive review of progress monitoring measures in mathematics).

After 4–6 data points are collected and graphed, each student's progress is then assessed. As discussed in Chapter 5, examples of decision-making rules include the 4-point rule or the trend line rule (*rti4success.org*). Using the 4-point rule, if the most recent 4 data points are below the goal line, an instructional change is implemented. If the most recent 4 points are above the goal line, the goal is raised. If points are both above and below the goal line, data collection is continued until a rule can be applied. The trend line rule is similar except that after 6 data points are collected, the trend of the data is calculated and the trend line is then compared to the goal line. If the trend line is less steep than the goal line, an instructional change is warranted. If the trend line is steeper than the goal line, the goal can be raised. If the trend line is parallel and close to the goal line, data collection is continued and no change is made.

If data indicate that an instructional change is needed, then the person responsible for intervention will need to administer a diagnostic test (or multiple diagnostics) to determine where intervention might be targeted. Examples of diagnostics in mathematics

> **Ongoing data collection that is valid and reliable is necessary to determine progress in mathematics over time, and diagnostic data can inform changes that may need to be made.**

include error analysis and mathematics interviews. For error analysis, students solve a page of problems reflecting the skill on which they have been working and then errors are categorized to determine where most errors are being made. For instance, errors might indicate that students are not paying attention to the sign, are using the wrong algorithm, or are starting in the wrong place. Mathematics interviews are similar, except that students talk through problems as they solve them, so a professional can assess *online processing* and identify where errors are being made. An example of a commercial diagnostic tool that has utility for teachers is the diagnostic intervention that is part of the mCLASS mathematics system from *Wirelessgeneration.com*. Developed by Herb Ginsburg at Teachers College, Columbia University, the diagnostic interview data can be collected via handheld technology. Students are asked to solve problems in various areas (commensurate with their grade level) and then are questioned about how they solved the problem and other ways that they could have solved the problem. The handheld device allows the administrator to document types of strategies the student uses (e.g., using paper, manipulatives, counting on, counting up, counting all) and then provides a mathematics profile for each student that details the student's strengths and areas of need, as well as potential activities on which the student (or group of students) could work. This tool provides an excellent way to determine the type of instructional change that might be necessary. The professional would use the results from the student's progress monitoring data as well as diagnostic data to determine the extent of the intervention, with very low, plateau-like data indicating the need for a more substantial change. See an example of a reading graph and changes in instruction in Figure 5.1 (Chapter 5).

SUMMARY

Similar to reading, as professionals consider how to instruct students in mathematics who are in Tier 2, it is important to continue to attend to the evidence that supports interventions, while also considering the length of time available for intervention as well as the resources (including staff) and materials that are available. In buildings where screening or benchmarking data indicate high numbers of students at Tiers 2 and 3, it is critically important to examine core mathematics instruction to determine if it is meeting the needs of students in the school and if it is being implemented with fidelity.

Mathematics research is much more limited than reading literature, but the high-quality reports published recently should provide greater insight into what education professionals need to do with students who are struggling. This chapter has provided suggestions for quality instructional routines when teaching Tier 2 students, methods to identify and track the progress of students who are in Tier 2, and examples of interventions that are either standard treatment protocols or are developed using a problem-solving model. Fidelity of intervention is of utmost importance; fidelity checklist samples are provided with many programs, and examples are also provided in this chapter. Additional resources are provided in Table 6.1.

TABLE 6.1. Evidence-Based Intervention Resources in Mathematics

Websites		Articles, books, reports
National Center on Response to Intervention *www.rti4success.org*	Doing What Works *dww.ed.gov/* Takes research-based practices and makes them into practical tools to use in the classroom.	Riccomini, P. J., & Witzel, B. S. (2010). *Response to intervention in math.* Thousand Oaks, CA: Corwin Press.
What Works Clearinghouse *wwc.ed.gov*		
Practice guides *Bestevidence.org*	Parent brochure for the NMP findings *www2.ed.gov/about/bdscomm/list/ mathpanel/parent_brochure.pdf*	National Math Advisory Panel report: *www2. ed.gov/about/ bdscomm/list/ mathpanel/index.html*
Program reviews *Interventioncentral.org* Evidence-based interventions in reading, mathematics, and behavior	Peer-Assisted Learning Strategies in Mathematics *kc.vanderbilt.edu/pals/*	
Center on Instruction *www.center-on-instruction.org/ index.cfm* Evidence-based resources in mathematics	Helping Your Child Learn Mathematics *www.ed.gov/parents/academic/help/ math/math.pdf*	
	Mathematics Curriculum Focal Points (NCTM) *nctm.org/standards/focalpoints. aspx?id=298*	
	Lesson Plans from NCTM *Illuminations.nctm.org*	

CHAPTER 7

Laying the Foundation for Tier 3 Supports

While the focus in this book, up to this point, has been on interventions for students in Tier 2, approximately 1–5% of children in the area of social behavior and 2–7% in the area of academic skills will not respond to Tier 2 interventions and will need more individualized assistance (Fuchs & Deshler, 2007; Sugai, 2011). Little research has been conducted on the use of Tier 3 interventions within the context of a continuum of supports (Scott, Alter, Rosenberg, & Borgmeier, 2010; Stecker, 2007). Fortunately, this is a topic of recent research efforts and professional writing (e.g., Bohanon, McIntosh, & Goodman, 2011b; Stecker, 2007).

This chapter presents additional information on how teams can determine responsiveness to Tier 2 interventions—a determination that is critical to providing more intense levels of support. Next, decision rules for moving to Tier 3 are discussed, followed by examples of evidence-based Tier 3 interventions and resources for obtaining more information on interventions. Challenges and issues related to Tier 3 follow. Finally, given the limited research in this area and the challenges that many practitioners, administrators, and researchers have faced in implementing tiered systems, we conducted brief interviews with experts on the topic. These interviews were conducted with individuals representing unique perspectives and are included at the end of the chapter. They underscore the essential systems-related pieces that must be in place when laying the foundation for Tier 3 interventions.

DETERMINING TIER 2 INTERVENTION RESPONSIVENESS

As discussed throughout this book, before moving to the next tier on the continuum, it is essential to verify that the interventions and supports at the current tier are being implemented with fidelity (McIntosh, Reinke, & Herman, 2010; Stecker, 2007). According to Sugai (2011), implementation fidelity is a critical and defining feature of tiered models. *Implemen-*

tation fidelity can be defined as "team-based structures and procedures [that] are in place to ensure and coordinate appropriate adoption and accurate and sustained implementation of the full continuum of intervention practices" (Sugai, 2011, p. 2). More resources for fidelity of implementation in academic areas can be found on the website for the National Center on Response to Intervention (*rti4success.org*), using the search term *fidelity*.

> As discussed throughout this book, before moving to the next tier on the continuum, it is essential to verify that the interventions and supports at the current tier are being implemented with fidelity.

In terms of social behavior Tier 2 and 3 supports, the Benchmarks for Advanced Tiers (BAT) were developed to assist in determining if key features are in place and if there are specific needs to address (see *www.pbis.org*). The BAT is described in Figure 7.1. Teams could use this or develop another checklist with similar items (e.g., see Figure 7.2). Teams can also choose to have an outside evaluator come in and examine their implementation fidelity of Tiers 2 and 3 supports. If this is desired, one tool available at *pbis.org* is the Individual Student Systems Evaluation Tool (ISSET), which is briefly described in Figure 7.3. An example of a treatment fidelity checklist in academics can be found in Figure 5.2 in Chapter 5 or on the Florida Center for Reading Research website (*fcrr.org*).

Regarding the specific intervention, the team guiding Tier 2 interventions should use fidelity of implementation checklists to determine if the intervention is being delivered as intended. The number of students who respond to secondary supports often depends on the quality of interventions selected at the secondary level and the extent to which they are implemented with fidelity (McIntosh et al., 2010). Form 7.1 in the Appendix is a sample checklist an observer could use for the check-in/check-out behavior education program intervention. Chapter 5 in this book provides an example of a checklist for fidelity of implementation of an academic intervention. If the intervention is being implemented as intended, then a

Description: The BAT is a tool that school teams can use to self-assess their current needs and strengths regarding implementation of Tier 2 and 3 supports. When outside evaluators have administered the ISSET, this information is used in the assessment as well. Teams rate specific items according to whether they are "not yet started" = 0, "partially in place" = 1, or "fully in place" = 2.
Purpose: The BAT measures the implementation status of Tiers 1, 2, and 3.
Procedure: Someone with experience using the BAT trains school teams involved with Tiers 2 and 3 on using the measure. The teams then use the measure to self-assess their implementation of specific supports. It is desired that teams complete the measure together; when this is not possible, the team needs to meet to determine agreement and discuss items rated differently. It is vital that the scores reflect consensus of members.
Application: After completing the BAT, teams use a template to create an action plan with specific timelines for establishing needed Tier 2 and 3 supports.

FIGURE 7.1. Benchmarks for Advanced Tiers (BAT). Based on Anderson, Childs, et al. (2010).

			Yes	No
	**Missouri Schoolwide Positive Behavior Support** **Tier 2 Action Plan Checklist** *The purpose of the inventory is to assist Tier 2 leadership teams in (1) assessing current status, (2) determining items to add to the team action plan, and (3) developing suggested artifacts and documentation to evaluate outcomes.*
colspan="3"	School:		Date:
	Feature	Evaluation	Yes	No
1. Tier 2 Team	1. A Tier 2 team, including an administrator, is identified to (a) develop a Tier 2 process in the school, (b) develop interventions, and (c) make decisions about students receiving small-group and/or targeted supports.	List of team members		
	2. Team roles and responsibilities are designated.	List of team members with assigned role and responsibility		
	3. The Tier 2 team meets at least every 2 weeks, and a schedule of meeting dates is developed.	Team meeting schedule		
	4. Meetings are organized and employ a standard format.	Copies of agenda		
	5. The Tier 2 team is formally provided information about systems, data, and practices required for implementation of Tier 2 supports.	Professional development calendar; attendance at MO SWPBS coach meetings and/or summer institute		
	6. The team conducts an audit to determine existing interventions that are readily available.	Copy of audit; list and description of interventions that are continually available		
	7. Team provides information, modeling, feedback, support, and recognition for staff that implement Tier 2 interventions.	Professional development schedule, faculty meeting agenda, or written documentation of procedures		
2. Student Identification Process	1. The school uses a data-based process for identifying students who need additional support.	Check each process used: ____ Screening instrument ____ Nomination form ____ Progress monitoring ____ ODR data ____ Classroom minor data ____ Academic indicators ____ Attendance		
	2. All school staff is trained in and knows the process for initiating additional support for students.	Written procedures and professional development schedule		
	3. The Tier 2 team systematically schedules time for review of data decision rules and/or screening results to identify students who are at-risk/nonresponsive to Tier 1 supports.	Team meeting minutes		
	4. Students identified for additional support have full access to Tier 1 supports.	Written procedures		
	5. The process for access to intervention is designed such that student/staff needing assistance receives support within 3–10 school days of identification.	Advanced tier data collection spreadsheet		

(cont.)

FIGURE 7.2. Fidelity and needs assessment tool. From Missouri Center for Schoolwide Positive Behavior Supports (2011b). Reprinted by permission.

	Feature	Evaluation	Yes	No
3. Function-based Matching Process	1. A system for collecting, reviewing, and documenting student data is established.	Written procedures		
	2. A brief process to identify function of behavior is established.	Written procedures or flow chart of process		
	3. A set of research-based interventions, which can be matched to function of concern, is readily available.	Description of each intervention available		
4. Intervention Implementation	1. Interventions are consistent with schoolwide expectations.	Description of interventions and/or copy of daily progress report (DPR)		
	2. Each intervention has written materials to describe the core features and purpose of the strategy.	Description of interventions that include: entry criteria, goal and purpose, method to monitor progress and exit criteria		
	3. A coordinator is designated for each intervention available and has time scheduled to complete responsibilities.	Description of interventions		
	4. Each intervention includes a formal process for teaching appropriate behaviors.	Teacher interview		
	5. Each intervention includes regular opportunities for students to perform appropriate behaviors.	Teacher interview		
	6. Implementation of intervention requires no more than 10 minutes per day from any staff, other than the coordinator.	Teacher interview		
	7. A process for teaching staff how to implement each intervention is in place.	Professional development schedule and/or faculty meeting agenda		
5. Monitoring Progress, Evaluating Outcomes, and Making Decisions	1. An information system is used to monitor the impact of interventions, and the system allows for daily collection of behavior ratings. Monitoring of data occurs weekly by the intervention coordinator and/or the Tier 2 team.	Individual student behavior rating graphs		
	2. Each intervention uses accurate and objective data for monitoring student progress and making decisions.	Individual student behavior rating graphs and/or written materials		
6. Strategies for Communication	1. Teachers of students participating in an intervention receive progress updates at least monthly.	Format for progress updates is identified and includes who is responsible for updates and how often they will be completed. Teacher interview		
	2. Faculty/staff is informed at least quarterly about the number of students receiving interventions and the progress of all.	Format for progress updates is identified and includes who is responsible for updates and how often they will be completed. Faculty/staff interview		
	3. There is a documented process for notifying and routinely updating family /guardian when a student is identified for and receives additional support.	Format for progress updates is identified and includes who is responsible for updates and how often they will be completed. Family interview		

FIGURE 7.2. *(cont.)*

Description: The ISSET is an evaluation tool that specifically measures the status of implementation at Tiers 2 and 3. It includes 35 items organized into three parts: Foundations, Targeted Interventions, and Intensive Individualized Interventions.

Procedure: An outside evaluator administers the ISSET. The complete evaluation typically takes 2-3 hours. The process includes two data sources: interviews (with an administrator, five staff members, and a team leader) and a systematic review of permanent products such as meeting minutes, targeted intervention descriptions currently available, ODR forms, etc.

Application: Summary scores are obtained for each part and the data are shared with teams.

FIGURE 7.3. Individual Student Systems Evaluation Tool (ISSET). Based on Anderson, Lewis-Palmer, et al. (2010).

student's responsiveness to the intervention can be determined. "Without considering fidelity of implementation, it is unknown whether students fail to respond to secondary supports or if staff have failed to provide adequate supports" (McIntosh et al., 2011, p. 5).

> **The number of students who respond to secondary supports often depends on the quality of secondary level interventions and the extent to which they are implemented with fidelity.**

In addition to collecting fidelity data, teams should also establish methods and procedures to monitor and improve intervention fidelity. These can include use of scripts, consultation, and data-based feedback (McIntosh et al., 2011). Sample scripts for teachers, implementers, and parents are included in Forms 7.2, 7.3, and 7.4 in the Appendix. The use of coaching is another potential way to support professionals' use of Tiers 2 and 3 interventions. Similar to performance feedback, coaching generally includes one professional observing another and supporting his or her use of interventions through goal setting, modeling, problem solving, and performance feedback (Reinke, Sprick, & Knight, 2008).

In addition to considering factors that support and deter fidelity of implementation, it is also important to consider those that impact sustainability of evidence-based practices in schools after their adoption. In a recent exploration of variables associated with schools that sustained implementation of a Tier 2 intervention, First Step to Success, several findings were noted (Loman, Rodriguez, & Horner, 2010). Significant differences were found between sustained and nonsustained implementers on variables related to how schools and teams built the foundational capacity to support implementation of First Steps to Success as well as how students were selected to receive the intervention. Interview responses of staff from schools also underscored the importance of district coordination, training, dedicated resources, coaches, and parent participation to support sustained implementation. Sustained implementers reported that student selection was also important (24%), and nonsustained implementers emphasized the importance of staff buy-in (63%). Only 7% of sus-

> In addition to collecting fidelity data, teams should also establish methods and procedures to monitor and improve intervention fidelity.

tained implementers similarly reported staff buy-in as an issue, so it is possible that nonsustained implementers did not fully secure and support buy-in over time.

DATA DECISION RULES FOR TIER 3

For both academic and social behavior progress monitoring, data decision rules are created by teams and used to make decisions regarding students who need more intensive supports. As discussed in Chapters 3, 4, 5, and 6, guidelines for determining who needs Tier 3 supports have been provided by research. Typically, making decisions for Tier 3 needs for

> For both academic and social behavior progress monitoring, data decision rules are created by teams and used to make decisions regarding students who need more intensive supports.

supports should follow an established period of progress monitoring. After this established period of time, student data are reviewed and the team can determine if students are progressing with the current level of support (Scott et al., 2010; Stecker, 2007).

EVIDENCE-BASED TIER 3 INTERVENTIONS

Tier 3 interventions typically involve extensive individualization of academic and behavioral goals. Another issue teams face when determining responsiveness to Tier 2 supports is creating decision rules regarding referral for evaluations for special education and related services. Referral for services may or may not be included in the top tier (Stecker, 2007; Sugai, 2011). One Tier 3 intervention that has the most research to date within the social behavior literature is functional behavior assessment. Table 7.1 lists available resources on functional behavior assessment for school professionals. Most children who have academic Tier 3 supports also need behavioral support, and most children with intensive behavioral needs also have academic needs for support. It is vital that school professionals ensure that individuals are trained to provide the level of support that children with Tier 3 needs require. These interventions may include functional behavior assessment, individual behavior plans, person-centered planning, wraparound services, and designing specific academic goals and benchmarks. In the area of academics, students may or may not receive an abbreviated assessment using standardized achievement or IQ tests as part of movement to Tier 3. In some schools, students receive intervention that is delivered in a smaller group and

> It is vital that school professionals ensure that individuals are trained to provide the level of support that children with Tier 3 needs require.

is more intense (explicit and systematic) than the Tier 2 intervention was. As indicated throughout the book, as children move up the triangle, there is a need for increased data collection and review (even weekly) and communication with families.

TABLE 7.1. Resources on Functional Behavior Assessments for School Professionals

Reference	Description
Bambara, L. M., & Kern, L. (2005). *Individualized supports for students with problem behaviors: Designing positive support plans.* New York: Guilford Press.	Focuses on designing positive behavior support plans for students. Provides strategies to address individual behavioral problems at all levels of severity. Details specific interventions that can be included in student behavioral plans.
Crone, D. A., & Horner, R. H. (2003). *Building positive behavior support systems in schools: Functional behavioral assessment.* New York: Guilford Press.	Presents a conceptual model and practical tools for meeting the challenges of severe problem behavior in elementary and middle school settings. Focuses on the development and implementation of team-based support plans for students who require intensive, individualized behavioral assessment and intervention.
IDEA *www.fape.org/idea/what_idea_is/osher/main.htm*	Prepared by the Center for Effective Collaboration and Practice: *An IEP Team's Introduction to Functional Behavioral Assessment and Behavior Intervention Plans* (2nd edition).
IRIS Center *iris.peabody.vanderbilt.edu/fba/chalcycle.htm*	Module for functional behavioral assessment. Explores the basic principles of behavior and the importance of identifying the reasons that students engage in problem behavior. Describes the steps for conducting a functional behavioral assessment and developing a behavior plan.
O'Neill, R., Horner, R., Albin, R., Sprague, J., Storey, K., & Newton, J. S. (1997). *Functional assessment and program development for problem behavior: A practical handbook.* Pacific Grove, CA: Brooks/Cole.	Includes a variety of strategies for assessing problem behavior situations. Presents a systematic approach for designing appropriate behavioral support programs.
PBIS *pbis.org/pbis_resource_detail_page.aspx?PBIS_ResourceID=887*	*Practical Functional Behavioral Assessment Training Manual for School-Based Personnel.* Designed to train school-based personnel with flexible roles in a school to conduct practical functional behavioral assessments.

(cont.)

TABLE 7.1. *(cont.)*

Reference	Description
Scheuermann, B. K., & Hall, J. A. (2008). *Positive behavioral supports for the classroom.* Upper Saddle River, NJ: Pearson Education.	Presents research-based strategies and techniques to help teachers and other professionals manage the behavioral challenges of students. Provides information on how to design effective preventive and management interventions for use in the classroom.
Umbreit, J., Ferro, J., Liaupsin, C., & Lane, K. (2006). *Functional behavioral assessment and function-based interventions: An effective, practical approach.* Columbus, OH: Pearson.	Provides a complete system for conducting functional-based assessments. Discusses step-by-step strategies for developing, implementing, and monitoring effective interventions.
Watson, T. S., & Steege, M. W. (2003). *Conducting school-based functional behavioral assessments: A practitioner's guide.* New York: Guilford Press.	A manual for school practitioners that provides the tools necessary to complete reliable and valid functional behavioral assessments and use them to plan effective interventions. Defines basic terms and procedures and describes in detail the process of working with individual students.
Witt, J. C., Daly, E. M., & Noell, G. (2000). *Functional assessments: A step-by-step guide to solving academic and behavior problems.* Longmont, CO: Sopris West.	Instructs school professionals in conducting best-practice functional assessments for academic and behavioral concerns. Uses a four-step model to help identify antecedents and consequences of behavior, interpret assessment data, develop strategies for reducing inappropriate behavior, and analyze and monitor student progress.

Note. Adapted from Newcomer (2010c). Copyright 2010 by Lori L. Newcomer. Reprinted by permission.

CHALLENGES AND ISSUES

Generally speaking, as children proceed to the top of the triangle, the extensiveness of resources needed to address their needs increases (Stecker, 2007; Stormont et al., 2008; Sugai, 2011). Children's movement to more intensive supports requires a corresponding increasing intensity of (1) resources that will need to be secured, (2) attention placed on investigating and changing essential environmental factors, and (3) attention to gathering and utilizing data for decision making (Bohanon et al., 2011b). As mentioned in Chapter 1, some researchers have called for increasing integration efforts to support alignment of multiple school initiatives. Some researchers have recommended the use of a technique referred to as "braiding" to unite complementary change models (Bohanon et al., 2011a). Teams are a logical driving force for these unifications and can work to integrate new initiatives within the existing models. "The process involves identifying how parallel systems, data, and practices may be combined into a coherent, unified set of daily responsibilities with a common language" (Bohanon et al., 2011a, p. 3).

INTERVIEWS

This chapter concludes with interviews of three individuals with different backgrounds, experiences, and expertise, who are currently involved in RTI and/or PBIS implementation efforts. The interviews were conducted electronically with a researcher, a state-level administrator, and a practicing school psychologist. We thought that professionals reading this book would like to hear from other professionals who are in the trenches of implementation efforts in different capacities. In addition to underscoring the important points from this chapter, the interviews may help readers find solace in knowing that others are dealing with the same issues, and learn more about how professionals in the field are working in the area of Tier 3 interventions.

Pamela M. Stecker, PhD

1. Provide some information about yourself. Specifically, how long have you been involved in research and teaching at the university level related to RTI, and what is your current title?

Currently, I am Professor of Special Education in the Eugene T. Moore School of Education at Clemson University in South Carolina. Although I have been discussing RTI as a schoolwide preventive framework in my courses and have used this model for working with schools in conjunction with the S.C. Department of Education's State Improvement Grant during the past decade, I have been involved in research, development, and instruction related to reliable and valid progress monitoring tools, particularly curriculum-based measurement (CBM), since the beginning of my graduate studies in the mid-1980s under Lynn and Doug Fuchs at Peabody College of Vanderbilt University. We initially examined the response of students with disabilities to instruction delivered in special education settings and found that teachers who used CBM to inform instructional decision making effected better achievement among their students than special educators who used their own methods for assessing student progress. Later, we followed students with disabilities into general education classrooms and monitored their response to instruction as well as the response of their typical peers. General education teachers expressed interest in monitoring the progress of all their students, and several federally funded grants supported efforts to help teachers conduct classwide progress monitoring, to use data to target students who appeared to need additional academic assistance, and to modify instruction to better meet the needs of individual students or groups of students. We worked to develop and validate some instructional practices that general education teachers could use to accommodate student academic diversity in their classrooms, such as peer-assisted learning strategies (PALS). The students of greatest concern, of course, were those individuals whose response to otherwise effective instruction was poor; that is, both their level of performance and rate of improvement were significantly discrepant from their peers. This dual discrepancy later became one method for identifying potential students with specific learning disabilities. Thus, we were involved in several areas of research that now have become common practice among many models of RTI. My interest in data-based decision making, specifically in teachers' use of data to formulate better instructional programs for students with disabilities or who are low performing and to evaluate the effect of that instruction for individual students, continues to this day.

2. What are some of the systems pieces that need to be in place for schools to effectively implement Tier 3 academic interventions?

I probably should describe first how I view Tier 3 within the context of RTI. Although many types of RTI models are implemented in schools today, I view Tier 1 services as instruction occurring in general education classrooms where strong core programs are in place and universal screening occurs. Teachers also may be delivering some targeted instructional practices. For example, teachers may use their initial data to design groupings of students for instructing particular subjects or skills, or teachers may choose to implement some supplementary instructional practices that are designed and validated as generally effective across a broad range of students, particularly if screening data indicate that the classroom has a large number of students that is low performing. By monitoring the progress of students, at least monitoring those students who are designated as low performing, teachers then can use the data to determine whether their Tier 1 instructional program is working in the desired manner or whether a particular student's inadequate response indicates the need for additional instruction.

These progress monitoring data provide a database for justifying Tier 2 instruction, which I view as supplemental instruction for small, homogeneous groups of students that is delivered in addition to the Tier 1 program. Although a variety of individuals may deliver this small-group instruction, progress monitoring data are collected and used to determine whether supplemental instruction, along with Tier 1 instruction, is producing the desired effect of improved student achievement. When possible, research-validated practices should be used for Tier 2 supplemental instruction, both because research supports that particular practice as generally effective for low-performing students in this subject and/or grade level and because school resources may be better allocated and managed if standardized interventions are implemented. Progress monitoring data are used to determine whether Tier 2 interventions can be discontinued or whether particular students need yet more intensive intervention. Of course, more than one round of Tier 2 supplementary instruction may be tried for particular students.

Both Tier 1 and Tier 2 educational programs fall under the auspices of general education. However, where I may differ from some current RTI school practices is that I view

Tier 3 services as special education. If a student has not responded adequately to practices considered to be generally effective in Tier 1 and, likewise, has not responded adequately to one or more rounds of supplementary instruction in Tier 2, especially if those practices have been demonstrated by research as likely to enhance both performance and progress among low-performing students, then a database has been developed to aid in the determination of a disability and to justify more intensive services. In other words, poor response to Tier 2 triggers special education evaluation. Of course, schools also must allow for a referral for special education evaluation to occur at any point in time within the RTI framework.

With that said, I see Tier 3 academic interventions as services provided as special education for individual students. Although these services sometimes can be provided within general education classrooms rather than in special education settings, these academic interventions have been developed by a team that includes at least one professional who has expertise in instructional practices for students with disabilities. Knowledge of research-based practices is important in designing interventions to address academic skills among students with disabilities. However, even research-based interventions may need to be tailored to meet the needs of individual students.

The use of progress monitoring data is critically important in the provision of these academic interventions. Progress monitoring data are used to evaluate student growth while a particular intervention is implemented. If the student's level of performance and rate of improvement are not adequate, then the academic intervention should be modified in one or more ways in an effort to better meet the individual student's needs. Of course, the data will help to answer the question of whether the modified instruction works better for the targeted student. In this way, teachers can use the database to determine which interventions appear to work better for particular students and to develop more effective instructional programs over time for individuals. These practices really lie at the core of special education intervention, in which progress monitoring data are used in true problem-solving fashion. Consequently, schools need to employ professionals who are knowledgeable about research-validated instructional practices and the use of scientifically based progress monitoring systems for data-based decision making.

Because RTI tiers encompass the provision of support for students at successive levels of instructional intensity, schools must recognize the exceedingly intensive nature of Tier 3 services in the allocation of instructional resources. Highly skilled teachers are needed to implement interventions and to evaluate their effectiveness. Although a number of system-level pieces need to be in place for an RTI model to function well, specific to Tier 3 are decisions about how a student qualifies for Tier 3 services and how long a student can receive such intensive service. For example, RTI is designed to provide flexibility among the tiers with movement in both directions. Issues that schools must address include not only the procedures to determine when a student needs more intensive assistance but what to do when a student appears to thrive in a more intensive tier but fails to progress satisfactorily when moved to a less intensive tier. Consequently, alignment and collaboration between general and special education are paramount. Additionally, schools must decide how parents should be kept informed of RTI procedures in general and must include parents in the provision of Tier 3 services.

3. What do you think are some challenges schools face when trying to build capacity for the use of Tier 3 interventions?

Schools face numerous decisions and challenges when trying to implement RTI as a schoolwide model, and Tier 3 interventions remain a critical component of this framework. Because RTI is designed as a preventive system, the goal is to have fewer students identified as needing Tier 3 services. The first order of business, then, is to help ensure implementation of high-quality instruction using evidence-based practices and curricula in Tier 1 classrooms and in Tier 2 preventive tutoring. However, data from tiered instruction can be used to help identify students with specific learning disabilities. The length and number of rounds of preventive instruction a student may receive should not delay the provision of special education services for students with disabilities who need them. Consequently, a critical challenge schools face when implementing RTI is to ensure that students who need special education services receive them in a timely fashion. Ongoing professional development is important for administrators and for teachers and service providers of all levels of tiered instruction.

4. How is your research/teaching related to the needs of children who need Tier 3 supports?

As a professor in special education, I work with undergraduate-, master-, and doctoral-level students to prepare future special educators as well as school and teacher leaders. Our special education programs at Clemson focus on the use of evidence-based practices, and I provide instruction in literacy and mathematics interventions and coursework focused especially on the needs of students with learning disabilities. I teach undergraduate and graduate students about progress monitoring in academic areas and the use of systematic decision rules for the formulation and evaluation of individualized education programs, but all of our faculty work hard to help our students become professionals who use data to drive educational decision making.

My current research efforts include collaboration with Anne Foegen of Iowa State University on an Institute of Education Sciences grant to develop a web-based tool for providing professional development to teachers about progress monitoring and for tracking student progress in algebra. We especially see the potential usefulness of this tool in aiding teachers of older students with learning disabilities to be more responsive to their students' instructional needs.

5. Do you have additional comments regarding considerations that are important to remember when laying the foundation for Tier 3 interventions?

Progress monitoring is central to RTI and critical for the development and ongoing evaluation of Tier 3 interventions. Although we have a variety of technically adequate tools to use with younger students, research is sparse in the area of reliable and valid progress monitoring systems for older students and in content-area subjects. However, having a set of tools that can be used frequently across the year to track student growth toward long-term goals is a necessary component for developing and modifying Tier 3 interventions.

Similarly, we know a great deal about effective instruction for elementary-age students with disabilities in academic areas, and more in reading than in mathematics, but we still have much more to investigate regarding interventions that are successful for older students. Consequently, implementation of RTI in middle and high schools becomes more challenging. Because time is of the essence for older students with disabilities, schools need to make sure that the students who need Tier 3 services get them quickly and that they are of sufficient intensity.

Mary Richter, PhD

1. Please provide some information about yourself, including how long you have been involved in statewide PBIS efforts and your current title.

I was a researcher and trainer for the University of Missouri Center for SW-PBS from 2002 to 2006. In the fall of 2006 the Missouri Department of Elementary and Secondary Education established funding for a state coordinator of the Missouri Schoolwide Positive Behavior Support (MO SW-PBS) initiative, and I accepted the position. The University of Missouri is the fiscal agent for my contract. The MO SW-PBS initiative is fortunate to be supported by the Missouri Department of Education and affiliated with the MU Center for SWPBS, which is led by Dr. [Tim] Lewis. In this way we are a part of statewide planning and provide direct service to schools throughout Missouri and are also able to be a part of innovative research associated with SW-PBS. Prior to 2002 I held a variety of positions in K–12 public education as a general and special education teacher and administrator. I think that having a diverse background has helped me consider SW-PBS application through a more comprehensive lens.

2. What are some of the systems pieces that need to be in place for schools to effectively implement Tier 3 academic and social behavior interventions?

Schools need to have effective and sustainable Tier 1 and Tier 2 systems in place before building Tier 3. Some of the important pieces that need to be established through these levels include:

- Building systems that provide adequate training and support for staff to understand the logic and framework of schoolwide PBS, and how to consistently apply it across all three tiers
- Assuring that schoolwide and classroom environments are structured to support all students
- Implementing practices to provide quality instruction in social and behavioral skills in schoolwide and classroom settings
- Providing training in data-based decision making so that staff can understand, analyze, and apply data to identify desired outcomes and how to reach them
- Formulating data-based decisions regarding how to objectively determine which students may be in need of more intensive supports

- Learning to understand the science of behavior and its key concepts (e.g., function of behavior, setting events, antecedent, setting, and skill or performance deficit)
- Establishing ongoing systems of communication with all stakeholders, including families, district-level personnel, and building-level staff
- Assuring that SW-PBS work fits with district- and building-level long-range planning (formal district goals and plans, alignment with state and federal guidelines)
- Determining necessary within-district and school supports to sustain SW-PBS at all three tiers
- Identifying within-district personnel to provide ongoing technical assistance and behavioral expertise
- Instituting systems of professional development within district- and building-level plans
- Collaborating with other agencies and initiatives as appropriate

3. What have been some challenges you have faced when trying to build capacity for the use of Tier 3 interventions?

School and district personnel understandably want to address the issues associated with students displaying more intense or chronic behavioral challenges. Helping them understand that the development of systems, data, and practices at Tiers 1 and 2 must come first has been a challenge. Now that more schools across the state have experienced why this is necessary, this challenge is becoming smaller, but it's still an issue we need to directly address.

Another challenge is developing a statewide system capable of scaling up training capacity, Tier 3 curriculum content, and technical support to address the needs and diversity of schools within Missouri. We have small rural K–8 or K–12 districts in more isolated geographic areas all the way to inner-city districts. We train staff for PreK through 12th grade. For these as well as a host of other reasons we need to concentrate on identifying the desired outcomes and the data we need to determine progress toward meeting them.

A third challenge is planning for long-term sustainability. We want to develop state systems that are realistic when we double or triple the number of schools we're serving. We also want to assist schools/districts to build systems that are comprehensive enough to meet Tier 3 needs with local supports. This means that we, as a state, need to use a problem-solving process to (a) identify the desired outcomes, (b) determine our current status, (c) review current resources, (d) prioritize and action plan, (e) implement the plan, (f) assess progress, and then (g) revise as indicated.

4. How is Missouri trying to meet the needs of children who need Tier 3 supports?

To date we've concentrated on direct training at Tiers 1 and 2 while also providing technical support for Tier 3. Tiers 1 and 2 training include progressively more sophisticated understanding of the science of behavior and that the same basic logic applies. It's the unit of analysis that changes; concentrating on building schoolwide, classroom, and Tier

2 systems for prevention and intervention provides the foundation for implementing Tier 3. The same problem-solving process we model as a state is taught to school- and district-level teams. We've also included increasingly sophisticated data analysis skills. Our Tier 3 training is based on the problem-solving model. The interventions we teach are within the context of the model.

Now we're preparing to implement Tier 3 training and are currently piloting it in two districts. The content has been determined after a multiyear process of learning from the national PBIS center, other SW-PBS states, and school districts with strong foundations for Tier 3 work. Some aspects of the expertise needed at Tier 3 are potentially beyond the resources of individual schools. This is another reason we encourage district-level adoption. Districts need to identify how to use their resources to structure supports across their schools so that students with the most intense needs can be successful.

We have been partnering with other agencies and initiatives within Missouri that also serve students and families with needs at the Tier 3 level. We are learning the structures and capabilities of our respective entities and considering how to best leverage our resources. We're also learning each other's language. For instance, there is more than one definition for *wraparound* and *person-centered planning*. As a group we understand that availability of resources and programs varies, but if we can build systems of communication and collaboration, then we can potentially provide more logical and sustainable systems of support for our staff and those we serve.

5. Do you have additional comments regarding considerations that are important to remember when laying the foundation for Tier 3 interventions?

Just as with other tiers of SW-PBS, districts will take the lead on determining how the framework we provide best fits with the systems they want to build and their resources. Our state initiative needs to help districts be aware of state and federal guidelines that may impact their decisions as well as how to address them within a proactive and comprehensive Tier 3 system. The system should include consideration of all stakeholders, who should be a part of building, implementing, and sustaining the system.

Sushama Nagarkar, NCSP

1. Please provide some information about yourself. Specifically, how long you have been involved in working in the schools and what is your current title?

I am a nationally certified school psychologist and have been working in the U.S. public school system for over 11 years now. I began my career as a school psychologist in southeast Louisiana and in 2006, post-Katrina, I moved to mid-Missouri to my current position. Prior to working in southeast Louisiana, I worked for several years with students and their families in India. The experiences between the two cultures and societies are very different. In India at that time, the medical model was very prevalent and there were no governmental mandates to provide education to students with disabilities; there are more directives now.

Working in the U.S. public school system has provided a whole different set of experiences.

2. What are some of the systems pieces that need to be in place for schools to effectively implement Tier 3 academic and social behavior interventions?

The effective implementation of Tier 3 academic and social behavior interventions has to be monitored at the building level by a problem-solving team. It does help when the school system has procedures in place that are well mapped out. In Louisiana, for example, the state guidelines for special education (called *Bulletin 1508* or the *Pupil Appraisal Handbook*) explain clearly the role of the building-level problem-solving team in facilitating the intervention process. Across the entire state, the problem-solving team is known as the *School Building Level Committee* (SBLC), the members are spelled out in Bulletin 1508, and the forms and documentation used by the different school districts are very similar. Thus it becomes easier to manage when students transfer in or out of schools or even districts. Essentially the organizational pieces are taken care of and all teams are on the same page, so to say.

If the state regulations do not direct school districts to map out their problem-solving procedures, it is imperative that school districts develop their own guidelines for all buildings to follow. When there are no districtwide systems in place, it becomes more difficult to implement interventions and assess student progress or lack thereof, particularly when students transfer in and out of buildings and when personnel, such as school psychologists, are moved from building to building. At each of the buildings to which I have been assigned, the problem-solving team has been different and has had a different set of procedures and data gathering mechanisms. School psychologists are well trained in guiding teams in the process of implementing and monitoring interventions; however, to do so becomes challenging when teams and processes across buildings are dissimilar.

The ground reality is that, regardless of district or building mandates, Tier 3 academic and social behavior interventions are a challenge to implement when personnel have not been adequately trained in the problem-solving process.

3. What have been some challenges you have faced when trying to build capacity for the use of Tier 3 interventions?

As just mentioned, one of the challenges has been not having an efficient problem-solving team in place. Another challenge is that the level of training and expertise needed to develop and implement interventions is lacking; thus fidelity of implementation becomes a huge issue. The third challenge is teacher buy-in. At some buildings, the divide between regular education and special education continues to exist. Some regular educators believe that when a student needs a Tier 3 type intervention, the student must be "special ed." and no longer their responsibility. In those situations, implementation of an intervention is very cursory, if at all. At times, it becomes a waiting game to the evaluation process.

4. How is your school and/or your school district trying to meet the needs of children who need Tier 3 supports?

During the present school year, the building administrators with whom I work are very data-driven and are intent on making sound data-based decisions for all students. It also helps that they are willing to think outside the box and challenge their building-level teams to do so as well. At one of my buildings, we have team meetings every few weeks and examine the grade-level data as well as individual student data. The students needing Tier 3 supports are very clearly being identified, and we are trying to use all available resources in the building and beyond it to help these students succeed. This is a work in progress, and it is slow. However, at the end of the day, students who are at risk for lack of instruction or cultural and economic disadvantage *are* making progress—and that is very exciting. Importantly, teachers feel validated.

5. Do you have additional comments regarding considerations that are important to remember when laying the foundation for Tier 3 interventions?

Several! The foundations at the building and district level (not necessarily in that order) have to be well laid out. There has to be training at the building/district level, and there has to be ongoing support to personnel who are actually implementing the interventions. I do believe that delivering Tier 3 interventions with fidelity and monitoring progress can be done by faculty and staff that are available in the buildings. It requires creative scheduling, planning, and ongoing training and support. School psychologists are well trained in facilitating the processes, helping with interpreting data, and are a valuable resource to these endeavors. Unfortunately, our expertise in these areas is not always tapped—for a multitude of reasons.

SUMMARY

This chapter presents information on determining when children may need the most intense level of supports, referred to as Tier 3. It is important that professionals do not move to this level until they have assessed fidelity of implementation of Tier 2 supports. Determining children's responsiveness to Tier 2 is a vital prerequisite to Tier 3 assignment, and a large part of their responsiveness can be attributed to the types of interventions selected and the fidelity with which they are implemented (McIntosh et al., 2010). There are many challenges and issues related to aligning systems to more clearly support transitioning from one level of support to another as children move up the triangle. It is imperative that systems are prepared to provide the necessary resources to support successful implementation of more intense support; often this includes making sure that personnel have the skills to support the selection of evidence-based practices. The brief interviews with experts on the topic underscore current trends and issues as well as the essential systems pieces that must be in place when laying the foundation for Tier 3 interventions.

Epilogue

There is much to be excited about regarding the evolving application of RTI methods within schools. As RTI scientific advances occur and school personnel become increasingly better equipped to implement these models, more schools will become places where all children can flourish. Because of practical and legal necessity, schools have traditionally placed high priority on providing services to students who exhibit the most extreme behavior and academic problems. RTI methods have helped schools both to improve the quality of supports for those most in need and also to use a framework for addressing the needs of all students. As schools build capacity to provide high-quality, responsive universal supports and also intensive individual supports mandated by federal law, sometimes students in the middle—those in the so-called yellow zone or Tier 2—get overlooked. The purpose of this book is to shine the light on this group of students, this essential tier of support in an RTI framework. We have attempted to describe the state-of-the-science Tier 2 supports for students showing subclinical but significant externalizing and internalizing behavior problems and academic deficits. These methods, when implemented properly, will lessen the overall burden on school professionals by reducing the number of children who progress to needing more intensive supports. Undoubtedly, Tier 2 methods will continue to evolve as we develop even more systematic and efficient methods for responding to students in need of modest supports. Our current methods described in this book give much reason for optimism and for believing that schools can help all children be successful even with limited resources.

Reproducible Forms

FORM 1.1

Developing a Matrix and Teaching Plan

To create a matrix, school teams need to do the following:	Date completed
1. Review examples from exemplary schools (*pbismissouri.org/exemplar.html*).	
2. Determine expectations that fit with school culture.	
3. Draft some expectations for staff to review.	
4. Draft specific rules (three to five per setting and expectation) based on problems (problem = student running in the hall is problematic, so one rule for the expectation to be safe in the hallway setting = walk).	
5. Solicit input from all staff.	
6. Revise.	
7. Develop a plan for teaching each rule under each expectation.	
8. Develop a plan for supporting each rule (prompts, reinforcement).	
9. Develop a plan for making data decision rules about student, staff, and environmental needs.	
10. Develop a plan for teaching new staff and children.	

Based on Stormont, Lewis, Beckner, and Johnson (2008).

From Melissa Stormont, Wendy M. Reinke, Keith C. Herman, and Erica S. Lembke. Copyright 2012 by The Guilford Press. Permission to photocopy this form is granted to purchasers of this book for personal use only (see copyright page for details).

Format and Procedures for Determining, Teaching, and Supporting Behavioral Expectations and Specific Rules across Settings

Expectations	Settings			
	All Settings	Classroom	Hallway	Cafeteria
Be Safe	Walk			
Be Kind				
Be Responsible				

From Melissa Stormont, Wendy M. Reinke, Keith C. Herman, and Erica S. Lembke. Copyright 2012 by The Guilford Press. Permission to photocopy this form is granted to purchasers of this book for personal use only (see copyright page for details).

General Student At-Risk Nomination Form

General Information

Student: _____   Parent/Guardian: _____

Referring Teacher(s): _____   Phone Number: _____

Address: _____   City/State/ZIP: _____

How and when was parent notified about referral?

_____

Reason for Referral (Primary Concern):

_____ Academic   _____ Behavioral   _____ Emotional

Please describe the specific concerns prompting this referral. What makes this student difficult to teach? List any academic, social, emotional, or other factors that you think negatively impact the student's performance.

_____
_____
_____
_____
_____
_____
_____

How do this student's academic skills compare to those of an average student in your classroom?

_____
_____
_____
_____
_____
_____
_____

(cont.)

From Melissa Stormont, Wendy M. Reinke, Keith C. Herman, and Erica S. Lembke. Copyright 2012 by The Guilford Press. Permission to photocopy this form is granted to purchasers of this book for personal use only (see copyright page for details).

In what settings/situations does the problem occur most often? _____

_____

In what settings/situations does the problem occur least often? _____

_____

What are the student's strengths, talents, or specific interests? _____

_____

What have you tried to resolve this problem?

_____

_____

_____

_____

How did it work?

_____

_____

_____

_____

When did you start the intervention? _____

When did you end the intervention? _____

From Newcomer (2010a). Copyright 2010 by Lori L. Newcomer. Reprinted by permission.

Cumulative Record Review

School: _____   Student: _____

Reviewed by: _____   Review Date: _____

Attendance	Grade 1	Grade 2	Grade 3	Grade 4	Grade 5	Grade 6	Grade 7	Grade 8	Total tardy/absent out of total days
Tardy									/
Absent									/

Has the student been retained? _____

If so, what grade(s)? _____

Support the student is receiving or has received (indicate year):

☐ Special education _____

☐ 504 _____

☐ Counseling _____

☐ ELL _____

☐ After-school programs _____

☐ Other: _____

MAP* or other scores	Grade 3	Grade 4	Grade 5	Grade 6	Grade 7	Grade 8
Reading/LangArt						
Math						

Referrals	Source (e.g., classroom, gym, lunchroom, specials)
# Office referrals to date:	
# ISS** days to date:	
# OSS*** Days to date:	
Health concerns:	Medications:

Notes:

*Missouri Assessment Program; **In-school suspension; ***Out-of-school suspension.

From Newcomer (2010b). Copyright 2010 by Lori L. Newcomer. Reprinted by permission.

From Melissa Stormont, Wendy M. Reinke, Keith C. Herman, and Erica S. Lembke. Copyright 2012 by The Guilford Press. Permission to photocopy this form is granted to purchasers of this book for personal use only (see copyright page for details).

Sample Initial Referral Form

Student: _____   Grade: _____   Date: _____

DOB: _____   Age: _____   Gender: _____

Referred by: _____   Classroom Teacher: _____

Check Primary Reason for Referral: ☐ CA   ☐ Math   ☐ Behavior

Primary Teacher concerns: (Measurable & Observable) **(Sample goal:)**

Parent's Name: _____   Retention: (Yes/No)   Which Grade: _____

Address: _____   Other Schools Attended: _____

Phone: _____   Vision: (Pass/Fail)   When? _____

Days Absent/Tardy/Early Out: __/__/__   Hearing: (Pass/Fail)   When? _____

Medical Diagnosis _____   (Ex., ADHD) Speech: (Pass/Fail) When? _____

Medications _____   Current Physician _____
(if applicable)   (if applicable)

****NOTE: Parents must be contacted by phone or in person <u>PRIOR</u> to SAT referral.

Parent Comments: Notes/Phone Calls/Emails/Meetings (Dates & Results)/Behaviors at home.

<u>Current Services Provided</u>: Check all those that apply

☐ Speech/Language	☐ Reading Improvement Plan	☐ SB 319 Tutoring	☐ A+
☐ ESL/ELL	☐ Reading Interventionist	☐ TA	☐ Health Care Plan
☐ 504 Plan	☐ Behavior Plan	☐ Triage	☐ Focus/Recovery
☐ Counselor Referral	☐ Other Plan		

Student Strengths:
Student Challenges:

Note: Complete information as applicable from most recent assessments.

(cont.)

From Melissa Stormont, Wendy M. Reinke, Keith C. Herman, and Erica S. Lembke. Copyright 2012 by The Guilford Press. Permission to photocopy this form is granted to purchasers of this book for personal use only (see copyright page for details).

Communication Arts

Primary Goals: (Measurable & Specific) **(Sample goal:)**

DIAL-3

Name: _____ Age: _____

Results: Motor: _____ Concepts: _____ Language: _____

Total: _____

Stanford 10

Date: _____ Grade: _____ Age: _____

Total Reading: ____ / ____ Total Language: ____ / ____ Listening: ____ / ____

Composite Score: ____ / ____

Most Current MAP Score Total CA Score: _____ Ach Level: _____ of Year _____

AIMSweb (check one) Fall _____ Winter _____ Spring _____ of Year _____
(Score AND Perf Summary Level—*e.g., Below Avg*)

LNF _____ LSF _____ PSF _____ NWF _____ R-CBM _____ MAZE _____

Fountas & Pinnell/Guided Reading Level _____ Grade Level Equiv _____

SRI Fall _____   Winter _____   Spring _____ of Year _____

(Lexile/Grade Level Equiv./Pred Ach Level)   (Lexile/Grade Level Equiv./Pred Ach Level)   (Lexile/Grade Level Equiv./Pred Ach Level)

DORA Fluency ____ Comprehension _____ Phonics _____ Word Recognition _____

Vocabulary _____ Spelling _____ High Frequency _____ Phonemic Awareness _____

Writing
Mechanics   ☐ Below Grade   ☐ On Grade Level ☐ Above Grade Level

Legibility/Fine Motor ☐ Below Grade   ☐ On Grade Level ☐ Above Grade Level

Language
Receptive   ☐ Below Grade   ☐ On Grade Level ☐ Above Grade Level

Expressive ☐ Below Grade   ☐ On Grade Level ☐ Above Grade Level

(cont.)

Current Accommodations & Results
Modifications & Results

Tried Interventions (name program)	Start Date	End Date	Frequency/ Duration of Intervention	Person Responsible for Delivery	Data Collection/ Frequency	Measured by Instrument & Assessment	Baseline Score	End Results
1.								
2.								
3.								

Bring to SAT meeting:
   Current grade card   *Previous grade card*
   District writing assessments/samples   *Phonemic Awareness Test*
   Literacy folder   *Running records*
   AIMSweb reports   *SRI reports*
   Student work samples

Math

Primary Goals: (Measurable & Specific) **(Sample goal:)**

Number Recognition: _____   Counts to: _____

Addition Facts   ☐ Below Grade   ☐ On Grade Level ☐ Above Grade Level

Subtraction Facts   ☐ Below Grade   ☐ On Grade Level ☐ Above Grade Level

Multiplication Facts   ☐ Below Grade   ☐ On Grade Level ☐ Above Grade Level

DIAL-3

Name: _____   Age: _____

Results: Motor: _____   Concepts: _____ Language: _____

          Total: _____

Stanford 10

Date: _____   Grade: _____   Age: _____

Total Math: _____   Composite Score: _____

(cont.)

Most Current MAP Score   Total CA Score: _____   Ach Level: _____ of Year _____

AIMSweb (check one) Fall _____ Winter _____ Spring _____ of Year _____
(Score AND Perf Summary Level—*e.g., Below Average*)

OC _____   NI _____   QD _____   MN _____   COMP ___   M-CAP _____   M-CBM _____

Please list two characteristics of learning style: *Ex: Kinesthetic, auditory, visual*

Current Accommodations & Results **Modifications & Results**

Tried Interventions (name program)	Start Date	End Date	Frequency/ Duration of Intervention	Person Responsible for Delivery	Data Collection/ Frequency	Measured by Instrument & Assessment	Baseline Score	End Results
1.								
2.								
3.								

Bring to SAT meeting:
  Current grade card
  Previous grade card
  Unit pre/post assessment(s)
  AIMSweb assessments

  Skill-based timed assessment(s)
  District assessments
  Cumulative file
  Student work samples

Behavior

Primary Goals: (Measurable & Specific) **(Sample goal:)**

(cont.)

Behavior Patterns	**Peers/Social/Affect**

Behavior Patterns
- Defiant
- Constant discipline
- Blaming/denying
- Fighting/outbursts
- Verbally aggressive
- Physically aggressive
- Cheating
- Lying
- Crying
- Obscene language
- Easily overstimulated
- Attention seeking
- Lack of organization skills
- Needs one-on-one redirection
- Easily distracted
- Short attention span
- Lack of work completion
- Recess/lunch concerns
- _____

Peers/Social/Affect
- Peer rejection
- Lack of friends
- Avoids peer contact
- Change in friends
- Sudden popularity
- Extremely negative
- Avoids contact with staff
- Unexplained grief
- Reports fears, nightmares
- Erratic behavior change
- Defensive, irritable
- Withdrawn
- Unwilling to communicate
- Impulsive
- _____
- _____
- _____

Core teachers' observations:

_____

_____

_____

_____

_____

CAMP/ENCORE teachers' observations:

_____

_____

_____

Parent observations:

_____

_____

_____

Note: Modified from an original provided by Raymore-Peculiar School District, Peculiar, Missouri.

FORM 1.6

Tier 2 Resource Needs Assessment

Tier 2 Need	In Place	Need Area
Team to support implementation		
Data-gathering systems to determine who needs Tier 2 supports		
Data-monitoring system to monitor children receiving Tier 2 supports		
Evidence-based Tier 2 interventions to support children—academic areas		
Evidence-based Tier 2 interventions to support children—social behavioral		
Additional training opportunities		
Resources to support implementation needs		

(cont.)

From Melissa Stormont, Wendy M. Reinke, Keith C. Herman, and Erica S. Lembke. Copyright 2012 by The Guilford Press. Permission to photocopy this form is granted to purchasers of this book for personal use only (see copyright page for details).

Tier 2 Need	In Place	Need Area
Mechanism for home–school communication		
Systems and practices to build capacity (e.g., train all teachers on specific interventions)		

Action Planning Based on Need Areas:

Target areas:

Next steps, including person responsible for each step:

Follow-up meeting:

FORM 1.7

Tier 2 Support Plan

Student: _____

Support needs	Interventions currently in place in school	Person responsible	Data to monitor progress

Copy if need more than four supports

(cont.)

From Melissa Stormont, Wendy M. Reinke, Keith C. Herman, and Erica S. Lembke. Copyright 2012 by The Guilford Press. Permission to photocopy this form is granted to purchasers of this book for personal use only (see copyright page for details).

Notes:

Data management system:

Meeting for progress review:

Discuss any family support needs:

Rubric for Examining Cultural Responsiveness of Academic and Behavior Support Teams

Understand the Cultural Context	
Your team has developed a rich picture of the cultural context of your classrooms and school through personal contact and experiences with the students and their families.	2
Your team has some understanding of the cultural context based on limited interactions with your students and their families.	1
Your team has not considered the many different aspects of culture and how cultural variables impact the way your students think and act.	0
Become Aware of Personal Assumptions	
Your team continually evaluates your values, assumptions, and worldviews and how they may impact your delivery of academic and behavior supports.	2
Your team examines your personal assumptions and how they compare to those of your students, but only infrequently.	1
Your team has not considered ways that your personal assumptions may impact delivery of academic and behavior supports.	0
Engage in Ongoing Collaboration	
Your team establishes ongoing collaborations with students and community members regarding the appropriateness of academic and behavior supports.	2
Your team discusses adaptations of academic and behavior supports with students and community members, but only at the beginning of support planning or only infrequently.	1
Your team has not established any collaborative relationships with students or community members about academic and behavior supports.	0
Make Specific Cultural Adaptations	
Your team has created lesson plans and behavior supports using language, examples, and assessment materials to match the life experiences of the students in your school.	2
Your team makes some adaptations to academic and behavior supports, but not in a comprehensive or planful way (e.g., making adaptations only during a lesson).	1
Your team has not made any efforts to adapt academic and behavior supports to the students in your school.	0

Based on Lopez, Edwards, Pedrotti, Ito, and Rasmussen (2002).

From Melissa Stormont, Wendy M. Reinke, Keith C. Herman, and Erica S. Lembke. Copyright 2012 by The Guilford Press. Permission to photocopy this form is granted to purchasers of this book for personal use only (see copyright page for details).

Survey on Parents' Opinions of Homework

Home learning: We like to do the following together:

- Go to the library
- Go to parks
- Take walks
- Go to the store
- Visit friends and relatives
- Read books
- Sing
- Go to the mall
- Listen to music
- Watch TV
- Play video games
- Find information on the Internet
- _____
- _____

If home learning activities were connected to the types of things you like to do together, would that make "homework" easier?

- Yes
- No

What are some challenges you have related to your child's homework?

- None
- Directions are not clear
- Time
- Child forgets to tell me
- Don't believe children this young should have homework
- Other: _____

How much homework do you think is appropriate for your child?

- 30 minutes/day
- 20 minutes/day
- 10 minutes/day
- 5 minutes/day
- 10–15 minutes a few times per week
- None

From Stormont (2007). Copyright 2007 by Pearson Education Inc. Reprinted by permission.

From Melissa Stormont, Wendy M. Reinke, Keith C. Herman, and Erica S. Lembke. Copyright 2012 by The Guilford Press. Permission to photocopy this form is granted to purchasers of this book for personal use only (see copyright page for details).

FORM 2.3

Homework on Social Behavior: General Format

Dear family of _____

Your child is working on _____

_____

The specific behaviors related to this skill include:

Please work on this skill when you _____

At school, I do the following when working with your child:
- **Remind** him/her of what he/she should do—see above.
- **Watch** his/her behavior.
- **Remind** him/her of what he/she should be doing if he/she makes a mistake.
- **Praise** him/her when he/she uses the skill correctly!
- **Understand** that this is something that requires teaching and support just like academics.

From Stormont (2007). Copyright 2007 by Pearson Education Inc. Reprinted by permission.

From Melissa Stormont, Wendy M. Reinke, Keith C. Herman, and Erica S. Lembke. Copyright 2012 by The Guilford Press. Permission to photocopy this form is granted to purchasers of this book for personal use only (see copyright page for details).

Ways for Family Members to Be Involved

I would like to be involved in my child's school in the following ways:

Volunteering and Fundraising:

Career Day speaking

Chaperoning on a field trip and assisting with student supervision

Clipping coupons or purchasing extra classroom supplies

Activities in the Classroom:

Reading with students in small groups

Attending classroom project presentations

Making or donating something for a class party

Joining the PTA:

Attend monthly meetings and stay informed

Contribute to fundraising ideas and activities

Helping to put together and host Back-to-School Night

At Home:

Discussing your child's school day with him/her

Being aware of your child's social development and academic progress

Helping with homework

Staying in contact with teachers and school personnel

Providing important details of your home life and culture to your child's teacher

Potential Obstacles I May Have:

Lack of time and/or flexibility

Financial responsibilities

Childcare

Taking time off from work

Transportation

Language barriers

Special needs (i.e., family members with disabilities)

From Melissa Stormont, Wendy M. Reinke, Keith C. Herman, and Erica S. Lembke. Copyright 2012 by The Guilford Press. Permission to photocopy this form is granted to purchasers of this book for personal use only (see copyright page for details).

Function Hypothesis Development and Planning Form

Student: _____ Date: _____

Antecedent	Behavior	Consequence	Possible Function/Purpose
What happens before the problem behavior?	What does the problem behavior look like?	What happens after the problem behavior?	Does the student receive **attention**, **obtain something**, or **avoid/escape** something?
Student Supports Needed (check off all that apply):	☐ Adult attention ☐ Peer attention ☐ Avoid aversive activity ☐ Avoid aversive social interaction	☐ Academic support ☐ Support with organizing ☐ Choices ☐ Reinforce replacement behavior	☐ Teach social behavior ☐ Teach cognitive coping ☐ Teach problem solving ☐ Home–school communication
Behavior(s) to Increase: What behavior(s) will replace the problem behavior to support student success?		Tier 2 Intervention: What Tier 2 intervention(s) was selected to support the student? Intervention provides needed supports? **Y N** (If no, how will needs be met?)	

From Melissa Stormont, Wendy M. Reinke, Keith C. Herman, and Erica S. Lembke. Copyright 2012 by The Guilford Press. Permission to photocopy this form is granted to purchasers of this book for personal use only (see copyright page for details).

Daily Behavior Card

Student: _____ Date: _____

☺	3 = Great	Goal:
☺	2 = OK	Points Earned:
☹	1 = Needs work	Goal Met? Y or N If yes, reward earned?

Goals & Expectations	Subject	Subject	Subject	Subject	Subject	Subject	Subject	Total Points
Goal 1: 1. 2.								
Goal 2: 1. 2.								
Goal 3: 1. 2.								
Total Points Earned							% Earned Today:	
Total Points Possible								

Parent Signature _____

(cont.)

From Melissa Stormont, Wendy M. Reinke, Keith C. Herman, and Erica S. Lembke. Copyright 2012 by The Guilford Press. Permission to photocopy this form is granted to purchasers of this book for personal use only (see copyright page for details).

Directions for using Daily Behavior Card:

1. At the end of each period the student will present the Daily Behavior Card to the teacher. The teacher should provide a score in the corresponding cell for each goal. To determine the appropriate score, the teacher should take into consideration the student's behavior only during that class period.

2. To render the scores consistent across teachers, it is important to reflect on the student's behavior. If the student had no problems, he or she should earn a 3, three times (one in each cell for each goal). If some behavior problems were observed, first determine which specific goal was affected. Next, determine the severity of the problem (severe = danger to others, minor = needed redirection) and the number of times it occurred. If the behavior was mild and occurred one or two times, the score should be a 2. If the behavior was severe or occurred more than two times, then the score should be a 1.

3. The teacher completes the form and provides feedback. If the student did not earn 3's across all goals, the teacher should briefly explain, in a nonemotional manner, how the student can increase the score. Additionally, the teacher can indicate in what area(s) the student did well and that he or she can get all 3's in the next class period.

4. At the end of the day, the classroom teacher tallies the points and percentage. If the goal is met, the reward should be provided immediately.

5. Send home the Daily Behavior Card for parent signature.

FORM 3.3

Behavior Tracking Form

Student: _____

Week: _____

Behavior to Decrease: _____

Behavior to Increase: _____

1. Mark a tally for each time the behavior to decrease occurs.
2. Earn a reward by meeting the goal or fewer tallies.

Monday	Tuesday	Wednesday	Thursday	Friday
Today's Goal:	Today's Goal:	Today's Goal:	Today's Goal:	Today's Goal:
Reward Earned? Y N	Reward Earned? Y N	Reward Earned? Y N	Reward Earned? Y N	Reward Earned? Y N

From Melissa Stormont, Wendy M. Reinke, Keith C. Herman, and Erica S. Lembke. Copyright 2012 by The Guilford Press. Permission to photocopy this form is granted to purchasers of this book for personal use only (see copyright page for details).

Pass System with Response Cost

Student:

Goal:

Passes can be used to:

Date:

Daily Passes Each pass not used = 5 pts/day	Monday ☐ Earned reward	Tuesday ☐ Earned reward	Wednesday ☐ Earned reward	Thursday ☐ Earned reward	Friday ☐ Earned reward
Points Earned					
Points Removed					
Pass #1					
Pass #2					
Pass #3					
Pts Rolled Over =					
Cumulative Points:					

Student Signature _____

Teacher Signature _____

189

From Melissa Stormont, Wendy M. Reinke, Keith C. Herman, and Erica S. Lembke. Copyright 2012 by The Guilford Press. Permission to photocopy this form is granted to purchasers of this book for personal use only (see copyright page for details).

Behavior Contract Template

Student:	Date:
Teacher/School Personnel:	Parent/Caregiver(s):

What behavior(s) will student work to increase?

1.

2.

3.

To track each time one of these behavior occurs, _____ will do the following:

(teacher/adult at school)

Daily Goal:

If _____ reaches this goal, s/he will choose one of the following:	List of daily reward choices:

Weekly Goal:

If _____ reaches this weekly goal, s/he will choose one of the following:	List of weekly reward choices:

I helped to create this contract, understand it, and agree to the terms of this behavior contract.

Student Signature: _____

I understand and agree to follow through with my part of this contract.

Teacher/School Personnel Signature: _____

I understand and agree to follow through with my part of this contract.

Parent/Caregiver Signature(s): _____

From Melissa Stormont, Wendy M. Reinke, Keith C. Herman, and Erica S. Lembke. Copyright 2012 by The Guilford Press. Permission to photocopy this form is granted to purchasers of this book for personal use only (see copyright page for details).

Mood Monitoring Form

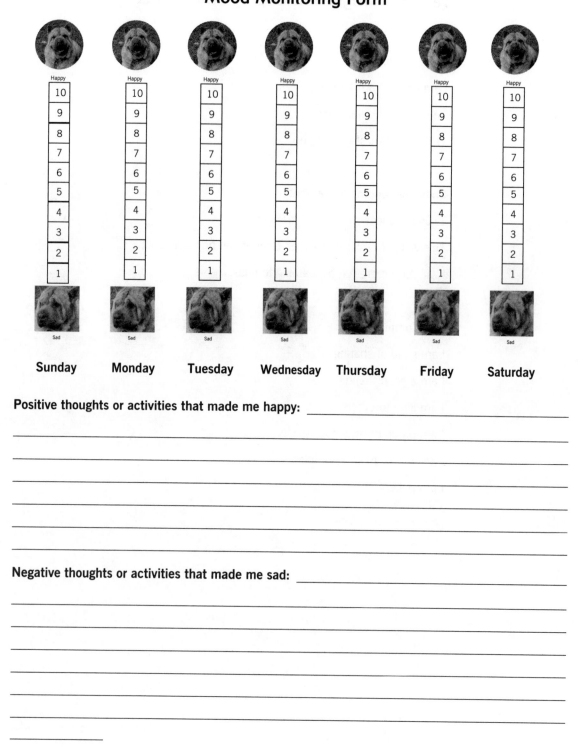

| | Sunday | Monday | Tuesday | Wednesday | Thursday | Friday | Saturday |

Positive thoughts or activities that made me happy: _____

_____

_____

_____

_____

_____

_____

Negative thoughts or activities that made me sad: _____

_____

_____

_____

_____

_____

_____

From Melissa Stormont, Wendy M. Reinke, Keith C. Herman, and Erica S. Lembke. Copyright 2012 by The Guilford Press. Permission to photocopy this form is granted to purchasers of this book for personal use only (see copyright page for details).

Self-Encouragement Coping Statements

Coping Statements

I can do this.

I am brave. I am strong.

I am safe. This will pass.

This is all part of growing up.

Challenge Coping Statements

Taking chances makes me stronger.

This will get easier and easier. Soon it will be automatic.

I will have more fun by learning to relax.

Self-Compliments

I am good at sharing.

I am a good friend.

I am kind to others.

I am proud of myself for trying.

I know how to solve problems.

I am patient.

From Melissa Stormont, Wendy M. Reinke, Keith C. Herman, and Erica S. Lembke. Copyright 2012 by The Guilford Press. Permission to photocopy this form is granted to purchasers of this book for personal use only (see copyright page for details).

Thought Detective

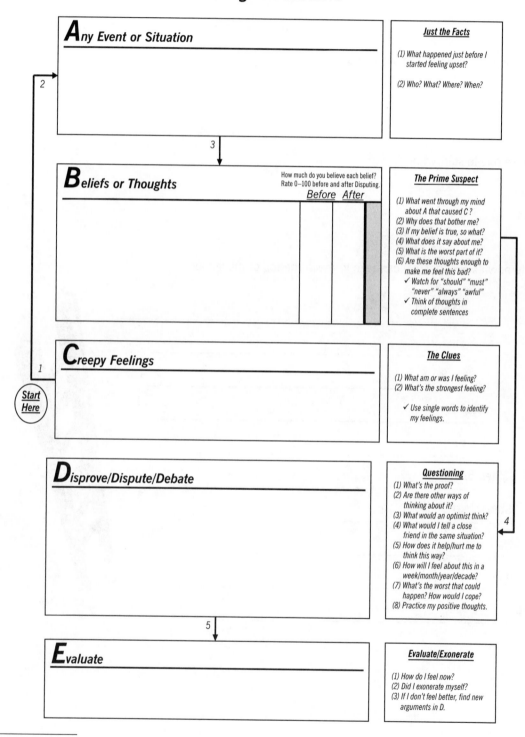

Any Event or Situation

Just the Facts

(1) What happened just before I started feeling upset?

(2) Who? What? Where? When?

2

3

Beliefs or Thoughts

How much do you believe each belief? Rate 0–100 before and after Disputing.

Before _After_

The Prime Suspect

(1) What went through my mind about A that caused C ?
(2) Why does that bother me?
(3) If my belief is true, so what?
(4) What does it say about me?
(5) What is the worst part of it?
(6) Are these thoughts enough to make me feel this bad?
✓ Watch for "should" "must" "never" "always" "awful"
✓ Think of thoughts in complete sentences

Creepy Feelings

The Clues

(1) What am or was I feeling?
(2) What's the strongest feeling?

✓ Use single words to identify my feelings.

1

Start Here

Disprove/Dispute/Debate

Questioning

(1) What's the proof?
(2) Are there other ways of thinking about it?
(3) What would an optimist think?
(4) What would I tell a close friend in the same situation?
(5) How does it help/hurt me to think this way?
(6) How will I feel about this in a week/month/year/decade?
(7) What's the worst that could happen? How would I cope?
(8) Practice my positive thoughts.

4

5

Evaluate

Evaluate/Exonerate

(1) How do I feel now?
(2) Did I exonerate myself?
(3) If I don't feel better, find new arguments in D.

From Melissa Stormont, Wendy M. Reinke, Keith C. Herman, and Erica S. Lembke. Copyright 2012 by The Guilford Press. Permission to photocopy this form is granted to purchasers of this book for personal use only (see copyright page for details).

Fear Hierarchy

One Step at a Time

What fears do you want to overcome?

Choose one to start with:

Write down steps that you can take to reach the top of the ladder:

Most Feared

Step 10: _____

Step 9: _____

Step 8: _____

Step 7: _____

Step 6: _____

Step 5: _____

Step 4: _____

Step 3: _____

Step 2: _____

Step 1: _____

Least Feared

From Melissa Stormont, Wendy M. Reinke, Keith C. Herman, and Erica S. Lembke. Copyright 2012 by The Guilford Press. Permission to photocopy this form is granted to purchasers of this book for personal use only (see copyright page for details).

Implementation Checklist for Check-In/Check-Out

Feature	Goal	Yes/No
Program Design	An intervention coordinator is identified.	
	The intervention coordinator has a flexible schedule at the beginning and end of the day, is in the school everyday, and is highly positive and liked by students.	
	A consistent location for checking in and checking out (CICO) is designated.	
	A maximum number of students that can be served at one time is determined.	
	Your school's name for the CICO program and the daily progress report (DPR) are identified.	
	At least two people who can substitute if the coordinator is absent are designated and trained.	
Daily Progress Report	Each DPR includes your schoolwide expectations.	
	Each DPR includes rules for meeting the schoolwide expectations or a blank space to write the replacement behavior under each expectation.	
	The DPR has a place to document the student's goal.	
	The DPR includes a rating section for each class period of the day.	
	The DPR has designated criteria for how points are earned and includes a range of possible points.	
	The DPR data are easy to total.	
	The DPR is age appropriate.	
Reinforcement System	Reinforcers are available daily for students who check in.	
	Reinforcers are available daily for students who check out.	
	Additional reinforcers are available for students who meet their daily or weekly point goal.	
Data Management	A data management system is available to store and summarize student point totals.	
	The intervention coordinator is trained to enter and graph the student data.	
	Student data are examined and reviewed on a regularly scheduled basis.	
	The intervention coordinator brings data to the Tier 2 team meetings.	
	Data are shared with the whole staff at least quarterly.	
	Data are shared with parents on a regular basis.	

(cont.)

From Missouri Center for Schoolwide Positive Behavior Supports (2008). Reprinted by permission in Melissa Stormont, Wendy M. Reinke, Keith C. Herman, and Erica S. Lembke (2012). Permission to photocopy this form is granted to purchasers of this book for personal use only (see copyright page for details).

Feature	Goal	Yes/No
Plans for Fading	Criteria for fading students off the intervention are established.	
	The self-management process is understood by student and participating teachers.	
	A plan for celebration when students graduate from Behavior Education Program (BEP)—CICO is designed.	
	Periodic checkups/supports are in place for students who graduate from the program.	
Staff Training	Staff is trained on BEP—CICO, including how to complete the DPR and types of feedback statements to make to students.	
	A Tier 2 team member is designated to model the process of rating students and providing feedback each time a new teacher begins to implement the program.	
	Individual coaching is available for teachers who need extra support to implement the program as planned.	
	Yearly booster sessions about the purpose and key features of the program are provided to staff.	
Student and Parent Training	A plan for introducing students to the program is developed. The plan includes an overview of the program, how to check in and check out daily, adding up the daily points, determining whether daily point goals are met, accepting feedback (both positive and corrective), and procedures for taking the DPR home, getting it signed, and bringing it back.	
	A plan for introducing parents to the program is developed and includes procedures for providing feedback to the child.	

FORM 7.2

Implementation Script: Classroom Teacher

Instructions

- Read the steps and consider your level of participation.
- Circle the "Y," which means "Yes," if you feel you understand and consistently complete the step.
- Circle the "N," which means "No," if you do not consistently use the step or if you do not understand how to complete a step.
- Circle the "NA," which means "not applicable," if a step was not necessary.

Component and Features	
Regular Teacher Feedback	
• Prompt student to come to chart (if necessary).	Y N NA
• Provide a comment about whether expectations were or were not met for that activity.	Y N
• Award a sticker/points if expectations were met OR tell student what to do differently if expectation not met.	Y N
• Use a positive tone throughout interaction.	Y N
Total Number of Y Circled =	
Percent Implemented (total Y / total number of features × 100) =	

From Missouri Center for Schoolwide Positive Behavior Supports (2011a). Reprinted by permission in Melissa Stormont, Wendy M. Reinke, Keith C. Herman, and Erica S. Lembke (2012). Permission to photocopy this form is granted to purchasers of this book for personal use only (see copyright page for details).

FORM 7.3

Implementation Script: Facilitator

Instructions

- Read the steps and consider your level of participation.
- Circle the "Y," which means "Yes," if you feel you understand and consistently complete the step.
- Circle the "N," which means "No," if you do not consistently use the step or if you do not understand how to complete a step.
- Circle the "NA," which means "not applicable" if a step was not necessary.

Component and Features	
Daily Check-In	
• Greet student.	Y N
• Help student select/get daily progress report.	Y N
• Remind student of expectations and/or goal for the day (precorrect).	Y N
• Help student put chart in designated location.	Y N
• Use a positive tone throughout interaction.	Y N
Daily Check-Out	
• Prompt student to check out (if necessary).	Y N NA
• Help student identify whether daily goal was met.	Y N
• Offer participation success reinforcer if goal was met OR deliver corrective feedback (what to do differently), encouragement ("You can do better tomorrow"), and offer participation reinforcer.	Y N
• Use a positive tone throughout interaction.	Y N
Data Collection and Progress Monitoring	
• Help student count the number of points earned (child and adult together).	Y N
• Calculate percentage of points earned (adult only).	Y N
• Offer to let student enter data on to spreadsheet.	Y N
• Show student his/her graph and discuss whether the data point is above or below the goal line.	Y N
• Provide comment to student about what to keep data points above the goal line.	Y N
• Use a positive tone throughout the interaction.	Y N

(cont.)

From Missouri Center for Schoolwide Positive Behavior Supports (2011b). Reprinted by permission in Melissa Stormont, Wendy M. Reinke, Keith C. Herman, and Erica S. Lembke (2012). Permission to photocopy this form is granted to purchasers of this book for personal use only (see copyright page for details).

Parent Communication (May be applicable in early childhood center or setting where parent picks up student at end of day.)		
• Greet the parent.	Y	N
• Give parent the programwide expectations card.	Y	N
• Tell whether the child met or did not meet goal for the day.	Y	N
• If the child met the goal, remind/prompt parent to provide a privilege OR if child did not meet goal, remind/prompt parent to review expectations/goal with the child.	Y	N
• Remind/prompt parent to sign and return the card the next morning.	Y	N
• Use a positive tone throughout the interaction.	Y	N
Total Number of Y Circled =		
Percent Implemented (total Y / total number of features × 100) =		

Implementation Script: Parent

Instructions

- Read the steps and consider your level of participation.
- Circle the "Y," which means "Yes," if you feel you understand and consistently complete the step.
- Circle the "N," which means "No," if you do not consistently use the step or if you do not understand how to complete a step.
- Circle the "NA," which means "not applicable," if a step was not necessary.

Component and Features	
Parent Participation	
Ask your child if the daily goal was met.	Y N
If goal was met, provide designated home acknowledgment.	Y N NA
If goal was not met, give corrective feedback and encouragement Ask: • "What do you need to do differently tomorrow?" • "Is there anything I can do to help you with this?" • "I know you can meet your goal tomorrow."	Y N NA
Sign the daily progress report and remind student to return it to school.	Y N
Keep interaction and instruction brief.	Y N
Use a positive tone throughout the interaction.	Y N
Total Number of Y Circled =	
Percent Implemented (total Y / total number of features × 100) =	

From Missouri Center for Schoolwide Positive Behavior Supports (2011c). Reprinted by permission in Melissa Stormont, Wendy M. Reinke, Keith C. Herman, and Erica S. Lembke (2012). Permission to photocopy this form is granted to purchasers of this book for personal use only (see copyright page for details).

References

Adams, K. S., & Christenson, S. L. (2000). Trust and the family–school relationship examination of parent–teacher differences in elementary and secondary grades. *Journal of School Psychology, 38*(5), 477–497.

American Academy of Child and Adolescent Psychiatry. (2010). Depression Resource Center. Retrieved January 14, 2011, from *www.aacap.org/cs/Depression.ResourceCenter#about*.

Anderson, C. M., Childs, K., Kincaid, D., Horner, R. H., George, H., Todd, A. W., et al. (2010). *Benchmarks for Advanced Tiers (BAT)*. Educational and Community Supports, University of Oregon & University of South Florida. Retrieved January 12, 2011, from *www.pbis.org/pbis_resource_detail_page.aspx?Type=4&PBIS_ResourceID=*.

Anderson, C. M., Lewis-Palmer, T., Todd, A. W., Horner, R. H., Sugai, G., & Sampson, N. K. (2007). *Checklist for Individual Student Systems (CISS)*. Educational and Community Supports, University of Oregon. Retrieved January 12, 2011, from *www.pbis.org/pbis_resource_detail_page.aspx?Type=4&PBIS_ResourceID=245*.

Anderson, C. M., Lewis-Palmer, T., Todd, A. W., Horner, R. H., Sugai, G., & Sampson, N. K. (2010). *Student Systems Evaluation Tool version 2.7 (ISSET)*. Educational and Community Supports, University of Oregon. Retrieved January 12, 2011 from *www.pbis.org/pbis_resource_detail_page.aspx?Type=4&PBIS_ResourceID=885*.

Artiles, A. J., & Trent, S. C. (1994). Overrepresentation of minority students in special education: A continuing debate. *Journal of Special Education, 27*(4), 410–437.

Asarnow, J. R., & Callan, J. W. (1985). Boys with peer adjustment problems: Social cognitive processes. *Journal of Consulting and Clinical Psychology, 53*(1), 80–87.

Atkins, M. S., McKay, M. M., Frazier, S. L., Jakobsons, L. J., Arvantis, P., Cunningham, T., et al. (2002). Suspensions and detentions in an urban, low-income school: Punishment or reward? *Journal of Abnormal Child Psychology, 30*(4), 361–371.

Ball, E. W., & Blachman, B. A. (1988). Phoneme segmentation training: Effect on reading readiness. *Annals of Dyslexia, 38*, 208–225.

Ball, E. W., & Blachman, B. A. (1991). Does phoneme awareness training in kindergarten make a difference in early word recognition and developmental spelling? *Reading Research Quarterly, 26*, 49–66.

Bambara, L. M., & Kern, L. (2005). *Individualized supports for students with problem behaviors: Designing positive support plans.* New York: Guilford Press.

Bandura, A. (1986). *Social foundations of thought and action: A social cognitive theory.* Englewood Cliffs, NJ: Prentice-Hall.

Barbour, C., Barbour, N. H., & Scully, P. A. (2005). *Families, schools and communities: Building partnerships for educating children* (3rd ed.). Upper Saddle River, NJ: Pearson, Merrill, Prentice-Hall.

Barrett, P. (2004). *FRIENDS for Life program: Group leader's workbook for children* (4th ed.). Brisbane, Queensland: Australian Academic Press.

Barrish, H. H., Saunders, M., & Wolf, M. M. (1969). Good behavior game: Effects of individual contingencies for group consequences on disruptive behavior in a classroom. *Journal of Applied Behavior Analysis, 2*(2), 119–124.

Beardslee, W. R., Keller, M. B., Lavori, P. W., Staley, J., & Sacks, N. (1993). The impact of parental affective disorder on depression in offspring: A longitudinal follow-up in a nonreferred sample. *Journal of the American Academy of Child and Adolescent Psychiatry, 32,* 723–730.

Beers, K. (2002). *When kids can't read: What teachers can do.* Portsmouth, NH: Heinemann.

Benazzi, L., Horner, R. H., & Good, R. H. (2008). Effects of behavior support team composition on the technical adequacy and contextual fit of behavior support plans. *The Journal of Special Education, 40,* 160–170.

Berger, E. H. (2000). *Parents as partners in education: Families and schools working together* (5th ed.). Upper Saddle River, NJ: Merrill Prentice-Hall.

Bishop, A. G. (2003). Prediction of first-grade reading achievement: A comparison of fall and winter kindergarten screenings. *Learning Disability Quarterly, 26,* 189–200.

Blachman, B. A., Ball, E., Black, R., & Tangel, D. (1994). Kindergarten teachers develop phoneme awareness in low-income inner-city classrooms: Does it make a difference? *Reading and Writing: An Interdisciplinary Journal, 6,* 1–17.

Blachman, B. A., Ball, E. W., Black, R., & Tangel, D. M. (2000). *Road to the code: A phonological awareness program for young children.* Baltimore: Brookes.

Blevins, W. (2006). *Phonics from A to Z: A practical guide* (2nd ed.). New York: Scholastic.

Blueprints for Violence Prevention. (2011). Retrieved January 21, 2011, from *www.colorado.edu/cspv/blueprints/index.html.*

Boesch, E. E. (1996). The seven flaws of cross-cultural psychology: The story of a conversion. *Mind, Culture, and Activity, 3,* 2–10.

Bohanon, H., McIntosh, K., & Goodman, S. (2011a). *Integrating behavior and academic supports within an RtI framework: General overview.* Behavior Support Series for the RtI Action Network. Retrieved January 21, 2011, from *www.rtinetwork.org/Learn/Behavior/ar/Integrating-Behavior-and-Academic-Supports-Within-an-RtI-Framework-General-Overview.*

Bohanon, H., McIntosh, K., & Goodman, S. (2011b). *Integrating behavior and academic supports within an RtI framework Part IV: Tertiary supports.* Behavior Support Series for the RtI Action Network. Retrieved January 21, 2011, from *www.rtinetwork.org/learn/behavior/integrating-academic-and-behavior-supports-tertiary-supports.*

Bradshaw, C. P., Mitchell, M. M., O'Brennan, L. M., & Leaf, P. J. (2010). Multilevel exploration of factors contributing to the overrepresentation of Black students in office disciplinary referrals. *Journal of Educational Psychology, 102*(2), 508–520.

Bryant, D. P., Bryant, B. R., Gersten, R., Scammacca, N., & Chavez, M. M. (2008). Mathematics intervention for first- and second-grade students with mathematics difficulties: The effects of tier 2 intervention delivered as booster lessons. *Remedial and Special Education, 29,* 20–32.

Burns, M. K., Griffiths, A., Parson, L. B., Tilly, W. D., & VanderHayden, A. (2007). *Response to Intervention: Research for practice.* Alexandria, VA: National Association of State Directors of Special Education.

Campbell, A., & Anderson, C. (2008). Enhancing effects of check in/check out with function-based support. *Behavioral Disorders, 33,* 233–245.

Carnine, D. W., Silbert, J., Kame'enui, E. J., & Tarver, S. G. (2010). *Direct instruction reading* (5th ed.). Boston: Merrill.

Chard, D. J., Clarke, B., Baker, S., Otterstedt, J., Braun, D., & Katz, R. (2005). Using measures of number sense to screen for difficulties in mathematics: Preliminary findings. *Assessment for Effective Instruction, 30*(2), 3–14.

Chard, D. J., Vaughn, S., & Tyler, B. (2002). A synthesis of research on effective interventions for building fluency with elementary students with learning disabilities. *Journal of Learning Disabilities, 35,* 386–406.

Children's Defense Fund. (2008). *The state of America's children.* Retrieved January 5, 2011, from *www.childrensdefense.org.*

Chorpita, B. F., & Daleiden, E. L. (2009). Mapping evidence-based treatments for children and adolescents: Application of the distillation and matching model to 615 treatments from 322 randomized trials. *Journal of Consulting and Clinical Psychology, 77*(3), 566–579.

Christenson, S. L., Thurlow, M. L., Sinclair, M. F., Lehr, C., Kaibel, C., Reschly, A. L., et al. (2008). *Check & Connect: A comprehensive student engagement intervention manual.* Available from *checkandconnect.org.*

Cicchetti, D., & Toth, S. (1998). The development of depression in children and adolescents. *American Psychologist, 53,* 221–241.

Clare, A. (2011). *Effects of the behavior education program combined with a family-centered intervention on antisocial behaviors in elementary school students.* Unpublished master's thesis. University of Missouri, Columbia.

Clarke, G. N., Hawkins, W., Murphy, M., Sheeber, L., Lewinsohn, P. M., & Seeley, J. R. (1995). Targeted prevention of unipolar depressive disorder in an at-risk sample of high school adolescents: A randomized trial of a group cognitive intervention. *Journal of the American Academy of Child and Adolescent Psychiatry, 34,* 312–321.

Clarke, B., & Shinn, M. R. (2004). A preliminary investigation into the identification and development of early mathematics curriculum-based measurement. *School Psychology Review, 33,* 234–248.

Cole, D. A., & Turner, J. E. (1993). Models of cognitive mediation and moderation in child depression. *Journal of Abnormal Psychology, 102,* 271–281.

Committee for Children. (1988). *Second Step: A violence prevention curriculum.* Seattle, WA: Author.

Cooper, J. D., Chard, D. J., & Kiger, N. D. (2006). *Struggling readers—interventions that work.* Scholastic: New York.

Cordori, M. (1987). A computer-based recording system for analyzing disciplinary referrals. *NASSP Bulletin, 71,* 42–43.

Coutinho, M., & Oswald, D. (2000). Disproportionate representation in special education: A synthesis and recommendations. *Journal of Child and Family Studies, 10,* 135–136.

Crone, D. A., Hawken, L., & Horner, R. (2010). Appendix C.3: BEP development and implementation guide. In *Responding to problem behavior in schools: The behavior education program* (2nd ed., pp. 207–209). New York: Guilford Press.

Crone, D. A., & Horner, R. H. (2003). *Building positive behavior support systems in schools: Functional behavioral assessment.* New York: Guilford Press.

Crone, D. A., Horner, R. H., & Hawken, L. S. (2004). *Responding to problem behavior in schools: The behavior education program.* New York: Guilford Press.

Cox, D. (2005). Evidence-based interventions using home–school collaboration. *School Psychology Quarterly, 20*(4), 473–497.

Dearing, E., Kreider, H., Simpkins, S., & Weiss, H. B. (2006). Family involvement in school and low-income children's literacy: Longitudinal associations between and within families. *Journal of Educational Psychology, 98*, 653–664.

Delquadri, J., Greenwood, C., Stretton, K., & Hall, R. (1983). The peer tutoring spelling game: A classroom procedure for increasing opportunity to respond and spelling performance. *Education and Treatment of Children, 6*, 225–239.

Deno, S. L. (1985). Curriculum-based measurement: The emerging alternative. *Exceptional children, 52*, 219–232.

Deno, S. L. (2003). Developments in curriculum-based measurement. *Journal of Special Education, 37*(3), 184–192.

Denton, C. A., & Vaughn, S. (2010). Preventing and remediating reading difficulties: Perspectives from research. In M. R. Shinn & H. M. Walker (Eds.), *Interventions for achievement and behavior problems in a three-tier model including RTI* (pp. 469–500). Bethesda, MD: National Association of School Psychologists.

Derman-Sparks, L. (2003). Developing antibias, multicultural curriculum. In C. Copple (Ed.), *A world of difference: Readings on teaching young children in a diverse society* (pp. 173–178). Washington, DC: National Association for the Education of Young Children.

Dexter, D. D., & Hughes, C. (2008). *Making decisions about adequate progress in tier 2.* RTI Action Network Web. National Center for Learning Disabilities site: *www.rtinetwork.org/learn/research/making-decisions-about-adequate-progress-intier-2.*

Diamond, L., & Thorsnes, B. J. (2008). *Assessing reading: Multiple measures* (2nd ed.). Novato, CA: Arena Press.

Dishion, T. J., McCord, J., & Poulin, F. (1999). When interventions harm: Peer groups and problem behavior. *American Psychologist, 54*(9), 755–764.

Dodge, K. A. (2006). Translational science in action: Hostile attributional style and the development of aggressive behavior problems. *Development and Psychopathology, 18*(3), 791–814.

Dodge, K. A., & Price, J. M. (1994). On the relation between social information processing and socially competent behavior in early school-aged children. *Child Development, 65*(5), 1385–1397.

Donahue, P. L., Voelkl, K. E., Campbell, J. R., & Mazzeo, J. (1999). *NAEP 1998 reading report card for the nation and states.* Washington, DC: U.S. Department of Education, Office of Educational Research and Improvement.

Dowhower, S. L. (1987). Effects of repeated reading on second grade transitional readers' fluency and comprehension. *Reading Research Quarterly, 22*, 389–406.

Drabman, R. S., Spitalnik, R., & O'Leary, K. (1973). Teaching self-control to disruptive children. *Journal of Abnormal Psychology, 82*(1), 10–16.

DuBois, D. L., Holloway, B. E., Valentine, J. C., & Cooper, H. (2002). Effectiveness of mentoring programs for youth: A meta-analytic review. *American Journal of Community Psychology, 30*(2), 157–197.

D'Zurilla, T. J., & Goldfried, M. R. (1971). Problem solving and behavior modification. *Journal of Abnormal Psychology, 78*(1), 107–126.

Ehri, L. C., Nunes, S. R., & Willows, D. M. (2001). Phonemic awareness instruction helps children learn to read: Evidence from the National Reading Panel's meta-analysis. *Reading Research Quarterly, 36*, 250–287.

Elliott, S., & Gresham, F. (2007). *Social Skills Improvement System Screening system.* Upper Saddle River, NJ: Pearson.

Epstein, J. L. (1995). School/family/community partnerships. *Phi Delta Kappan, 76*, 702–712.

Esler, A. N., Godber, Y., & Christenson, S. L. (2002). Best practices in supporting home–school collaboration. In A. Thomas & J. Grimes (Series Eds.), *Best practices in school psychology IV* (Vol. 1, pp. 389–411). Bethesda, MD: National Association of School Psychologists.

Fairbanks, S., Sugai, G., Guardino, D., & Lathrop, M. (2007). Response to Intervention: Examining classroom behavior support in second grade. *Exceptional Children, 73*(3), 288–310.

Fantuzzo, J., Manz, P., Atkins, M., & Meyers, R. (2005). Peer-mediated treatment of socially withdrawn maltreated preschool children: Cultivating natural community resources. *Journal of Clinical Child and Adolescent Psychology, 34*, 320–325.

Fantuzzo, J., Tighe, E., & Childs, S. (2000). Family involvement questionnaire: A multivariate assessment of family participation in early childhood education. *Journal of Educational Psychology, 92*, 367–376.

Feil, E. G., Severson, H., & Walker, H. M. (1998). Screening for emotional and behavioral delays: The early screening project. *Journal of Early Intervention, 21*, 252–266.

Fish, M. C. (2002). Best practices in collaborating with parents of children with disabilities. In A. Thomas & J. Grimes (Eds.), *Best practices in school psychology IV* (Vol. 1, pp. 363–376). Bethesda, MD: National Association of School Psychologists.

Foegen, A. (2000). Technical adequacy of general outcome measures for middle school mathematics. *Diagnostique, 25*, 175–203.

Foegen, A., Jiban, C., & Deno, S. (2007). Progress monitoring measures in mathematics: A review of the literature. *Journal of Special Education, 41*(2), 121–139.

Foegen, A., Olson, J. R., & Impecoven-Lind, L. (2008). Developing progress monitoring measures for secondary mathematics: An illustration in algebra. *Assessment for Effective Intervention, 33*(4), 240–249.

Fowler, R. C., & Corley, K. K. (1996). Linking families, building community. *Educational Leadership, 53*(7), 24–26.

Friedberg, R. D., & McClure, J. M. (2002). *Clinical practice of cognitive therapy with children and adolescents: The nuts and bolts.* New York: Guilford Press.

Fuchs, D., & Deshler, D. D. (2007). What we need to know about responsiveness to intervention (and shouldn't be afraid to ask). *Learning Disabilities Research and Practice, 22*, 129–136.

Fuchs, D., & Fuchs, L. S. (2006). Introduction to responsiveness-to-intervention: What, why, and how valid is it? *Reading Research Quarterly, 41*, 92–99.

Fuchs, D., Fuchs, L. S., & Vaughn, S. (Eds.). (2008). *Response to intervention: A framework for reading educators.* Newark, DE: International Reading Association.

Fuchs, L. S., Fuchs, D., Finelli, R., Courey, S. J., & Hamlett, C. L. (2004). Expanding schema-based transfer instruction to help third graders solve real-life mathematical problems. *American Educational Research Journal, 41,* 419–445.

Fuchs, L. S., Fuchs, D., & Hollenbeck, K. H. (2007). Extending responsiveness to intervention to mathematics at first and third grades. *Learning Disabilities Research and Practice, 22*(1), 13–24.

Fuchs, L. S., Fuchs, D., & Karns, K. (2001). Enhancing kindergartener's mathematical development: Effects of peer-assisted learning strategies. *Elementary School Journal, 101,* 495–510.

Fuchs, L. S., Fuchs, D., Powell, S. R., Seethaler, P. M., Cirino, P. T., & Fletcher, J. M. (2008). Intensive intervention for students with mathematical disabilities: Seven principles of effective practice. *Learning Disability Quarterly, 31,* 79–92.

Fuchs, L. S., Fuchs, D., Prentice, K., Burch, M., & Paulsen, K. (2002). Hot Math: Promoting mathematical problem solving among third-grade students with disabilities. *Teaching Exceptional Children, 31,* 70–73.

Fuchs, L. S., Fuchs, D., Yazdian, L., & Powell, S. R. (2002). Enhancing first-grade children's mathematical development with peer-assisted learning strategies. *School Psychology Review, 31,* 569–584.

Fuchs, L. S., Hamlett, C. L., & Fuchs, D. (1998). *Monitoring basic skills progress: Basic math computation* (2nd ed.) [Computer program manual]. Austin, TX: Pro-Ed.

Fuchs, L. S., Hamlett, C. L., & Fuchs, D. (1999). *Monitoring basic skills progress: Basic math concepts and applications* [Computer program manual]. Austin, TX: Pro-Ed.

Gersten, R., Beckmann, S., Clarke, B., Foegen, A., Marsh, L., Star, J. R., et al. (2009). *Assisting students struggling with mathematics: Response to Intervention (RtI) for elementary and middle schools* (NCEE 2009-4060). Washington, DC: National Center for Education Evaluation and Regional Assistance, Institute of Education Sciences, U.S. Department of Education. Retrieved from *ies.ed.gov/ncee/wwc/publications/practiceguides.*

Gersten, R., Chard, D., Jayanthi, M., Baker, S., Morphy, S. K., & Flojo, J. (2008). *Teaching mathematics to students with learning disabilities and other learning difficulties: A meta-analysis of the intervention research.* Portsmouth, NH: RMC Research Corporation, Center on Instruction.

Gersten, R., Compton, D., Connor, C. M., Dimino, J., Santoro, L., Linan-Thompson, S., et al. (2009). *Assisting students struggling with reading: Response to intervention and multi-tier intervention for reading in the primary grades. A practice guide* (NCEE 2009-4045). Washington, DC: National Center for Education Evaluation and Regional Assistance, Institute of Education Sciences, U.S. Department of Education. Retrieved from *ies.ed.gov/ncee/wwc/publications/ practiceguides.*

Ginsburg, G. (2009). The Children Anxiety Prevention Study: Intervention model and primary outcomes. *Journal of Consulting and Clinical Psychology, 77,* 580–587.

Gottman, J. (1997). *The heart of parenting: Raising an emotionally intelligent child.* New York: Simon & Schuster.

Gresham, F. (2005). Response to Intervention: An alternative means of identifying students as emotionally disturbed. *Education and Treatment of Children, 28,* 328–344.

Gresham, F., & Elliot, S. (1990). *Social Skills Rating System.* Upper Saddle River, NJ: Pearson.

Gresham, F., & Elliott, S. (2007). *Social Skills Improvement System Rating Scale.* Upper Saddle River, NJ: Pearson.

Haager, D., Dimino, J. A., & Windmueller, M. P. (2007). *Interventions for reading success.* Baltimore: Brookes.

Haager, D., Klingner, J., & Vaughn, S. (2007). *Evidence-based reading practices for response to intervention*. Baltimore: Brookes.

Harris-Murri, N., King, K., & Rostenberg, D. (2006). Reducing disproportionate minority representation in special education programs for students with emotional disturbances: Toward a culturally responsive response to intervention model. *Education and Treatment of Children, 29*(4), 779–799.

Hawken, L. S., Adolphson, S., MacLeod, K., & Schumann, J. (2009). Secondary-tier interventions and supports. In W. Sailor, G. Sugai, R. H. Horner, & G. Dunlap (Eds.), *Handbook of positive behavior support* (pp. 395–420). New York: Springer.

Hawken, L. S., Pettersson, H., Mootz, J., & Anderson, C. (2005). *The Behavior Education Program: A check-in, check-out intervention for students at risk*. New York: Guilford Press.

Herman, K. C., Borden, L., Reinke, W., & Webster-Stratton, C. (in press). The impact of the incredible years parent, child, and teacher training programs on children's co-occurring internalizing symptoms, *School Psychology Quarterly*.

Herman, K. C., Lambert, S., Reinke, W., & Ialongo, N. (2008). Low academic competence in first grade as a risk factor for depressive cognitions and symptoms in middle school. *Journal of Counseling Psychology, 55*(3), 400–410.

Herman, K. C., Reinke, W., Parkin, J., Traylor, K., & Agarwal, G. (2009). Childhood depression: Rethinking the role of the school. *Psychology in the Schools, 46*, 433–446.

Herman, K. C., Reinke, W. M., Stormont, M., Puri, R., & Agarwal, G. (2010). Using prevention science to promote children's mental health: The founding of the Missouri Prevention Center. *The Counseling Psychologist, 38*(5), 652–690.

Henderson, A., & Berla, N. (1994). *A new generation of evidence: The family is critical to student achievement*. Columbia, MD: National Committee for Citizens in Education.

Herrera, C., Grossman, J. B., Kauh, T. J., Feldman, A. F., McMaken, J., & Jucovy, L. (2007). *Making a difference in schools: The Big Brothers/Big Sisters school-based mentoring impact study*. Philadelphia, PA: Public/Private Ventures.

Hershfeldt, P. A., Sechrest, R., Pell, K. L., Rosenberg, M. S., Bradshaw, C. P., & Leaf, P. J. (2009). Double-check: A framework of cultural responsiveness applied to classroom behavior. *TEACHING Exceptional Children Plus, 6*(2), 2–18.

Hill, N. E., & Craft, S. A. (2003). Parent–school involvement and school performance: Mediated pathways among socioeconomically comparable African-American and Euro-American families. *Journal of Educational Psychology, 95*, 74–83.

Hinshaw, S. P. (1992). Academic underachievement, attention deficits, and aggression: Comorbidity and implications for intervention. *Journal of Consulting and Clinical Psychology, 60*(6), 893–903.

Honig, B., Diamond, L., & Gutlohn, L. (2008). *Teaching reading sourcebook* (2nd ed.). Novato and Berkeley, CA: Arena Press and Consortium on Reading Excellence.

Horner, R. H., Sugai, G., & Todd, A. W. (2001). "Data" need not be a four-letter word: Using data to improve schoolwide discipline. *Beyond Behavior, 11*(1), 20–26.

Horner, R. H., Sugai, G., Todd, A. W., & Lewis-Palmer, T. (2005). Schoolwide positive behavior supports: An alternative approach to discipline in schools. In L. Bambara & L. Kern (Eds.), *Individualized supports for students with problem behaviors: Designing positive behavior plans* (pp. 359–390). New York: Guilford Press.

Ialongo, N. S., Edelsohn, G., & Kellam, S. G. (2001). A further look at the prognostic power of young children's reports of depressed mood. *Child Development, 72*, 736–747.

Ingram, M., Wolfe, R., & Lieberman, J. (2007). The role of parents in high-achieving schools serving low-income, at-risk populations. *Education and Urban Society, 39*(4), 479–497.

International Reading Association. (2002). *Family–school partnerships: Essential elements of literacy instruction in the United States.* A position statement of the International Reading Association. Newark, DE: Author.

Jitendra, A. K. (2007). *Solving math word problems: Teaching students with learning disabilities using schema-based instruction.* Austin, TX: Pro-Ed.

Jitendra, A. K., Griffin, C. C., McGoey, K., Gardill, M. C., Bhat, P., & Riley, T. (1998). Effects of mathematical word problem solving by students at risk or with mild disabilities. *Journal of Educational Research, 91,* 345–355.

Johnson, E., Mellard, D. F., Fuchs, D., & McKnight, M. A. (2006). *Responsiveness to intervention (RTI): How to do it.* Lawrence, KS: National Research Center on Learning Disabilities.

Jones, R. T., & Kazdin, A. E. (1975). Programming response maintenance after withdrawing token reinforcement. *Behavior Therapy, 6*(2), 153–164.

Kalberg, J. R., Lane, K. L., & Menzies, H. M. (2010). Using systematic screening procedures to identify students who are nonresponsive to primary prevention efforts: Integrating academic and behavioral measures. *Education and Treatment of Children, 33*(4), 561–584.

Kame'enui, E. J., & Simmons, D. C. (2003). *Planning and Evaluation Tool for Effective Schoolwide Reading Programs—Revised* (PET-R). Institute for the Development of Educational Achievement, College of Education, University of Oregon, Eugene.

Kaminski, R. A., Stormshak, E. A., Good, R. H., & Goodman, M. R. (2002). Prevention of substance abuse with rural Head Start children and families: Results of Project STAR. *Psychology of Addictive Behaviors,16,* S11–S26.

Kamphaus, R., & Reynolds, C. (2007). *Behavioral and emotional screening system.* Circle Pines, MN: AGS.

Kauffman, J., & Landrum, T. (2009). *Characteristics of emotional and behavioral disorders of children and youth* (9th ed.). Boston: Pearson/Merrill.

Kea, C., Campbell-Whatley, G. D., & Richards, H. V. (2004). *Becoming culturally responsive educators: Rethinking teacher education pedagogy.* Denver, CO: National Center for Culturally Responsive Educational Systems.

Kellam, S. G., Ling, X., Merisca, R., Brown, C., & Ialongo, N. (1998). The effect of the level of aggression in the first grade classroom on the course and malleability of aggressive behavior into middle school. *Development and Psychopathology, 10*(2), 165–185.

Kellam, S. G., & Rebok, G. W. (1992). Building etiological theory through developmental epidemiologically based preventive intervention trials. In J. McCord and R. E. Tremblay (Eds.), *Preventing antisocial behavior: Interventions from birth through adolescence.* (pp. 162–195). New York: Guilford Press.

Keller, M., Lavori, P., Beardslee, W. R., Wunder, J., & Ryan, N. (1991). Depression in children and adolescents: New data on "undertreatment" and a literature review on the efficacy of available treatments. *Journal of Affective Disorders, 21,* 163–171.

Kelley, M. L., & Stokes T. F. (1984). Student–teacher contracting with goal setting for maintenance. *Behavior Modification, 8*(2), 223–244.

Kendall, P. C., Furr, J., & Podell, J. (2010). Child-focused treatment of anxiety. In J. R. Weisz and A. E. Kazdin (Eds.), *Evidence-based psychotherapies for children and adolescents* (2nd ed., pp. 45–60). New York: Guilford Press.

Klerman, G. L., & Weissman, M. M. (1989). Increasing rates of depression. *Journal of the American Medical Association, 261*, 2229–2235.

Klingner, J. K., & Vaughn, S. (2000). The helping behaviors of fifth-graders while using collaborative strategic reading (CSR) during ESL content classes. *TESOL Quarterly, 34*, 69–98.

Klingner, J. K., Vaughn, S., Argüelles, M. E., Hughes, M. T., & Ahwee, S. (2004). Collaborative strategic reading: "Real world" lessons from classroom teachers. *Remedial and Special Education, 25*, 291–302.

Klingner, J. K., Vaughn, S., Dimino, J., Schumm, J. S., & Bryant, D. (2001). *From clunk to click: Collaborative strategic reading.* Longmont, CO: Sopris West.

Klingner, J. K., Vaughn, S., & Schumm, J. S. (1998). Collaborative strategic reading during social studies in heterogeneous fourth-grade classrooms. *Elementary School Journal, 99*, 3–21.

Kovacs, M. (1991). *Children's Depression Inventory.* North Tonowanda, NY: Multi-Health Systems.

Krezmien, M. P., Leone, P. E., & Achilles, G. M. (2006). Suspension, race, and disability: Analysis of state-wide practices and reporting. *Journal of Emotional and Behavioral Disorders, 14*, 217–226.

Kusche, C. A., & Greenberg, M. T. (1994). The PATHS (Promoting Alternative Thinking Strategies) curriculum. South Deerfield, MA: Channing-Bete.

LaBerge, D., & Samuels, S. J. (1974). Toward a theory of automatic information processing in reading. *Cognitive Psychology, 6*, 292–323.

Ladson-Billings, G. (1992). Reading between the lines and beyond the pages: A culturally relevant approach to literacy teaching. *Theory Into Practice, 31*(4), 312–320.

Landsverk, R. A. (Spring, 1995). *Families, communities, schools, learning together 2: Families in education packet.* Madison, WI: Wisconsin Department of Public Instruction.

Lane, K. L., Wehby, J. H., Robertson, E. J., & Rogers, L. A. (2007). How do different types of high school students respond to schoolwide positive behavior support programs? *Journal of Emotional and Behavior Disorders, 15*, 3–20.

Last, C. G., Francis, G., & Strauss, C. C. (1989). Assessing fears in anxiety-disordered children with the Revised Fear Survey Schedule for Children. *Journal of Clinical Child Psychology, 18*, 137–141.

Last, C. G., Hersen, M., Kazdin, A. E., Orvaschel, H., & Perrin, S. (1991). Anxiety disorders in children and their families. *Archives of General Psychiatry, 48*, 928–934.

Lee, Y. Y., Sugai, G., & Horner, R. (1999). Using an instructional intervention to reduce problem and off-task behaviors. *Journal of Positive Behavior Interventions, 1*(4), 195–204.

Lehr, C. A., Sinclair, M. F., & Christenson, S. L. (2004). Addressing student engagement and truancy prevention during the elementary years: A replication study of the Check & Connect model. *Journal of Education for Students Placed At Risk, 9*(3), 279–301.

Lembke, E. S. (2010). Raymore–Peculiar School District 2010–2011 student assistance team initial referral form.

Lembke, E. S., & Foegen, A. (2009). Identifying early numeracy indicators for kindergarten and first-grade students. *Learning Disabilities Research and Practice, 24*(1), 12–20.

Lembke, E. S., McMaster, K. L., & Stecker, P. M. (2009). The prevention science of reading research within a response-to-intervention model. *Psychology in the School, 47*(1), 22–35.

Lewinsohn, P. M., Rohde, P., & Seeley, J. R. (1998). Treatment of adolescent depression: Frequency of services and impact on functioning in young adulthood. *Depression and Anxiety, 7*, 47–52.

Lewinsohn, P. M., Rohde, P., Seeley, J., Klein, D., & Gotlib, I. (2003). Psychosocial functioning of young adults who have experienced and recovered from major depressive disorder during adolescence. *Journal of Abnormal Psychology, 112*, 353–363.

Lochman, J. E. (1995). Screening of child behavior problems for prevention programs at school entry. *Journal of Consulting and Clinical Psychology, 63*, 549–559.

Lochman, J. E., Barry, T. D., & Pardini, D. A. (2003). Anger control training for aggressive youth. In A. E. Kazdin & J. R. Weisz (Eds.), *Evidence-based psychotherapies for children and adolescents* (pp. 263–281). New York: Guilford Press.

Lochman, J. E., Boxmeyer, C. L., Powell, N. P., Barry, T. D., & Pardini, D. A. (2010). Anger control training for aggressive youths. In J. R. Weisz & A. E. Kazdin (Eds.), *Evidence-based psychotherapies for children and adolescents* (2nd ed., pp. 227–242). New York: Guilford Press.

Lochman, J. E., & Curry, J. F. (1986). Effects of social problem-solving training and self-instruction training with aggressive boys. *Journal of Clinical Child Psychology, 15*(2), 159–164.

Lochman, J. E., Wells, K. C., & Lenhart, L. A. (2008). *Coping power: Child group program, facilitator guide.* New York: Oxford University Press.

Loman, S., Rodriguez, B., & Horner, R. (2010). Sustainability of a targeted intervention package: First step to success in Oregon. *Journal of Emotional and Behavioral Disorders, 18*(3), 178–191.

Lopez, S. J., Edwards, L. M., Pedrotti, J. T., Ito, A., & Rasmussen, H. N. (2002). Culture counts: Examinations of recent applications of the Penn Resiliency Program. *Prevention & Treatment, 5*, Article 12.

MacMillan/McGraw Hill (2005). *Treasures reading.* New York: Author.

Maguin, E., & Loeber, R. (1996). How well do ratings of academic performance by mothers and their sons correspond to grades, achievement test scores, and teachers' ratings? *Journal of Behavioral Education 6*(4), 405–425.

March, J. S., Parker, J. D. A., Sullivan, K., Stallings, P., & Conners, C. K. (1997). The Multidimensional Anxiety Scales for Children (MASC): Factor structure, reliability and validity. *Journal of the American Academy of Child and Adolescent Psychiatry, 36*, 554–565.

Marston, D., Muyskens, P., Lau, M., & Canter, A. (2003). Problem-solving model for decision making and high-incidence disabilities: The Minneapolis experience. *Learning Disabilities Research and Practice, 18*, 187–200.

McCurdy, B., Kunsch, C., & Reibstein, S. (2007). Tier II prevention in the urban school: Implementing the Behavior Education Program. *Preventing School Failure*, 12–19.

McIntosh, K., Bohanon, H., & Goodman, S. (2011). *Integrating academic and behavior supports within an RtI framework, Part 3: Secondary supports.* Retrieved January 21, 2011, from *www.rtinetwork.org/learn/behavior/integrating-academic-and-behavior-supports.*

McIntosh, K., Campbell, A., Russell-Carter, D., & Dickey, C. (2009). Differential effects of a Tier Two behavior intervention based on function of problem behavior. *Journal of Positive Behavior Interventions, 11*(2), 82–93.

McIntosh, K., Campbell, A., Carter, D., & Zumbo, B. (2009). Concurrent validity of office discipline referrals and cut points used in schoolwide positive behavior support. *Behavioral Disorders, 34*, 100–113.

McIntosh, K., Reinke, W. M., & Herman, K. C. (2010). Schoolwide analysis of data for social behavior problems: Assessing outcomes, selecting targets for intervention, and identifying need for support. In G. Gimpel-Peacock, R. Ervin, E. J. Daly, & K. Merrell (Eds.), *Practical handbook of school psychology: Effective practices for the 21st century* (pp. 135–156). New York: Guilford Press.

McMaster, K. L., Fuchs, D., Fuchs, L. S., & Compton, D. L. (2005). Responding to nonresponders: An experimental field trial of identification and intervention methods. *Exceptional Children, 71*, 445–463.

McWayne, C., Hampton, V., Fantuzzo, J., Cohen, H. L., & Sekino, Y. (2004). A multivariate examination of parent involvement and the social and academic competencies of urban kindergarten children. *Psychology in the Schools, 41*(3), 363–377.

Mercer, C. D., & Mercer, A. R. (2005). *Teaching students with learning problems* (7th ed.). Upper Saddle River, NJ: Pearson.

Merikangas, K. R., He, J. H., Burstein, M., Swanson, S. A., Avenevoli, S., Cui, L., et al. (2010). Lifetime prevalence of mental disorders in U.S. adolescents: Results from the National Comorbidity Survey Replication—Adolescent Supplement (NCS-A). *Journal of the American Academy of Child and Adolescent Psychiatry, 49*(10), 980–989.

Merrell, K. W. (2008a). *Behavioral, social, and emotional assessment of children and adolescents* (3rd ed.). New York: Routledge/Taylor & Francis.

Merrell, K. W. (2008b). *Helping students overcome depression and anxiety* (2nd ed.). New York: Guilford Press.

Merrell, K. W., Carrizales, D., Feuerborn, L., Gueldner, B. A., & Tran, O. K. (2007). *Strong Kids—3–5: A social and emotional learning curriculum.* Baltimore: Brookes.

Merrell, K. W., & Gueldner, B. A. (2010). *Social and emotional learning in the classroom: Promoting mental health and academic success.* New York: Guilford Press.

Merrell, K. W., Parisi, D., & Whitcomb, S. A. (2007). *Strong Start—Grades K–2: A social and emotional learning curriculum.* Baltimore: Brookes.

Merrell, K. W., & Walters, A. S. (1998). *Internalizing Symptoms Scale for Children.* Austin, TX: Pro-Ed.

Merrell, K. W., Whitcomb, S. A., & Parisi, D. A. (2009). *Strong Start—Pre-K: A social and emotional learning curriculum.* Baltimore: Brookes.

Miller, D., DuPaul, G., & Lutz, J. G. (2002). School-based psychosocial interventions for childhood depression: Acceptability of treatments among school psychologists. *School Psychology Quarterly, 17*, 78–99.

Missouri Center for Schoolwide Positive Behavior Supports. (2008). *Missouri Schoolwide positive behavior supports.* Columbia: University of Missouri.

Missouri Center for Schoolwide Positive Behavior Supports. (2011a). *Implementation script—classroom teacher.* Columbia: University of Missouri.

Missouri Center for Schoolwide Positive Behavior Supports. (2011b). *Implementation script—facilitator.* Columbia: University of Missouri.

Missouri Center for Schoolwide Positive Behavior Supports (2011c). *Implementation script—parent.* Columbia: University of Missouri.

Mitchell, B. S., Stormont, M., & Gage, N. (in press). Tier two interventions within the context of school-wide positive behavior support. *Behavior Disorders.*

Moats, L. (2000). *Speech to print: Language essentials for teachers.* Baltimore: Brookes.

Mullis, I. V. S., Martin, M. O., Gonzalez, E. J., & Chrostowski, S. J. (2004). *TIMSS 2003 international mathematics and science study at fourth and eighth grade.* Boston: International Association for the Evaluation of Educational Achievement. Retrieved January 21, 2011, from *timss. bc.edu/pdf/t03_download/TO3INTLMATRPT.*

Muñoz, R. F., Le, H., Clarke, G., & Jaycox, L. (2002). Preventing the onset of major depression. In I. H. Gotlib & C. L. Hammen (Eds.), *Handbook of depression* (pp. 343–359). New York: Guilford Press.

Nakasato, J. (2000). Data-based decision making in Hawaii's behavior support effort. *Journal of Positive Behavior Interventions, 2*(4), 247–251.

National Assessment of Educational Progress (2009). *The Nation's Report Card: Mathematics 2009.* National Center for Education Statistics.

National Center for Culturally Responsive Educational Systems (2005). Cultural considerations and challenges in Response-to-Intervention models. Retrieved from *www.nccrest.org/PDFs/rti.pdf?v_document_name=Culturally%20Responsive%20RTI.*

National Center for Culturally Responsive Educational Systems (2011). Culturally responsive Response-to-Intervention. Retrieved from *www.nccrest.org/RTI/A1/Academy%201%20powerpoint%20ver%201.1%20FINAL%20kak.ppt.*

National Center for Education Statistics. (2010). Figure 11. Average scores and achievement-level results in NAEP mathematics for fourth-grade public school students, by state jurisdiction: 2009. *The Nation's Report Card: Mathematics 2009.* Retrieved from *nces.ed.gov/nationsreportcard/pdf/main2009/2010451.pdf.*

National Center on Response to Intervention. (2010). *Essential components of RTI: A closer look at response to intervention.* Washington, DC: U.S. Department of Education, Office of Special Education Programs.

National Institute of Child Health and Human Development. (2000). *Report of the National Reading Panel. Teaching children to read: An evidence-based assessment of the scientific research literature on reading and its implications for reading instruction* (NIH Publication No. 00–4769). Washington, DC: U.S. Government Printing Office.

National Institute of Child Health and Human Development, National Institutes of Health, & Department of Health and Human Services. (2001). *Put reading first: The research building blocks for teaching children to read.* Washington, DC: U.S. Government Printing Office.

National Mathematics Advisory Panel. (2008). *Foundations for success: The final report of the National Mathematics Advisory Panel.* Washington, DC: U.S. Department of Education.

National Research Council and Institute of Medicine. (2009). Preventing mental, emotional, and behavioral disorders among young people: Progress and possibilities. Washington, DC: National Academic Press.

Newcomer, L. (2010a). *General student at risk nomination form. Tier 2 Interventions.* Unpublished Report/manuscript.

Newcomer, L. (2010b). *Cumulative record review. Tier 2 Interventions.* Unpublished Report/manuscript.

Newcomer, L. (2010c). *Functional assessment linking FBA to function-based intervention plans.* Unpublished Report/manuscript.

Newman-Gonchar, R., Clarke, B., & Gersten, R. (2009). *A summary of nine key studies: Multi-tier intervention and response to interventions for students struggling in mathematics.* Portsmouth, NH: RMC Research Corporation, Center on Instruction.

O'Connor, R. E., Notari-Syverson, A., & Vadasy, P. F. (2005). *Ladders to literacy: A kindergarten activity book* (2nd ed.). Baltimore: Brookes.

O'Donnell, D. A., Schwab-Stone, M. E., & Muyeed, A. Z. (2002). Multidimensional resilience in urban children exposed to community violence. *Child Development, 73*(4), 1265–1282.

O'Neill, R., Horner, R., Albin, R. W., Sprague, J., Storey, K., & Newton, J. S. (1997). *Functional assessment and program development for problem behavior: A practical handbook* (2nd ed.). Pacific Grove, CA: Brooks/Cole.

Ortiz, S. O., & Flanagan, D. P. (2002). Best practices in working with culturally diverse children and families. In A. Thomas & J. Grimes (Series Eds.), *Best practices in school psychology* (Vol. 1, pp. 337–351). Bethesda, MD: National Association of School Psychologists.

OSEP Center on Positive Behavioral Interventions and Supports. (2004). *School-wide positive behavior support: Implementers' blueprint and self-assessment.* Eugene, OR: Author.

Overton, S. (2005). *Collaborating with families: A case study approach.* Upper Saddle River, NJ: Pearson Merrill Prentice-Hall.

Pahl, K. M., & Barrett, P. M. (2010). Interventions for anxiety disorders in children using group cognitive behavioral therapy with family involvement. In J. R. Weisz and A. E. Kazdin (Eds.), *Evidence-based psychotherapies for children and adolescents* (2nd ed., pp. 61–79). New York: Guilford Press.

Patterson, G. R., & Capaldi, D. M. (1990). A mediational model for boys' depressed mood. In J. Rolf, A. S. Masten, D. Cicchetti, K. H. Nuechterlein, & S. Weintraub (Eds.), *Risk and protective factors in the development of psychopathology* (pp. 141–163). Cambridge, UK: Cambridge University Press.

Patterson, G. R., Reid, J. B., & Dishion, T. J. (1992). *Antisocial boys.* Eugene, OR: Castalia Press.

Pfeiffer, S., & Reddy, L. (1998). School-based mental health programs in the United States: Present status and a blueprint for the future. *School Psychology Review, 27,* 84–96.

Positive Behavioral Interventions and Supports. (2011). *Figure: Supporting social competence and academic achievement.* Retrieved January 12, 2011, from *www.pbis.org/school/default.aspx.*

Positive Behavior Interventions and Supports. (2011). Practical functional behavioral assessment training manual for school-based personnel. Retrieved January 10, 2011, from *pbis.org/pbis_resource_detail_page.aspx?PBIS_ResourceID=887.*

RAND Reading Study Group. (2002). *Reading for understanding: Towards an R & D program in reading comprehension.* Santa Monica, CA: RAND.

Rapee, R. M., Wignall, A., Spence, S. H., Cobham, V., & Lyneham, H. (2008). *Helping your anxious child* (2nd ed.). Oakland, CA: New Harbinger Press.

Rathvon, N. (2008). *Effective school interventions: Evidence-based strategies for improving student outcomes* (2nd ed.). New York: Guilford Press.

Reid, J. B., Patterson, G. R., & Snyder, J. (2002). *Antisocial behavior in children and adolescents: A developmental analysis and model for intervention.* Washington, DC: American Psychological Association.

Reinke, W. M., & Herman, K. C. (2002). Creating school environments that deter antisocial behaviors in youth. *Psychology in the Schools, 39*(5), 549–560.

Reinke, W. M., Herman, K. C., Petras, H., & Ialongo, N. S. (2008). Empirically derived subtypes of child academic and behavior problems: Co-occurrence and distal outcomes. *Journal of Abnormal Child Psychology, 36*(5), 759–770.

Reinke, W. M., Herman, K. C., & Sprick, R. (2011). *Motivational interviewing for effective classroom management: The classroom check-up.* New York: Guilford Press.

Reinke, W. M., Lewis-Palmer, T., & Martin, E. (2007). The effect of visual performance feedback on teacher use of behavior-specific praise. *Behavior Modification, 31*(3), 247–263.

Reinke, W. M., Sprick, R., & Knight, J. (2008). Coaching classroom behavior management. In J. Knight (Ed.), *Coaching Approaches and Perspectives.* Thousand Oaks, CA: Corwin Press.

Reinke, W. M., Stormont, M., Herman, K. C., Puri, R., & Goel, N. (2011). Supporting children's mental health in schools: Teacher perceptions of needs, roles, and barriers. *School Psychology Quarterly, 26,* 1–13.

Reinke, W. M., & Walker, H. M. (2006). Deviant peer influences in programs for youth: Problems and solutions. In K. A. Dodge, T. J. Dishion, and J. E. Lansford (Eds.), *Deviant peer effects in education* (pp. 122–140). New York: Guilford Press.

Resch, J. A., Mireles, G., Benz, M., Grenwelge, C., Peterson, R., & Shang, D. (2010). Giving parents a voice: A qualitative study of the challenges experienced by parents of children with disabilities. *Rehabilitation Psychology, 55*(2), 139–150.

Resnick, L. B., & Hall, M. W. (1998). Learning organizations for sustainable education reform. *Journal of the American Academy of Arts and Sciences, 127*(4), 89–118.

Reynolds, C. R., & Kamphaus, R. W. (2004). *Behavior Assessment Scale for Children* (2nd ed.). Circle Pines, MN: AGS.

Riccomini, P. J., & Witzel, B. S. (2010). *Response to intervention in math.* Thousand Oaks, CA: Corwin Press.

Richards, H., Brown, A., & Forde, T. (2007). Addressing diversity in schools: Culturally responsive pedagogy. *Teaching Exceptional Children, 23,* 64–68.

Richter, M. M. (2008). *The relationship between principal leadership skills and school-wide positive behavior support: An exploratory study.* Unpublished dissertation. Columbia: University of Missouri.

Riley, R. W. (1994). Ingredient for success: Family involvement. *Teaching PreK–8, 25,* 12.

Roberts, M. L., Marshall, J., Nelson, J. R., & Albers, C. A. (2001). Curriculum-based assessment procedures embedded within functional behavioral assessments: Identifying escape-motivated behaviors in a general education classroom. *School Psychology Review, 30*(2), 264–277.

Rosenbaum J. F., Biederman J., Bolduc, E. A., Hirshfeld, D. R., Faraone, S. V., & Kagan J . (1992). Comorbidity of parental anxiety disorders as risk for childhood-onset anxiety disorders in inhibited children. *American Journal of Psychiatry, 149,* 475–481.

Samuels, S. J. (1988). Decoding and automaticity: Helping poor readers become automatic at word recognition. *Reading Teacher, 41,* 756–760.

Samuels, S. J. (1997). The method of repeated readings. *Reading Teacher, 41,* 403–408.

Sandomierski, T., Kincaid, D., & Algozzine, B. (2007). Response to intervention and positive behavior support: Brothers from different mothers or sisters with different misters? *Positive Behavioral Interventions and Supports Newsletter, 4*(2), 1–4.

Scheuermann, B., & Hall, J. (2008). *Positive behavioral supports for the classroom.* Upper Saddle River, NJ: Pearson Education.

Schneider, M. B., Friedman, S. B., & Fisher, M. (1995). Stated and unstated reasons for visiting a high school nurses's office. *Journal of Adolescent Health, 16,* 35–40.

Scott, T. M. (2001). A schoolwide example of positive behavioral support. *Journal of Positive Behavior Interventions, 3*(2), 88–94.

Scott, T. M., Alter, P. J., Rosenberg, M., & Borgmeier, C. (2010). Decision-making in secondary and tertiary interventions of school-wide systems of positive behavior support. *Education and Treatment of Children, 33*(4), 513–535.

Seagull, E. A., & Weinshank, A. B. (1984). Childhood depression in a selected group of low-achieving seventh-graders. *Journal of Child Clinical Psychology, 13,* 134–140.

Shinn, M. R., & Walker, H. M. (Eds.). (2010). *Interventions for achievement and behavior problems in a three-tier model including RTI.* Bethesda, MD: National Association of School Psychologists.

Shores, R. E., Jack, S. L., Gunter, P. L., Ellis, D. N., DeBriere, T. J., & Wehby, J. H. (1993). Classroom interactions of children with behavior disorders. *Journal of Emotional and Behavioral Disorders, 1*(1), 27–39.

Shure, M. B. (1992). *I Can Problem Solve: An interpersonal cognitive problem-solving program.* Champaign, IL: Research Press.

Skiba, R. J., Michael, R. S., Nardo, A. C., & Peterson, R. L. (2002). The color of discipline: Sources of racial and gender disproportionality in school punishment. *Urban Review, 34*(4), 317–342.

Skiba, R. J., Peterson, R. L., & Williams, T. (1997). Office referrals and suspension: Disciplinary intervention in middle schools. *Education and Treatment of Children, 20*(3), 295–315.

Skiba, R. J., Simmons, A. B., Ritter, S., Gibb, A. C., Rausch, M. K., & Cuadrado, J. (2008). Achieving equity in special education: History, status, and current challenges. *Exceptional Children, 74,* 264–288.

Smith, C. A., & Stormont, M. (in press). Building an effective school-based mentoring program. *Intervention in School and Clinic.*

Snow, C. E., Burns, S. M., & Griffin, P. (1998). *Preventing reading difficulties in young children.* Washington, DC: National Academies Press.

Sprague, J. R., & Walker, H. M. (2005). *Safe and healthy schools: Practical prevention strategies.* New York: Guilford Press.

Sprague, J. R., Walker, H. M., Stieber, S., Simonsen, B., Nishioka, V., & Wagner, L. (2001). Exploring the relationship between school discipline referrals and delinquency. *Psychology in the Schools, 38,* 197–206.

Stark, K. D., Rouse, L. W., & Kurowski, C. (1994). Psychological treatment approaches for depression in children. In W. M. Reynolds & H. F. Johnston (Eds.), *Handbook of depression in children and adolescents: Issues in clinical child psychology* (pp. 275–307). New York: Plenum Press.

Stark, K. D., Simpson, J., Schnoebelen, S. Hargrave, J., Glenn, R., & Molnar, J. (2006). *Therapists' manual for ACTION.* Broadmore, PA: Workbook.

Stecker, P. M. (2007). Tertiary intervention: Using progress monitoring with intensive services. *Teaching Exceptional Children, 39*(5), 50–56.

Stein, M., Kinder, D., Silbert, J., & Carnine, D. (2006). *Designing effective mathematics instruction: A direct instruction approach* (4th ed.). Upper Saddle River, NJ: Pearson.

Stein, M., Kinder, D., Zapp, K., & Feuerborn, L. (2010). Promoting positive math outcomes. In M. R. Shinn & H. M. Walker (Eds.), *Interventions for achievement and behavior problems in a three-tier model including RTI* (pp. 469–500). Bethesda, MD: National Association of School Psychologists.

Stormont, M. (2007). *Fostering resilience in young children at risk for failure: Strategies for K–3.* Upper Saddle River, NJ: Pearson.

Stormont, M., Beckner, R., Mitchell, B., & Richter, M. (2005). Supporting successful transition to kindergarten: General challenges and specific implications for students with problem behavior. *Psychology in the Schools, 42*(8), 765–778.

Stormont, M., Lewis, T. J., Beckner, R., & Johnson, N. W. (2008). *Implementing positive behavior support systems in early childhood and elementary settings.* Thousand Oaks, CA: Corwin Press.

Stormont, M., Reinke, W. M., & Herman, K. C. (2011). Teachers' knowledge of evidence-based interventions and available school resources for children with emotional or behavioral problems. *Journal of Behavioral Education, 20,* 138–147.

Stormont, M. A., & McCathren, R. B. (2008). Nowhere to turn: The young face of homelessness. In D. Capuzzi & D. R. Gross (Eds.), *Youth at risk: A prevention resource for counselors, teachers, and parents* (pp. 435–455). Alexandria, VA: American Counseling Association.

Stormont, M., Reinke, W. M., & Herman, K. C. (in press). Teacher characteristics and ratings for evidence-based behavior interventions. *Behavior Disorders.*

Stormont-Spurgin, M. (1997). I lost my homework: Strategies for improving organization in students with AD/HD. *Intervention in School and Clinic, 32,* 270–274.

Sugai, G. (2007). Promoting behavioral competence in schools: A commentary on exemplary practices. *Psychology in the Schools, 44*(1), 113–118.

Sugai, G. (2011). *School-wide positive behavior support and response to intervention.* Retrieved January 21, 2011, from *www.rtinetwork.org/learn/behavior/schoolwidebehavior.*

Sugai, G., Horner, R., & Todd, A. (2000). *Effective behavior support: Self-assessment survey.* Eugene, OR: University of Oregon.

Sugai, G., Lewis-Palmer, T., Todd, A., & Horner, R. (2001). *School-wide evaluation tool (SET).* Eugene, OR: OSEP Center for Positive Behavioral Supports, University of Oregon.

Sugai, G., Sprague, J. R., Horner, R. H., & Walker, H. M. (2000). Preventing school violence: The use of office discipline referrals to assess and monitor school-wide discipline interventions. *Journal of Emotional and Behavioral Disorders, 8*(2), 94–101.

Swick, K. J. (1995). What parents really want from family involvement programs. *Day Care and Early Education, 22*(3), 20–23.

The Center for Effective Collaboration and Practice (1998). *An IEP team's introduction to functional behavioral assessment and behavior intervention plans* (2nd ed.). Retrieved January 31, 2011, from *www.fape.org/idea/what_idea_is/osher/main.htm.*

The IRIS Center. (2011). Module for functional behavioral assessment. Retrieved January 31, 2011, from *iris.peabody.vanderbilt.edu/fba/chalcycle.htm.*

Therrien, W. J. (2004). Fluency and comprehension gains as a result of repeated reading: A meta-analysis. *Remedial and Special Education, 25,* 252–261.

Tilly, W. D., III. (2002). Best practices in school psychology as a problem-solving enterprise. In A. Thomas & J. Grimes (Eds.), *Best practices in school psychology* (4th ed., pp. 21–36). Bethesda, MD: National Association of School Psychologists.

Tobin, T. J., Sugai, G., & Colvin, G. (2000). Using disciplinary referrals to make decisions. *NASSP Bulletin, 84,* 106–117.

Torgesen, J. K. (2002). The prevention of reading difficulties. *Journal of School Psychology, 40,* 7–26.

Torgeson, J. K., & Hudson, R. F. (2006). Reading fluency: Critical issues for struggling readers. In S. J. Samuels & A. E. Fartstup (Eds.), *What research has to say about fluency instruction* (pp. 130–158), Newark, DE: International Reading Association.

Tseng, W. S., & Streltzer, J. (Eds.). (2004). *Cultural competence in clinical psychiatry.* Washington, DC: American Psychiatric Association.

Turnbull, A., Turnbull, R., Erwin, E., & Soodak, L. (2006). *Families, professionals, and exceptionality: Positive outcomes through partnership and trust* (5th ed.). Upper Saddle River, NJ: Pearson.

Umbreit, J., Ferro, J., Liaupsin, C., & Lane, K (2006). *Functional behavioral assessment and function-based interventions: An effective, practical approach.* Columbus: Pearson Education.

U.S. Census Bureau. (2000). Table DP-2: Profile of Selected Social Characteristics—2000. Washington, DC: Author.

U.S. Department of Education. (2007). *Reading first: Student achievement, teacher empowerment, national success.* Retrieved from *www.ed.gov/nclb/methods/reading/readingfirst.html.*

Vadasy, P. F., & Sanders, E. A. (2004). *Sound Partners: Research summary.* Seattle, WA: Washington Research Institute.

Vasquez, M. (2010). Ethics in multicultural counseling. In J. G. Ponterotto, J. M. Casas, L. A. Suzuki, & C. M. Alexander (Eds.), *Handbook of multicultural counseling* (4th ed.). Thousand Oaks, CA: Sage.

Vaughn, S., & Linan-Thompson, S. (2004). *Research based methods of reading instruction, grades K–3.* Alexandria, VA: Association for Supervision and Curriculum Development.

Vaughn, S., Linan-Thompson, S., & Hickman, P. (2003). Response to instruction as a means of identifying students with reading/learning disabilities. *Exceptional Children, 69,* 391–409.

Vaughn, S., Wanzek, J., Woodruff, A. L., & Linan-Thompson, S. (2007). Prevention and early identification of students with reading disabilities. In D. Haager, J. Klingner, & S. Vaughn (Eds.), *Evidence-based reading practices for response to intervention* (pp. 11–27). Baltimore: Brookes.

Velluntino, F. R., Scanlon, D. M., Sipay, E. R., Small, S., Chen, R., Pratt, A., et al. (1996). Cognitive profiles of difficult-to-remediate and readily remediated poor readers: Early intervention as a vehicle for distinguishing between cognitive and experiential deficits as basic causes of specific reading disability. *Journal of Educational Psychology, 88,* 601–638.

Walker, H. M., Stiller, B., Golly, A., Kavanagh, K., Severson, H., & Feil, E. (1997). *First Step to Success: Helping young children overcome antisocial behavior (an early intervention program for grades K–3).* Longmont, CO: Sopris West.

Walker, B., Cheney, D., Stage, S., Blum, C., & Horner, R. (2005). Schoolwide screening and positive behavior supports: Identifying and supporting students at risk for school failure. *Journal of Positive Behavior Interventions, 7*(4), 194–204.

Walker, H. M. (2004). Commentary: Use of evidence-based intervention in schools: Where we've been, where we are, and where we need to go. *School Psychology Review 33*(3), 398–407.

Walker, H. M., Horner, R. H., Sugai, G., & Bullis, M. (1996). Integrated approaches to preventing antisocial behavior patterns among school-age children and youth. *Journal of Emotional and Behavioral Disorders, 4*(4), 194–209.

Walker, H. M., Seeley, J. R., et al. (2009). A randomized controlled trial of the first step to success early intervention: Demonstration of program efficacy outcomes in a diverse, urban school district. *Journal of Emotional and Behavioral Disorders, 17*(4), 197–212.

Walker, H. M., & Severson, H. H. (1992). *Systematic screening for behavior disorders.* Longmont, CO: Sopris West.

Watson, T., & Steege, M. (2003). *Conducting school-based functional behavioral assessments: A practitioner's guide.* New York: Guilford Press.

Webster-Stratton, C. (1999). *How to promote children's social and emotional competence.* Thousand Oaks, CA: Sage.

Webster-Stratton, C. (2010). *How to promote children's social and emotional competence.* London: Paul Chapman.

Webster-Stratton, C., & Hammond, M. (1997). Treating children with early-onset conduct problems: A comparison of child and parent training interventions. *Journal of Consulting and Clinical Psychology, 65*(1), 93–109.

Webster-Stratton, C., & Herman, K. C. (2008). The impact of parent behavior management training on child depressive symptoms. *Journal of Counseling Psychology, 55,* 473–484.

Webster-Stratton, C., Mihalic, S., Fagan, A., Arnold, D., Taylor, T., & Tingley, C. (2001). *Blueprints for violence prevention, Book 11: The incredible years parent, teacher, and child training series*. Boulder, CO: Center for the Study and Prevention of Violence.

Weinstein, C. S., & Mignano, A. J. (2003). *Elementary classroom management: Lessons from research and practice* (3rd ed.). Boston: McGraw-Hill.

Whaley, A. L., & King, K. E. (2007). Cultural competence and evidence-based practice in mental health services. *American Psychologist, 62*, 563–574.

What Works Clearinghouse. (2011). Retrieved January 21, 2011, from *ies.ed.gov/ncee/wwc*.

White-Blackburn, G., Semb, S., & Semb, G. (1977). The effects of a good-behavior contract on the classroom behaviors of sixth-grade students. *Journal of Applied Behavior Analysis, 10*(2), 312.

Williams, R. L., & Anandam, K. (1973). The effect of behavior contracting on grades. *Journal of Educational Research, 66*(5), 230–236.

Witt, J., Daly, E., & Noell, G. (2000). *Functional assessments: A step-by-step guide to solving academic and behavior problems*. Longmont, CO: Sopris West.

Wright, J. A., & Dusek, J. B. (1998). Compiling school base rates for disruptive behaviors from student disciplinary referral data. *School Psychology Review, 27*(1), 138–147.

World Health Organization. (2004). *Prevention of mental disorders: Effective interventions and policy options—summary report*. Geneva: Author.

Yarbrough, J. L., Skinner, C. H., Lee, Y. J., & Lemmons, C. (2004). Decreasing transition times in a second grade classroom: Scientific support for the timely transitions game. *Journal of Applied School Psychology, 20*(2), 85–107.

Zentall, S. S., Harper, G. W., & Stormont-Spurgin, M. (1993). Children with hyperactivity and their organizational abilities. *Journal of Educational Research, 87*(2), 112–117.

Zins, J. E., Bloodworth, M. R., Weissberg, R. P., & Walberg, H. J. (2004). The scientific base linking social and emotional learning to school success. In J. E. Zins, R. P. Weissberg, M. C. Wang, & H. J. Walberg (Eds.), *Building academic success on social and emotional learning: What does the research say?* (pp. 3–22). New York: Teachers College Press.

Index

Page numbers followed by *f* or *t* indicate figures or tables.